Restructuring the Hold

Restructuring the Hold

Optimizing Private Equity and Portfolio Company Partnerships

Thomas C. Anderson
Mark G. Habner

WILEY

Published by John Wiley & Sons, Inc., Hoboken, New Jersey.

Published simultaneously in Canada.

No part of this publication may be reproduced, stored in a retrieval system, or transmitted in any form or by any means, electronic, mechanical, photocopying, recording, scanning, or otherwise, except as permitted under Section 107 or 108 of the 1976 United States Copyright Act, without either the prior written permission of the Publisher, or authorization through payment of the appropriate per-copy fee to the Copyright Clearance Center, Inc., 222 Rosewood Drive, Danvers, MA 01923, (978) 750-8400, fax (978) 646-8600, or on the Web at www.copyright.com. Requests to the Publisher for permission should be addressed to the Permissions Department, John Wiley & Sons, Inc., 111 River Street, Hoboken, NJ 07030, (201) 748-6011, fax (201) 748-6008, or online at www.wiley.com/go/permissions.

Limit of Liability/Disclaimer of Warranty: While the publisher and author have used their best efforts in preparing this book, they make no representations or warranties with respect to the accuracy or completeness of the contents of this book and specifically disclaim any implied warranties of merchantability or fitness for a particular purpose. No warranty may be created or extended by sales representatives or written sales materials. The advice and strategies contained herein may not be suitable for your situation. You should consult with a professional where appropriate. Neither the publisher nor author shall be liable for any loss of profit or any other commercial damages, including but not limited to special, incidental, consequential, or other damages.

For general information on our other products and services or for technical support, please contact our Customer Care Department within the United States at (800) 762-2974, outside the United States at (317) 572-3993, or fax (317) 572-4002.

Wiley publishes in a variety of print and electronic formats and by print-on-demand. Some material included with standard print versions of this book may not be included in ebooks or in print-on-demand. If this book refers to media such as a CD or DVD that is not included in the version you purchased, you may download this material at http://booksupport.wiley.com. For more information about Wiley products, visit www.wiley.com.

Library of Congress Cataloging-in-Publication Data

Names: Anderson, Thomas C., author. | Habner, Mark G., author.
Title: Restructuring the hold : optimizing private equity and portfolio
   company partnerships / Thomas C. Anderson & Mark G. Habner.
Description: Hoboken, New Jersey : Wiley, [2021] | Includes index.
Identifiers: LCCN 2020027480 (print) | LCCN 2020027481 (ebook) | ISBN
   9781119635185 (hardback) | ISBN 9781119635215 (adobe pdf) | ISBN
   9781119635208 (epub)
Subjects: LCSH: Private equity. | Mutual funds.
Classification: LCC HG4751 .A56 2021 (print) | LCC HG4751 (ebook) | DDC
   332.6—dc23
LC record available at https://lccn.loc.gov/2020027480
LC ebook record available at https://lccn.loc.gov/2020027481

Cover Design: Wiley
Cover Images: © William Dodge Stevens/Alamy Stock Photo,
              © binkski/Getty Images
Author Photos: © Jovanka Novakovic

Printed in the United States of America.

SKY10021917_102320

This book is dedicated to our families.

To my wife, Jean, whom I've loved since our high school days; and to our children, Benjamin, Caroline, Elizabeth, Catherine, and Samuel. Thank you for your unceasing love and support. I'd be remiss if I didn't mention Bear our black Labrador and constant family companion. – Tom

To my lovely wife, Pamela; my beautiful twin boys, Colin and Ryan; and my parents, Jill and Wayne. Like many of us, my family has been an integral component to every accomplishment I've been fortunate to achieve and supportive in every failure I have accepted. – Mark

Contents

List of Figures

Foreword

Restructuring *the Hold* is an invaluable read for anyone engaging with private equity for the first time, as well as for those who've had previous experiences with private equity. I'm a big fan of PE – but private equity done right. This book provides a roadmap for doing private equity the right way.

Over the years, I've experienced each of the primary types of business ownership structures, including a large public corporation, small startup enterprise, private family-run business, and a private equity-sponsored company. I'm convinced that private equity is the most efficient and the most rewarding for building great businesses. Let me explain why I think this by telling my PE story and explain how the concepts laid out in *Restructuring the Hold* are so relevant today.

After graduation, I joined a large multinational public company and gained a great deal of experience as a young professional. While I enjoyed the work, I became intrigued with the idea of self-employment. After four years and two promotions, I resigned at the young age of 26 to start a carpet-cleaning franchise. My friends and colleagues thought I was nuts.

During the next several years, I worked hard and expanded my franchise to include three different brands, each achieving top performance within the franchise holding company. At 37, I was invited to become president of one of the brands. I sold my businesses and moved my family to Waco, Texas, where the company was headquartered. I was soon promoted to COO and president of the overall multibranded international business. While technically a public company (with the onerous reporting and expectations of posting ever-positive quarterly results), the founder's family still owned a controlling interest. Perhaps not surprisingly, the family had become somewhat risk-averse following their early success and was increasingly hesitant to make good bets to further grow the business. It was the worst of both worlds.

Eventually, the family decided to sell the business. It was 2003, and at that time PE was not widely known in the franchising community. We were intrigued and listened to the private equity firm suitors, and after research and reference checking we sold the business to our first-choice firm. Over the many years that followed and to this day, we've been private equity-owned and have transitioned through three increasingly successful investment periods and currently are on our fourth. With each year, we've achieved impressive growth and increased profitability, enabling us to continuously provide better experiences for our customers, our franchise owners, and our employees.

Neighborly is now fully 20 times bigger (and better) than we were in 2003. But it was during this last full investment period between 2014 and 2018 where we achieved the fastest growth and created the most value – that was the investment period where Tom Anderson and his colleagues partnered with me and my team to drive the most positive change our company has ever seen. During those four years, Neighborly expanded exponentially through our implementing a broad value creation program of organizational improvement, operational efficiencies, organic growth, and add-on acquisitions. Together during that time, we more than tripled the enterprise value of Neighborly and provided investors much more than that in the form of cash-on-cash financial returns.

Our team achieved truly extraordinary accomplishments by implementing many of the principles and practices described in *Restructuring the Hold*. Listed below are just a few of the accomplishments we made together:

Partnership. Tom and I, as well as his colleagues and my leadership team in general, developed a very natural operational cadence that was simply invaluable. Together we established an efficient and effective – and enjoyable – working rhythm of remote and in-person interactions, constantly communicating and (almost) always on the same page. Together we built the kind of partnership described in *Restructuring the Hold*. It felt to us like our equity partners were simply an extension of our leadership team in Waco.

Organization. Early in the investment period, we worked together to carefully evaluate every leadership role with respect to our strategies and carefully made necessary adjustments over time through promotions, replacements, and other changes. We created new opportunities for the most capable and increased the size of the corporate team to enhance our franchisee-supporting capability and capacity, adding over 30 percent to the ranks. Over the course of the investment period, we fully transitioned from what had still largely been a legacy family business to a full-contingent professional leadership and support team capable of running a much larger business. Thank goodness, too, because we've continued our new growth trajectory to this day with that team.

Operations. We jointly evaluated all aspects of our business and enhanced the most important and least efficient, for instance, transitioning from a large in-house IT infrastructure maintaining old homegrown systems to an outsourced best-of-breed approach, and establishing an efficient online recruiting system benefiting our thousands of franchisees. We also knew in our hearts that building a new corporate office would be justified, and because of our trusting relationship, our equity partners were fully supportive, and the result has been more than what we'd hoped for.

Growth. We utilized the same value creation process described in the book to jointly prioritize and implement dozens of growth initiatives in addition to operating and organizational initiatives. In the course of doing so, we canceled some in-flight initiatives and business concepts that, in retrospect, were ill-conceived, and created a plethora of new capabilities, including new branding and messaging, new lead generation and call-center infrastructure, and an entirely new cross-brand marketing approach focused on a new concept we created together, called "Neighborly." In fact, from its success we changed the name of the company to Neighborly.

Expansion. Our equity partners were not only supportive but enthusiastic about helping us grow aggressively through acquisitions. Where we'd made only one acquisition in the previous few years, during this investment period we acquired and integrated 10 add-on companies. Internationally, our business had faced three years of increasing losses in Europe. Where other private equity firms might have simply forced us to shut it down, Tom and his colleagues worked with us on a new strategy, starting with simply to "make a buck" in Europe. Rather than shutting it down, we carefully "doubled-down" – hiring great EU leaders, acquiring two new businesses, and achieving scale economies so that today our European business represents a very profitable and growing part of our story.

My management team and I have learned much from our private equity sponsors. The simple truth of the matter is that you cannot grow 20 times in size by continuing to execute what you currently know how to do. As you scale, different systems, different tools, and different methodologies must be deployed to sustain that growth. If that's not done, growth stalls, and that's the first step toward decline. Our PE sponsors have continuously helped us not only to avoid a stall but to actively sustain and accelerate growth.

Since becoming a PE CEO veteran, I have spoken with CEOs who have not had the same positive experience we've had. Now, perhaps we have been lucky, but we made much of our own luck – we were careful in checking out potential suitors, we worked hard to understand our sponsors' objectives, and most of all, we were committed to establishing successful collaborative partnerships. Together, we all achieved what we'd intended, and then some.

Tom Anderson was the PE operator I partnered with during that particularly impressive four-year sprint I described. In *Restructuring the Hold,* he and his co-author Mark Habner do a masterful and entertaining job laying out the high value-creating concepts that he and I together honed and lived for four years. Fifteen years ago – at the beginning of my "Year 0" with private equity – it sure would have been nice to have had the benefit of reading Tom and Mark's book *Restructuring the Hold*. Who knows how much even further and faster we could have gone?

Mike Bidwell
CEO, Neighborly

Preface

"Just think of how much more we could have done if we'd known what to expect earlier!" is a phrase management teams have said to us time and again later in the hold period. "You should write this all down."

And so we did.

But our reasons for writing this book go well beyond simply accelerating the understanding by portfolio company management teams of what the hold period could be like. We decided to write *Restructuring the Hold* because we wanted to make a broader impact across more companies, more management teams, and more individuals than what we could otherwise by working only with a handful of portfolio companies at any given time.

And we wanted that impact to be much more than improved financial outcomes. To be clear, investor returns are *the* endgame. You'll not find a single recommendation in the pages that follow that doesn't focus on optimizing financial outcomes. But with any luck, we've designed *Restructuring the Hold* to achieve much more than that.

This book is about a bigger mission than just the bottom line. It's about improving outcomes in the broadest sense. It's about helping business leaders – portfolio company leadership and equity partners alike – feel that important sense of pride in building something of considerable and sustainable value. It's about creating opportunity – better products and services, better careers and leaders, and better relationships. It's about marrying character and capability to establish constructive partnerships and (hopefully) life-long friendships.

It's also meant to make the case for focusing on fundamentals. The challenges businesses face today are proliferating like never before. Global instability, domestic politics, environmental crises, and worldwide pandemics all generate serious obstacles for companies everywhere. But despite the changing economic climate, sound business practices remain constant. By focusing on the fundamentals, business leaders – and particularly those of middle-market portfolio companies – are better prepared to not only weather these storms but actually thrive in the new economic conditions, no matter what circumstances they encounter.

We believe in leading lives according to strong moral codes. These perpetuate within companies as core values representing fundamental beliefs. Values represent what a company stands for, who they are, and how they act. Core values serve as a steadfast barometer for the entire team, consistently guiding behavior, decisions, and actions.

In the pages that follow you'll not only see us articulate our vision of purposeful, practical, and principled leadership during the hold period, but present our core values through the words of others and give voice to them in narrative form. To us, the characters that populate the novels of Ernest Hemingway and John Steinbeck personify those values and bring them to life. Both authors crafted individuals who embrace their own codes of authenticity, integrity, and compassion, illustrating courageous and empathetic souls as well as strong and stoic achievers. We also created the story of GrammCo to show how these core values manifest themselves in the lived experience of an imagined hold period. In starting each chapter with a quote from Hemingway or Steinbeck as well as a vignette from the story of GrammCo, we hope not only to persuade you of the importance of these values but show them in action. These are the values we aspire to emulate, and we hope that comes across in *Restructuring the Hold*.

About the Authors

Tom Anderson and Mark Habner are co-authors for the book. Both have long been recognized as industry-leading practitioners in the private equity operating space. Tom and Mark have worked together in various capacities in private equity for over 12 years.

Thomas C. Anderson

Tom serves private equity-owned companies in very active hands-on chairman and board director roles, helping CEOs accelerate sustainable growth and prepare for successful transactions.

From 2013 to 2020, Tom was an operating partner at The Riverside Company, a global private equity firm making control investments in growing middle-market businesses. At any given time, Tom served as chairman of the board for three to five companies, typically for the duration of each hold from diligence through exit. Tom earned the reputation for developing strong collaborative partnerships with executive teams to plan and accelerate company performance and exit value.

Before Riverside, Tom was an operating partner with Sun Capital, serving interim leadership and EBITDA growth acceleration roles across portfolio companies in both the US and Europe. Prior to that, he was a director with the restructuring firm AlixPartners, where he led company-wide transformation programs for private equity sponsored portfolio companies. These included growth strategies, merger integrations, and company turnarounds.

Tom started his career as an industrial engineer for First Brands Corporation. He graduated from Virginia Polytechnic Institute & State University with a BS in Industrial Engineering & Operations Research, subsequently earning an MS from Rensselaer Polytechnic Institute and an MBA from Georgetown University. Tom lives in Charlotte, NC, with his wife of almost 30 years. Together they have five children.

Mark G. Habner

Mark is currently CEO of BeckWay Group, an operating company dedicated to providing operating governance and EBITDA growth support during the entire hold period. BeckWay Group is retained by a small set of middle-market private equity firms and their portfolio companies.

The BeckWay Group operating platform provides hands-on operating leadership, cloud-based deployment technologies, and hard-to-find talent acquisition capabilities. Embracing a strong set of core values, BeckWay Group works side-by-side with management teams to increase and accelerate exit value throughout the hold period.

Previously, Mark was a senior managing director at SSA & Company, an operations consulting firm, where he led the organization's five capability practices. Before that role, Mark was a partner with the Australian private equity firm RMB Capital Partners. He began his career with Booz, Allen, & Hamilton, a strategic management consulting firm.

Mark lives in the New York metro area with his wife and twin sons. He is chairman of the University of Tasmania Foundation (USA) and a member of YPO. Mark earned his bachelor of commerce and bachelor of laws (honors) degrees from the University of Tasmania in 1992. He earned an MBA with distinction from the Kellogg Business School at Northwestern University in 1997.

Acknowledgments

In addition to our families, we'd like to thank our friends and colleagues who supported us during the many months of this exciting endeavor, especially our writing coach and editor, Dr. D. Olson Pook, for his numerous enthusiastic reviews and constant encouragement, and private equity communications specialist Mark Wiskup for his early direction-setting advice for how to get started.

I'd like to express long-overdue appreciation to those who hired and mentored me early in my career, particularly John Strasburg and Joe Owen. A big thank-you to each of my friends and colleagues over the years, including those most recently at The Riverside Company. My deepest appreciation to the executives with whom I've worked for their partnership and friendship, particularly CEOs John Sypek, Mike Bidwell, Chris Fitzgerald, Carl Will, Jeff Leone, Mike Sinoway, Girisha Chandraraj, Michael Saunders, Michael Fiore, and Linda Heasley. **– Tom**

I'd like to thank my friends and colleagues from RMB Capital, where I got my start in private equity, and the teams of our many portfolio companies and firms who provided the all-important portfolio support services. Thank you to Phil Latham, Derek Prout-Jones, Martin Keyser, Matt McLellan, and Mark Wilson for your patience, guidance, and partnership. I particularly would like to acknowledge my friend and mentor, Ken Shabanee. – **Mark**

And finally, we would like to thank our colleagues at BeckWay Group. They have built an organization with the highest values and integrity. It is a pleasure and honor to work as part of this team, and where we keep learning every day. Thank you to Colin Garner, Danyell Lance, and Scott Burke for being with us from the start.

Introduction

Private equity as an investment class has skyrocketed in recent years, both globally and domestically. If you're not directly or indirectly involved in private equity today, there's a good chance you soon will be.

Before the 1980s, private equity was a new and largely unknown phenomenon. Today it represents one of the largest asset classes available to institutional investors, private investors, and management teams alike. In the US alone, a few thousand private equity firms control over 50,000 companies through some combination of direct investment, board control, and operational involvement.

Over the years, private equity firms have acquired a reputation for being ruthless, possessing a single-minded focus on their own profits at the expense of the companies and their employees they acquire. Even today, over 30 years after its release, we still hear plenty of references to the chart-topping 1987 movie *Wall Street*. Michael Douglas's character Gordon Gekko sanctimoniously purchases and dismantles companies with the single goal of lining his own pockets. "It's not a question of enough, pal," he lectures his idealistic young protégé, "it's a zero-sum game: Somebody wins, somebody loses." His philosophy is pithily summed up in the film's most memorable line: "Greed is good."

Douglas's portrayal of Gekko is of course a caricature, but distrust over the motives of private equity still runs wide and deep, even among well-informed and seasoned business professionals. The image seems universally ingrained: fancy-suited, hard-talking, ruthless investors buying, breaking up, and brokering companies for personal gain, brutally and heartlessly manhandling employees and their families without regard to the consequences of their actions. Many continue to doubt the intentions of private equity firms claiming to seek win–win outcomes in which everyone shares in a better and more profitable future.

The investing world has certainly spawned its share of Gekko-like characters leveraging junk bonds or pursuing other means to aggressively finance disreputable deals. But in its short history, private equity has matured quickly, embodying more professionalism and proficiency today than ever before – and more competition, too. Gone are the days where firms could buy a company at a low multiple of earnings price, leverage it through taking on lots of debt, loosely monitor the investment through quarterly board meetings, and sell the company a few years later at a higher exit multiple – all but guaranteeing exceptional returns. To succeed in private equity today, investors and management teams must work together to improve and grow businesses rather than financially engineer them.

More and more investors are searching harder than ever to find and buy promising companies, and the billions of "dry powder" dollars available for investment only serves to intensify competition. To differentiate in a very crowded and oversubscribed field, fund variations continue to proliferate based on company size, industry, investment horizon, and asset quality. One area of particular interest to growth-minded investors is the middle-market, loosely defined as those companies with annual revenues between $10 million and $1 billion, most of which will be sold at least once during the next dozen years.

Due to interest and competition, private equity firms that target the middle-market can no longer count on proprietary deal flow, transaction acumen, financial engineering, and multiple expansion to achieve even reasonable (let alone outsized) returns. It's now all about growing businesses: crafting strategies, building management teams, improving infrastructure, and actively driving value throughout the typical three- to seven-year hold period.

The need for understanding how to successfully navigate the hold period is undeniable. Achieving growth in earnings (EBITDA, or earnings before interest, taxes, depreciation, and amortization) today requires active operational involvement from private equity and accelerated and innovative action from the portfolio company. Yet while a great deal of ink has been spilled over the necessity of increased hands-on investor involvement and even more on management team effectiveness, very little has been said about the intersection of the two. What's missing in the conversation is an explanation about why it's important to have collaborative and constructive partnerships between private equity principals and portfolio company executives – and how to get there.

Restructuring the Hold: Optimizing Private Equity and Portfolio Company Partnerships illuminates an improved approach to private equity investing that centers on more productive and profitable working relationships and practices among management teams, equity partners, and boards of directors. Vastly different in concept and execution from the extremes of either the traditional hands-off approach or the equally ineffective we-tell-you-do method, *Restructuring the Hold* spells out how to develop a dynamic collaborative partnership based on trust and accountability between private equity principals and portfolio executives.

By examining how a truly collaborative partnership would develop and implement effective practices over the course of the hold period, *Restructuring the Hold* explains how management teams and their private equity partners can and should work together to achieve an efficient operating rhythm, accelerate sustainable EBITDA growth, and ultimately optimize exit value – benefiting investors and private equity firms as well as portfolio company management, company employees, and their families. *Restructuring the Hold* therefore serves four primary goals:

Elevate portfolio company expectations for constructive partnerships with their private equity firm that leverages each of their complementary capabilities throughout the hold period.

Encourage private equity firms to continuously up their game through embodying core values and better governing practices when collaborating with their portfolio companies.

Empower portfolio company executives and equity partners to establish and execute an aggressive Value Creation Program based on attitude and capability that focuses on the hold period endgame.

Achieve accelerated sustainable earnings growth and optimize enterprise value through authentic relationships, constructive partnerships, clear accountabilities, and better operating practices.

Built on a chapter by chapter explanation of the typical steps within the hold period, *Restructuring the Hold* illustrates how private equity and portfolio companies can form constructive partnerships and implement better practices to optimize the outcomes for everyone.

Core Audience

The lessons of *Restructuring the Hold* are applicable across the wide spectrum of private equity and other business sectors. It's relevant to anyone interested in how to establish more productive and more profitable working relationships and practices between and among management teams, private equity investors, and board directors. Whether you're a limited or general partner associated with a private equity firm, a banker at an investment or commercial institution, an individual investor in alternative asset classes, an executive at a portfolio company, or just someone interested in this essential business sector, *Restructuring the Hold* will reshape your thinking about how private equity and portfolio companies can and should work together to reconfigure outdated and ineffective approaches to hold periods.

The book is particularly suited for investors, executives, and managers associated and working with the portfolio companies of middle-market private equity firms. If you find yourself in one or more of the following groups, *Restructuring the Hold* will help you create sustainable value in your businesses:

Sooners. Executives and managers soon to be part of the private equity world because their companies will soon be sold to private equity. These folks wonder what they should expect and what's about to "happen to me." Sooners don't know whether they should be excited or looking for another job.

Improvers. Executives and managers already part of a private equity sponsored portfolio company. These individuals might want to better understand what's happening to them or might want to improve their game, their relationship with the private equity partners, and their careers as well.

Again-ers. Executives and managers who have had one or more previous experiences with private equity, resulting in either positive or less-than-stellar experiences. These are the ones interested in making their next go-round not only financially successful but personally and professionally rewarding.

Board directors. The board of directors for a portfolio company is interested in providing more insightful guidance to their executive teams during the hold and in advising management teams on how to best work within their new ownership structures to drive the best performance possible.

Investors. Partners and other principals in private equity firms themselves, interested in establishing more personally, professionally, and financially rewarding partnerships with their portfolio company executives and management teams.

Professional service providers. Accountants, attorneys, consultants, and other providers working directly with private equity portfolio companies who would benefit from having a deeper understanding of their customers and the opportunities and challenges that occur during the hold period.

Educators. College professors, business school instructors, executive coaches, industry speakers, and other educators interested in helping their charges better understand the private equity space and prepare for and improve their business careers.

Emulators. Executives and managers of public, family, or closely held businesses interested in leveraging the practices employed by collaborative private equity and portco teams to accelerate value in a compressed time frame and achieve a new trajectory.

Organization of the Book

Restructuring the Hold shows private equity principals and portfolio company executives how to work together to restructure their approach to hold periods. It is not about the bookends of private equity – the "before" of evaluating opportunities, transacting deals, and financing investments, or the "after" of hiring sell-side investment bankers, building sales presentations, and executing portfolio company exits. It's a close look at the hold period – the time from when the private equity firm buys a company to the day it's sold – when most of the value is created. How that happens – the nuts-and-bolts of value generation – is what this book is all about.

Restructuring the Hold is organized into 12 chapters. After introducing the ins and outs of private equity and the principles underlying constructive partnerships, each of the subsequent chapters corresponds to a particular time period – critical milestones marking progress during the typical private equity hold period. If properly managed, the consternation of the first month gives way to optimism and guarded enthusiasm in the next two. *Restructuring the Hold* then looks at the dynamics of each of the next three quarters, where bumps in the road inevitably occur while growth momentum increases. This sets the stage for a discussion of years two and three, where internal infrastructure is improved, sales growth is accelerated, and external acquisitions are integrated. It concludes with a chapter devoted to the exit where the company is sold. Each chapter identifies challenges and goals for the time period under consideration and focuses on how management and private equity can work in concert to achieve the best possible outcomes.

The framework for each chapter consists of three primary components:

Narrating the hold. At the beginning of each chapter, we check in with the story of Gramm Company, a fictitious but illustrative composite of a typical middle-market portfolio company that recently has been sold to Patterson Lake Capital – a similarly fictitious forward-thinking private equity firm keen to help GrammCo's management team grow the company during the hold period. Each vignette sets the stage for the content of the chapter, focusing on the frustrations and excitement experienced by a management team under new ownership and the steps that key principals from a private equity firm take to forge genuine partnerships during the hold period.

Explaining the hold. Each chapter then looks closely at the typical challenges and opportunities facing the partnership during the time period in question. This part of each chapter looks specifically at how private equity firms and portfolio companies can leverage their constructive partnership and shared goals to overcome the distinct obstacles in their way at a given point in time during the hold period and implement effective practices that drive lasting gains in EBITDA value.

Picturing the hold. Accompanying the subsections of each chapter are illuminating graphics that offer an illustrated framework of the business content discussed. These illustrations serve as helpful guides to the ideas discussed in the chapter and offer a snapshot of better practice frameworks that readers can apply to their own situation.

Through the combination of helpful illustrations, applicable better practice frameworks, and a very typical days-in-the-life story, *Restructuring the Hold* offers a 360-degree portrayal of how to successfully navigate the hold period to optimize outcomes.

Chapter 1
Private Equity

"... it's our land. We measured it and broke it up. We were born on it, and we got killed on it, died on it. Even if it's no good, it's still ours. That's what makes it ours – being born on it, working it, dying on it. That makes ownership, not a paper with numbers on it."

– John Steinbeck, *Grapes of Wrath*

The Gramm Company (GrammCo) designs and manufactures heavy-duty all-terrain service vehicles (ASV) for rugged and remote deployments, primarily serving the North American pipeline, transmission, and forestry industries. Headquartered in Denver and employing around 300 people, the company retains a fabrication plant outside the city as well as service depots in Houston, Calgary, and Las Vegas. After 20 years founder Russ Gramm stepped back from the day-to-day, handing the reigns to Dianne Franklin three years ago.

(continued)

(*continued*)

Originally a mechanical engineer from Poly Tech, Dianne spent her formative professional years in Big Oil. An entrepreneur at heart who loves hiking and camping, it didn't take much for Russ to convince her to leave the fancy glass corporate buildings of downtown Houston to move to Colorado and serve as CEO of a middle-market company with $165 million in revenues enjoying 15 percent net profit margins.

Patterson Lake Capital is a private equity firm based in Chicago specializing in middle-market acquisitions. With $750 million currently invested across seven portfolio companies, Patterson Lake is particularly active in the industrial and business services space. Among its small but dedicated staff, Patterson Lake has an investing partner and an operating partner specifically associated with the GrammCo deal, each well-respected and in the prime of their careers. They love what they do and do it well – finding valuable middle-market companies and helping them grow.

Operating Partner Shed Cooper started as an engineer in the aerospace industry out west, and after working his way through b-school he moved east and progressed through several successful executive roles in the automotive space, then served five years as CEO of a national distributor before transitioning to private equity. Shed has been at Patterson Lake for seven years now.

Olivia Charles Gleason – Ocie – has been with Patterson Lake for almost twice as long as Shed. Ocie joined the firm after cutting her teeth at a well-known Wall Street I-bank. Though she attended business school in Boston, she's become a committed Midwesterner and loves Chicago. Like Shed, she's married with kids and has figured out how to balance raising a family and traveling for work.

Throughout this book, we'll regularly check in with the happenings at GrammCo and Patterson Lake Capital as their worlds quickly come together. We'll watch as they form an authentic collaborative partnership and note the intentional steps they took to get there. We'll see them grow and optimize the enterprise value of the company despite the challenging headwinds facing private equity. Most importantly, we'll see how they navigate together the various ups and downs of the investment period, growing their own capacities and abilities and the company's bottom line in ways they never would have imagined.

The Asset Class

Although this book will not investigate the entire investment cycle and inner workings of private equity, it's helpful to start with a brief overview. A snapshot of the private equity asset class not only presents the opportunity to introduce and explain the terminology we'll be using but also provides a useful framework for understanding why this book's focus is on the operational side of the investment period.

Private equity is the idea of investing capital to acquire an ownership stake in an existing established business, with the expectation of realizing future profits when the company is sold to another party. Private equity is different from venture capital, which is a term most often used for capital applied to accelerate new startups or early-stage businesses. By contrast, the term *private equity* has typically been used to indicate an ownership stake in more established organizations. It's worth noting these distinctions have blurred somewhat as both venture capital and private equity have become increasingly competitive and investors seek investment opportunities in both markets.

The Players in Private Equity

Limited partners (LPs) are the individuals and institutions (e.g., pension funds, endowments, insurance companies, sovereign wealth entities, etc.) who provide investment equity. LPs are the investors in the fund, which is managed by a private equity group (PEG). In other words, they provide the capital that the private equity firms use to invest. LPs are typically not involved in the day-to-day activities of the general partner. They simply select the private equity firms and funds in which they want to invest, monitor performance remotely, and expect sufficient returns on their capital. For larger private equity firms, the limited partners are often large institutional investors, while for smaller firms, they might be high-net-worth individuals or family funds. Often, a private equity firm will raise their funds from dozens of limited partners, including both institutional and private money.

Private equity group (PEG) is the catchall term we will use in this book to refer to the terms *general partner, private equity firm, buyout firm,* and *private equity fund* synonymously. While there are differences in definition and scope among these concepts such that the term PEG is not a perfect fit, those differences need not concern us here. What is consistent is that the PEG decides (within prearranged bounds) where to invest the limited partners' money. It does this by accumulating portfolio companies and monitoring and influencing those investments over time to optimize performance. The PEG decides when to sell or "exit" each company in its portfolio so that they can provide sufficient returns to the investors.

Portfolio companies are purchased with LP equity and augmented with debt capital as determined by the PEG. Each portfolio company (or *portco*) in the PEG's portfolio represents an individual investment. The PEG monitors and manages each investment to optimize returns to the limited partners. The LPs may have investments in specific portfolio companies, in the broader portfolio of companies, or both. Either way, each company in the portfolio is critical to the performance of the entire fund. If fund performance is poor, meaning that one or more portcos underperform, the PEG will have a hard time attracting future capital from LPs, thereby risking the PEG's ability to continue investing and operating.

Professional services firms such as accountants, attorneys, and consultants are employed to guide and support portfolio company performance improvement. Typically, it's the portco that retains the service providers, but the PEG will have a say in their selection and provide guidance and steering to those providers.

Commercial banks provide the debt capital (the leverage on investment equity), enabling the PEG to invest in bigger opportunities and more of them. While the PEG will certainly play a big role in bank selection and relationships, each portfolio company will incur the debt on its balance sheet. Servicing that debt through high monthly interest payments is often a fresh hurdle for companies new to the private equity world. Throughout the hold period, the portco and PEG will work to pay down the debt, reducing monthly interest expense and also increasing the future net exit value when the company is later sold.

Participants in private equity and their roles are summarized in Figure 1.1.

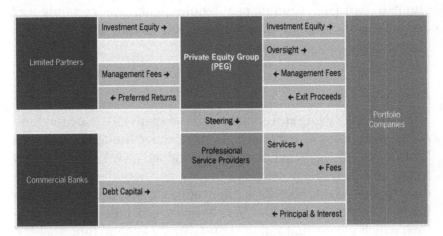

Figure 1.1 Private Equity Participants

Private Equity Groups: Firms, Funds, and Process

There are many PEG variants in the private equity space. Many firms are small, having fewer than a dozen people focused on a single specific sector, but others are quite large with hundreds of employees investing across multiple sectors. Regardless of its size and focus, most PEGs typically have four core functions and organizes themselves accordingly:

Fundraising. Responsible for investor relations (IR) and courting limited partners. The PEG raises a new fund every few years, during which time the IR team is particularly busy.

Investing. Responsible for investment and exit decisions, as well as for structuring and securing sufficient equity and debt funding for each deal. The investing team typically has the most people in the PEG, ranging from new associates to partners with lengthy tenures.

Operating. Responsible for operational oversight of the portfolio companies. The PEG's operating team is usually quite small, consisting of very experienced practitioners, typically former CEOs and executives or senior expert consultants.

Administrating. Responsible for overall fund administration, accounting, and reporting on investment performance to the limited partners. Compliance requirements are certainly not insignificant, and fund administration is an important but behind-the-scenes player.

Risk and Return

The process of raising and operating a fund spans all these functions. A PEG will begin by explaining to prospective limited partners its investment strategy (including sector, industry, size, or geography focus) and seek to convince the limited partners that investing in their fund is a better bet for higher returns than investing in other funds. A recent trend is for PEGs to operate as independent sponsors, which means that rather than raising a general fund that targets a particular sector, they seek funds from limited partners on a deal-by-deal basis.

Funds vary in size, with $50 million on the smaller side to $1 billion or more representing a larger fund. The firm then deploys the raised equity, leveraging it with debt capital to buy new portfolio companies (and any additional supporting acquisitions) over the next few years. The PEG works with its portfolio companies during each hold period to build and grow the businesses and then harvests returns by selling companies after typical portco hold periods of three to seven years. Successful PEGs provide top quartile (or at least sufficient) returns to their LPs, allowing them to raise additional funds and begin the cycle again.

As an asset class, private equity has many characteristics that increase its risk profile. Lower- and middle-market portfolio businesses often had been privately held and therefore lack a history of broad and deep scrutiny. Nor is the investment liquid – once purchased, there is not a readily accessible market to sell, and there is limited visibility regarding timing and potential future valuation at time of sale. Selling or exiting the investment, therefore, requires significant and unpredictable time, effort, and cost, yet returns are anything but guaranteed. The time horizon for the investment is also not insignificant – several years where the investor's money is locked up in the fund.

Offsetting the increased risk profile is the opportunity for superior returns compared to other asset classes. Because of the risk, LPs require higher returns than they would for lower risk or more liquid investments. The corresponding rate of return may be in the double digits, likely double or more the rate they might receive from other less risky investment opportunities. For instance, a reasonable return for an LP may be two-times cash-on-cash after a reasonable hold period (receiving back twice what they invested).

Measuring Success

For startups or turnarounds, cash is king, but in the private equity space EBITDA rules. Earnings before interest, taxes, depreciation, and amortization is a useful, simple, but admittedly inexact proxy for operating cash flow and overall performance. It's used to support evaluations of company core business performance without including further complicating factors associated with financing, tax treatment, and accounting regulations. EBITDA is a PEG's primary indicator of the overall enterprise value for any given company.

Another indicator of overall enterprise value is referred to as the *multiple*. To arrive at a purchase price for a company, the buyer and seller agree to a normalized EBITDA as well as a multiplier to arrive at the purchase price. Although the objectivity of EBITDA is arguably debatable, the appropriate multiple associated with a company is far more subjective. Determining the multiple is an inexact science but certainly involves evaluating the general growth prospects of the industry, specific growth prospects for the company, and overall risk profile. All other factors being equal, higher growth potential and lower risk means higher multiples.

Challenges and Headwinds

The dramatic proliferation of the private equity asset class, and therefore the inevitable maturing of the class, has led to an intensification of both external and internal challenges over the past several years.

Lots of suitors, lots of money. More and more capital, particularly big institutional capital, is now targeted at private equity. Competition for big lucrative deals has driven larger private equity firms to increasingly look down market in search of attractive (if not proprietary) deals from smaller companies. Proprietary deals have become even more scarce, and auctioned deals are increasingly being bid up. The resulting supply–demand imbalance has served to drive purchase prices up, and multiples on EBITDA paid for companies have increased from low- to mid-single digits to often well into double digits, depending on the specific sector. It's simply costing more money to buy companies – particularly good ones.

Performance requirements. Because of competition and higher prices, portfolio company performance improvement and real growth over the investment period is even more critical. Higher purchase prices translate directly to the need for higher portfolio company performance to achieve the same return that investors enjoyed only a handful of years ago. No longer can PEGs rely on financial engineering and multiple accretion to provide sufficient returns. The pressure to improve portfolio company performance and accelerating growth has never been higher.

Lower fees, higher scrutiny. Since the early days of private equity, the model has been such that the PEG receives two forms of compensation from the LPs – management fees and carried interest, or *carry* (the fee the PEG receives based on realized investment returns above a certain hurdle rate to the LPs). Management fees and the effective carry component paid by LPs to the PEG have consistently shrunk over the years as the private equity market has matured and competition increased.

These challenges point to the biggest opportunities in the private equity space. Having paid a premium for the portfolio company in today's competitive market, PEGs need to maximize value like never before. It should come as no surprise that the place where the biggest gains can be achieved is in restructuring the hold period – improving how PEGs and portcos work together to grow EBITDA (through both commercial and operational actions), increase the exit multiple (through enhancing portco infrastructure and enabling future opportunities), while continuously paying down company debt. A collaborative partnership between private equity firms and their portfolio companies represents a critical differentiator in achieving future success and outsized returns for LPs, PEGs, and management teams alike.

The Middle-Market

The middle-market represents one of the most important and also dynamic segments of the US economy. It also underscores the essence of the American character: large, growing, and everchanging. It is for these reasons the middle-market is not just an important but also a value-laden investment space. It represents a significant opportunity for investors and management teams to still achieve the growth necessary to realize significant gains in future valuation and the returns investors seek.

Defining the Middle-Market

To better understand the world of private equity investing, PEGs and service providers segment the space in a variety of ways. The logic for segmenting is to help identify organizations that may have similar needs and constraints, making it easier to target and service those companies. One way to segment is by industry – industrials, consumer products, healthcare services, and so on. Another is by relative company health – growing, mature, underperforming, troubled, and such. A third widely used classification relates to size in terms of annual revenue of the company.

The term *middle-market* is one common size segment, but there is no hard-and-fast definition as to what a middle-market company is. Depending on whom you ask, the middle-market can include companies ranging anywhere from $10 million to $1 billion in revenue. Because that range is quite large, you'll often hear people segment the middle-market into thirds – lower, middle, and upper-middle-market – based on company revenue (illustrated in Figure 1.2).

Private equity firms and service providers working in the middle-market space will often specify their focus area. Some will pursue a wide lens, targeting the middle-market generally, whereas others have a specific target like "underperforming manufacturing companies in the lower-middle-market." When we speak of the middle-market throughout this book, we're specifically referring to PEG-owned companies focused on improvement and growth; not steady run-for-cash (lifestyle) businesses, but companies that are going somewhere, having started smaller with the intention of growing bigger.

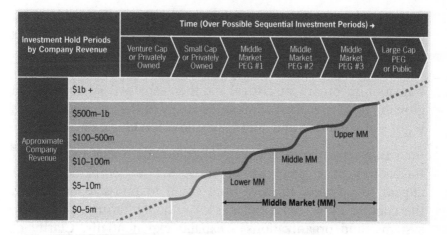

Figure 1.2 Progression Through Multiple Investment Periods

Middle-Market Characteristics

Companies in the middle-market are a bit like adolescents. They're maturing but not quite there yet. Because they are still growing, they can be awkward and gangly. Middle-market companies can be both restless and reckless at the same time, and things change quickly for them. As a result, they represent risky but possibly rewarding propositions. With the right guidance, they will "graduate" and go on to enjoy future success, but without it they could also total the family car.

We find that middle-market companies (and particularly growth-oriented lower-middle) tend to share certain characteristics that set them apart from both small- and large-cap companies. While the features we describe below are quite typical, no one middle-market company necessarily possesses them all. Yet the combination of these factors makes the middle-market space an important one for investors because these characteristics present the biggest opportunity to build and grow even better companies.

Individuals matter disproportionately. Perhaps more than with larger companies, every single manager and executive in a middle-market company can have an impact on company success. Those with great attitudes and lots of ability shine and shine brightly. Correspondingly, the other extremes are just as noticeable. No one can hide in the middle-market. Decisions about creating a new role, top-grading an existing employee, or transitioning others are critical and time-sensitive. Fortunately, in growing middle-market companies, many of the key role changes require augmenting and adding positions too long delayed.

Increasing complexity emerges. Middle-market companies find themselves at a precipice of sorts. While companies might appear to progress linearly from small to mid-size, in reality, the complexity of those businesses – their offerings, processes, systems, and organizations – expand exponentially. Clarity of vision becomes critical at these moments. Small companies can perhaps be all things to all people within their confined space, but middle-market companies need to define not only what they are but (just as important) what they are not. Too much new complexity too fast can quickly crater a company. For middle-market companies, complexity is front and center, and important make-or-break decisions must be made, fraught with risk, opportunity, and reward.

Change is intense, feedback is immediate. In much larger companies, most change occurs slowly, having to work its way across lots of people, geographies, and processes, spreading up and down the ranks and organizational layers. But change in a middle-market company happens quickly. It usually only takes a matter of hours to get feedback on change – both positive and negative – and companies begin feeling the impact of that change in just days. Even small changes can be surprisingly consequential in middle-market companies. They are like a tightly wound spring, and any movement can result in fast and eventful effects.

Sustainable infrastructure is needed. In the early days of a company's history, the focus of the founder or leader was solely on growth. When it became a small market company, the focus shifted to defining and honing offerings and generating sales and cash flow to sustain continued expansion. These companies were small enough to manage by line-of-sight. But as companies grow in size, systems and processes need to be formalized and management and reporting structures codified. Building appropriate sustainable infrastructure early in a new investment period to enable continued and accelerated growth is very important in the middle-market.

Commercial sophistication builds. Having become more complex, middle-market companies begin to address that complexity and build sustainable infrastructure. As they mature, they also realize they cannot be "all things to all people," and increasingly organize and formalize themselves commercially, specifically what they offer and to whom. They begin to get their arms around market and customer segmentation, portfolio management, and price management. They become more sophisticated in how they address the marketplace – their branding and marketing, message specificity and differentiation, sales and support team capabilities and assignments, and a variety of processes and tools to simplify commerce and make things easier for their customers.

Acquisitions require incorporation. Where smaller companies have neither the infrastructure nor the stable and repeatable processes to effectively absorb an add-on company, middle-market companies are coming of age and can begin to consider finding, buying, and integrating add-on acquisitions. Each add-on company might offer an extension of the "platform" portfolio company's current offerings, or it might have the same or similar offering in a new geography. The add-on might provide needed resources and new capabilities, or it might just be more of the same, but with consolidation opportunities to leverage a single corporate and back-office infrastructure.

Change must be coordinated. Because of the new complexity, need for improved infrastructure, and the increasing commercial sophistication, middle-market companies have been and will be increasingly implementing changes and enhancements to their business at an accelerated rate. There will be a lot of moving parts and a lot of activity, in addition to running the day-to-day. These companies are typically not used to managing a company-wide transformation effort, which is really what we're talking about. There are or soon will be a significant number of initiatives now needing to be actively prioritized, resourced, coordinated, and managed – a new reality for a new foundational capability.

The Investment Cycle

While no two private equity firms are exactly alike (and in fact many PEGs are fairly unique), most follow a relatively consistent investment cycle: finding and evaluating promising portfolio companies, buying the ones they like and can afford to pay for, building and growing those companies, and eventually selling them to finish off the investment cycle (as shown in Figure 1.3).

Finding Opportunities

Finding promising investment opportunities is the first phase of the investment cycle. Scouring the marketplace to find companies for sale is not difficult; the challenge lies in uncovering potential

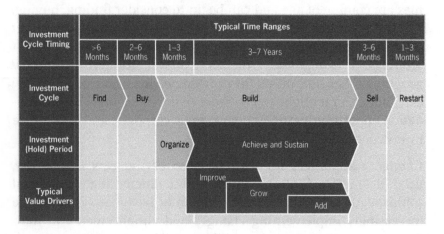

Figure 1.3   Investment Cycle Overview

portfolio companies that meet specific investment mandates or targeted types of opportunities. To find the right companies to buy, the investing partners in a PEG will typically work with business development professionals and attend industry conferences to expand their knowledge and contact base in and near the space they look to invest.

The Buy Phase

The buy phase arrives when a target company has been found and needs to be evaluated through management meetings and due diligence. This typically proceeds under a letter of intent (LOI) and requires a significant investment of time from both the buyer as well as seller's management team in response to questions and information requests. When the equity team decides they want to proceed with an offer, they finalize their deal thesis – a detailed document substantiating why they want to buy this company and how they plan to realize sufficient returns to investors – then solicit consensus from a broader investment committee within the PEG. Once obtained, they strategize purchase offer details, including pricing, terms, funding, timing, and so forth, and proceed to negotiate the purchase. Once the deal is solidified, it may be only days or weeks until ownership is transferred.

The Build Phase

The longest phase is the build phase corresponding with the hold period. This is the most important component of the entire investment cycle and where the magic happens. The hold – which in truth is more accurately characterized as the *investment period* and what we'll call it from this point forward – is when equity partners work jointly with portfolio company executives and their management teams to establish a vision, organize and execute initiatives, integrate acquisitions, and grow the bottom line and add value to the company. In many respects, the investment period is the very opposite of holding still.

This period consists of preparing and organizing for the investment period, followed by achieving substantial and sustainable
growth, and finally showing or demonstrating that new as well
as future value to potential buyers. Building the business and
enhancing value is particularly hard work, typically requiring a
combination of infrastructure improvement, commercial growth,
and hopefully add-on acquisitions.

Sell and Reward

The final two phases are sell and reward. The PEG investment team
will decide when is the right time to sell the company. Various
considerations are included in the decision process, including value
creation achieved and opportunities remaining for the company,
length of time the business has been held, market conditions for
selling, likelihood of a buyer at the price that has been set, and so
on. Once sold, the private equity team then returns the principal to
the investors and shares the net gains with them, the PEG, and the
management team as well.

As seen in Figure 1.2, the buying and selling cycle may occur
several times for a single company as it progresses through new
venture or privately held status, to small-cap PEG ownership,
then one or more middle-market PEGs (lower, middle, and
upper-middle-market) and continuing to large-cap PEG or public
company status (of course, sometimes the next buyer is not another
fund, but another company interested in the portfolio company
as a strategic add-on acquisition). Regardless of who the buyer is,
once a favorable transaction is complete, the original investors and
management team are rewarded for their financial support and a
job well done.

The Motivation

There are considerable financial incentives for all the players in private equity – LPs, PEGs, and management teams – when portfolio
companies perform well and grow. To understand them fully let's

Portfolio Company ($ millions)	EBITDA	Transaction	Debt @ 50%	Equity		
				LP & GP	Portco	Total
Beginning EBITDA	$25m	$25m				
Purchase Multiple		10x				
Purchase Price		$250m	$125m	$125m	$0m	$125m
New Capability	$(5m)					
Improvement	$10m					
Organic Growth	$10m					
Add-Ons	$10m		$50m			
EBITDA Growth	$25m					
Debt Paydown			$(75m)			
Ending EBITDA	$50m	$50m				
Exit Multiple		12x				
Exit Price (& Ownership %)		$600m	$(100m)	91%	9%	$500m
Distributed Proceeds				$455m	$45m	$500m
Cash-on-Cash Return & Value Creation				3.6 x		$375m

Figure 1.4   Investment Period Economics

walk through a simplified story of a representative investment cycle described in Figure 1.4 to describe what happens between a hypothetical PEG, its limited partners, and a representative middle-market portco.

Investment Economics

The PEG does its due diligence and settles on a company it would like to purchase. It negotiates to buy the portco (a $25m EBITDA company) for a purchase price of the multiple 10× EBITDA ($250m), funding half with equity and half with debt. For the equity portion, it used $125m from the fund it had recently raised from LPs and financed the remaining $125m with new debt placed on the portfolio company's balance sheet.

Working together, the PEG and portco management team accomplish quite a bit of growth during the investment period. Early on under the direction and with the support of the PEG, the portco invested in additional leadership and capabilities totaling $5m in new annual operating expenses. Together they also undertook a series of internal improvement initiatives over the next five years, resulting in a total recurring annualized bottom-line benefit of $10m. They also completed various organic growth initiatives totaling another $10m of annualized bottom-line growth.

Around the middle of the investment period, the portco used accumulated cash and additional debt to make two small add-on purchases, adding a total of $10m of incremental EBITDA to the platform. Throughout the investment period, the company generated enough cash flow from operations to periodically pay down its debt to a remaining balance of $100m.

All these factors have contributed to the growth and long-term sustainability of the portco during the five-year investment period. It improved its infrastructure and capabilities, became more efficient, and grew organically as well as inorganically through acquisitions. The company fully doubled its EBITDA from $25m to $50m.

With another round of fundraising on the horizon, the PEG decides to sell the portco to provide a nice return to its LPs as well as justify raising more money so that it can continue to buy new platform companies. The PEG hires an investment bank to help prepare and position the company for sale and manage the selling process.

After several lengthy management presentations and detailed information sharing, the PEG receives three impressive offers. With input from portco management, the PEG selects a buyer and proceeds with the details of the sale transaction, including negotiations regarding pricing, terms, and conditions. Because of the portfolio company's impressive growth record and remaining opportunities, scaled and stable infrastructure, and skilled management team, the buyer was willing to pay "two turns" more than what the PEG originally paid – 12× EBITDA instead of 10×. The company was therefore sold for $600m, or 12× its $50m EBITDA. After paying off the remaining $100m debt, the transaction results in proceeds of $500m, representing a $375m gain over the original equity investment of $125m.

In this scenario, the investors realized a healthy 3.6× gross cash-on-cash return, receiving $455m in return for their original $125m investment. Of the $455m, investors paid the PEG $50m in the form of carried interest, which the PEG then applied toward operating expenses and firm-wide incentives. The portfolio company management team – specifically those having been awarded stock options early in the investment period – received a total of $45m (9%) of the proceeds.

After proceeds are distributed and the company keys are handed over, a new investment period begins with new owners – meaning that in addition to their exit proceeds the portfolio management team has earned the opportunity to do it all over again. Assuming continued growth rates from the new higher starting point, this next investment period could be even more lucrative for the portco team.

In addition to financial rewards, the nonfinancial rewards for both the PEG and portco management are also extremely fulfilling, because successfully navigating the investment period is an exciting challenge, offering unparalleled career growth opportunities and a deep sense of accomplishment from creating lasting value.

Equity Value Creation

Private equity groups communicate to prospective limited partners the breakdown of how they create equity value. The three typical primary sources for value creation during the investment period are debt reduction, multiple expansion, and EBITDA growth. Often (and certainly preferably), a portfolio company investment will generate equity value from all three categories. Sometimes an investment will realize value from only two or perhaps only one source, while the other sources remain stagnant or even deteriorate. While EBITDA growth is cause for particular pride, what matters at the end of any specific individual investment is the final total return on investment to the LPs.

Because the three categories are interrelated, teasing out the precise contribution from each is challenging; nevertheless, it is valuable to understand the relative contribution from each equity value driver category:

Debt reduction remains a viable and appropriate use of excess operating cash flows for value creation. Unlike other financial engineering methods used by some in the 1970s and 1980s, including risky deal structures, excessive incentives, aggressive accounting, and overextended leverage, debt reduction remains a sound strategy. PEGs utilize leverage, taking on debt in addition to equity, to fund the purchase of a business and then pay down that debt during the investment period. Similar to the benefit homeowners receive when paying off a portion of their mortgage, debt reduction is a smart strategy for investment period value creation.

Multiple expansion is realized when a buyer pays a higher multiple of earnings than did the seller previously. When the private equity space was in its infancy, it was much easier for PEGs to find a great private deal and buy a business at a relatively lower multiple and count on it to rise over time. Yet with the maturation of private equity, such "proprietary" deals are much less common, and purchase multiples are nowadays strongly influenced by the competitive market. When multiples across the private equity industry are rising, tailwinds are with the investors. But when multiples are stagnant or dropping, headwinds are strong and increases the need to achieve other equity value drivers to offset the loss from multiple contraction.

EBITDA growth therefore is usually the key today to creating equity value. The financial crisis of 2008 was an event that really brought commercial and operations improvement into focus as the third and arguably the most important value driver. Growing and improving businesses is the best bet for increasing the underlying value of an investment, thereby encouraging buyers to "pay up" for an attractive business.

Figure 1.5 offers a hypothetical example of relative value creation from each of the three sources described above. In this example, EBITDA growth from a combination of new capabilities, internal efficiencies, organic revenue growth, and new add-on acquisitions drove the most equity value – roughly six times the value created from both debt reduction and multiple expansion.

Value Creation ($ millions)	Buy	Relative Value Creation by Source			Sell
		Debt Reduction	Multiple Expansion	EBITDA Growth	
EBITDA	$25m	$25m	$25m	$55m	$55m
Multiple	10x	10x	12x	10x	12x
Enterprise Value	$250m	$250m	$300m	$550m	$660m
Debt	$125m	$75m	$125m	$125m	$75m
Equity	$125m	$175m	$175m	$425m	$585m
Equity Value Creation	–	> $50m	> $50m	> $300m	$460m

Note:
■ Blue highlighted boxes in source columns refer to the primary changed field to reflect relative impact

Figure 1.5 Value Creation by Source

Despite the clear advantages of focusing on EBITDA growth, PEGs and portcos have often struggled to significantly improve it and therefore have failed to reach their potential as a constructive partnership during the investment period. The reasons for this are many, and understanding and overcoming them is not easy. Indeed, as the title of this book suggests, *Restructuring the Hold* is the necessary next step in the evolution of the PEG and portco relationship to successfully grow and add value to portfolio companies. Doing so requires rethinking how PEGs and portcos can work collaboratively and complementarily to achieve these outcomes. That story is the focus of the rest of the book.

Chapter 2

New Ownership

Driving down Colorado Route 301 Monday morning, GrammCo CEO Dianne Franklin caught herself smiling with pride. After Russ Gramm handed her the reins three years ago, Dianne and her team continued to grow the business without missing a beat. Three years of double-digit expansion is certainly something to be proud of, and when Russ said he was ready to sell, Dianne knew the growth she had shepherded was a major factor. She smiled as she recalled the bankers using the phrase "monies moved" when the transaction was completed. Some of that money had also moved into her bank account; not enough to make her want to retire, but certainly enough to permit a little

(continued)

(*continued*)

accentuated head-bobbing as she belted out Springsteen's *Born to Run.*

As the final chords drift away, Dianne's attention turned to her executive team. The last several weeks had been a very trying time for those few "in the know." While continuing to keep a close eye on the running of the business, they had to prepare and present GrammCo for sale. They put in even longer than usual hours, giving presentations, attending dinners, responding to questions from half a dozen different potential buyers, and posting reams of diligence information to the virtual data room as the suitors increasingly asked for more and more minutia.

The team did a great job and had told the story of GrammCo well. While staying outwardly focused, Dianne knew they were worried about what the future would bring. Now it had arrived in the form of new ownership – and private equity owners at that. While no one on her team had worked for a portfolio company of a private equity firm before, all of them had heard stories of sharp-elbowed Wall Street types running their firms from their phones and cutting costs from their spreadsheets at their big-city offices back east.

Dianne had concerns of her own. She was confident in her role as CEO going forward – her new equity partners had made sure of that – but something else nagged at her: Big Brother. As Patterson Lake's operating partner now responsible for GrammCo, Shed Cooper was their new chairman of the board and therefore her new boss. *Shed said he likes to be involved and that he'll be on-site quite a bit,* Dianne mused. *I wonder just what that really means ...*

She had a sense of what *involved* meant from the diligence he and the investment partner Ocie Gleason did on GrammCo. They had listened more intently to GrammCo's presentations, had more questions, and asked for more information than any other prospective buyer. Both Shed and Ocie had an easy manner to them and Dianne already had established a good rapport with both. It was clear to her that the equity partners at Patterson Lake would be hands-on. But would they let her run the company she had been so ably helming for the past three years?

She knew she had a lot to learn about what it meant to run a company during an investment period, while Shed and Ocie clearly knew their stuff, having done it many times before. Patterson Lake was plainly a principled organization that expected accountability. But if accountability was only viewed through the lens of the short-term bottom line, it would lead to cutting corners. She had seen GrammCo's competition do the same, and knew GrammCo's preeminence in the market was in no small part due to their people, the fact that they did not cut corners, and the value they offered their customers.

Was it too much to hope that Shed saw things the same way? She had inklings that he did and had the same approach to leadership as she did: to help the people around you grow and flourish. One thing was certain: She knew that her success depended on a close partnership with Shed, Ocie, and everyone else at Patterson Lake.

The Ideal Partnership

Restructuring the Hold is premised on establishing solid and rewarding relationships between the PEG and portfolio company management. As CEO Dianne Franklin illustrates in our GrammCo narrative, there's not a universal understanding of what that entails. It's worth pausing then to consider what a productive versus unproductive relationship looks like – both the strengths and benefits of a constructive partnership and the different ways it can go off the rails.

Constructive Partnerships

Constructive partnerships are effective and rewarding because there is close alignment in a shared attitude of *collaboration* and a recognition that each team brings complementary *capabilities*. Collaborative attitudes are based on trust, where the PEG and portco feel free to have open and candid discourse, sometimes spirited but always respectful. Both teams have realistic expectations of the other and appreciate the other's capabilities. They take active steps to continuously nurture their relationship, realizing collaboration serves to optimize enterprise value.

PEGs with a collaborative mindset take the time to truly understand their portcos, including what formed the basis for the company's past successes as well as what inspires each management team member going forward. They ask provocative questions, introduce better practices and proven frameworks for creating value, illuminate opportunities for growth while mitigating risks, and support their portcos where and when needed – all the while appreciating that it's the portco running the company and not the PEG. These PEGs know when and, where to poke and prod, and just as important, know when and where to quietly take a back seat and let management do their thing.

Portcos who value collaboration similarly take the time to understand their PEG partners and the private equity investment cycle. They grasp what's important to PEGs as they work to provide sufficient returns to their investors within an expected investment period. These portcos appreciate the unique perspectives of their PEG and are receptive to their active involvement leveraging their experience in facilitating value creation. They realize that only together will they maximize exit value. And like their PEG partners, collaborative portcos know when and where to accept pushback and direction in the spirit of a genuine constructive partnership.

Destructive Partnerships

Destructive partnerships represent the negative extreme, where neither PEG nor portco authentically collaborates with the other or truly values the other's capabilities. Relationships are strained and sometimes contentious, as PEGs resort to being prescriptive and heavy-handed while portcos opt for being closeminded, defensive, or even passive-aggressive. In these cases, neither PEG nor portco bring their best or accept the best from the other.

When this happens, whether from the beginning of the investment period or emerging during it, trust between the PEG and portco plummets and one or both stop listening to the other. Team spirit, individual drive, and personal ownership falter – sometimes significantly. Both PEG and portco are unable to leverage each other's capabilities and therefore fail to create the value they would have otherwise had they collaborated.

A destructive PEG/portco partnership does not necessarily mean the enterprise value will not grow. But it does mean that the growth won't be nearly as much as it otherwise could have been, and the investment period certainly won't be as enjoyable as it could have been for either the PEG or the portco – a sad and disappointing outcome but one that is avoidable as well.

Partnership Matrix

As shown in Figure 2.1, constructive PEG/portco partnerships enjoy collaborative attitudes and complementary capabilities. Destructive partnerships have contentious attitudes and separate, nonleveraged capabilities. But if attitudes are collaborative but capabilities limited and uncomplementary, they have a superficial partnership – they get along great but don't bring much to the party. And in situations where capabilities are significant and complementary but attitudes are contentious, the PEG and portco miss out on the opportunity to work together to drive real value.

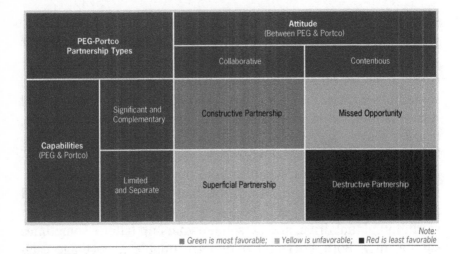

PEG-Portco Partnership Types		Attitude (Between PEG & Portco)	
		Collaborative	Contentious
Capabilities (PEG & Portco)	Significant and Complementary	Constructive Partnership	Missed Opportunity
	Limited and Separate	Superficial Partnership	Destructive Partnership

Note:
■ *Green is most favorable;* ■ *Yellow is unfavorable;* ■ *Red is least favorable*

Figure 2.1   PEG/Portco Partnership Types

Anticipating Management Sentiment

The early days of the investment period are particularly critical ones – maybe the most critical. What happens during these first days and weeks sets the stage for the next few years. And while a stage once set can be reset, it's easier to begin working from the same script.

For the management team under new private equity ownership, the early days are often characterized by a general uneasiness about what the future might hold and anxiety about future relationships with the individuals associated with the private equity firm. Specific roles may change and business direction may be altered, but however that is manifested, management realizes that the status quo no longer exists.

Effective stage-setting by the PEG relies on open-mindedness, attention to relationships, and expectation setting. Making generalized or hasty assumptions, engaging in opaque maneuvers, or taking hardline stands are especially problematic at this point, and only serve to erode any trust that had been building since diligence started. It's important for the PEG and portco alike to invest the time to understand each other and to understand roles and expectations going forward.

One of the most important aspects of the investment period is grasping how it typically unfolds from the portfolio company's perspective. The ability by the PEG to anticipate the sentiments experienced by the portco team over time is important, enabling the riding out of lows and leveraging highs. Collaborative PEGs have both the desire as well as the competencies to help their portfolio company management teams work through the change, understanding that transitioning to new ownership can be unsettling. They grasp the natural change cycle of such a transition and work carefully with their management teams to help them settle into the new ownership model. They distinguish themselves from those PEGs who either haven't the compassion or the capabilities to support their management teams to get through the rough patches and lack the patience for management concerns as they transition to a new owner.

Once the transaction is completed, the management team will generally experience a range of emotions. The rollercoaster typically lasts several months and progresses through a series of up and down sentiments and outlooks regarding company and career prospects. Figure 2.2 illustrates the typical change curve experienced by a portfolio company management team during this time.

Preacquisition

The initial feelings of anxiety and even disorientation start at due diligence for those who are aware of a likely sale. That sentiment spreads to other observant employees as they notice increased closed-door meetings, unexplained executive absences, and strange visitors asking lots of questions. As word gets out of an impending sale, many in the company find themselves in limbo, waiting for the sale and worrying about the future. They wonder if they'll enjoy working for new owners and whether their roles within the company will change. Most people don't like change, particularly change they had no part in initiating.

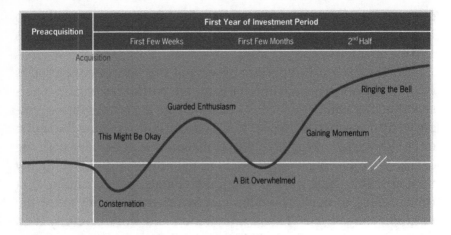

Figure 2.2 First-Year Management Sentiment

Consternation (Chapter 3)

For the first several weeks of the investment period, there is plenty of nervousness and confusion, particularly around the role of the PEG and their operational involvement, as well as possible changes to the leadership structure. Savvy PEGs will spend time clarifying the expectations as well as the opportunities of the investment period and defining the key roles and responsibilities of both the PEG and the portco. An essential element of this phase is properly onboarding all the key players together, setting expectations, and getting to know each other. Particularly during the first month or so, PEG and portco leadership spend a lot of time together and begin (at least subconsciously) to establish and reinforce a shared set of core values that will guide decisions and actions going forward.

This Might Be Okay (Chapter 4)

Typically following the first few weeks of the investment period, consternation begins to subside as portco management starts to feel comfortable with the new ownership. PEG and portco have gotten to know each other a bit, and in the case of collaborative PEGs it's starting to look like the movies about private equity were wrong. This period is characterized by several key fundamental activities – intentionally working to establish trusting relationships, achieving a common understanding of the baseline and goals for the investment period, and putting in place basic reporting that will serve to keep everyone on the same page. During this period, both the PEG and the portco teams begin to feel that they are going to be successful working together – and might even enjoy themselves in the process.

Guarded Enthusiasm (Chapter 5)

Around (give or take) three months into the investment period, the management team typically becomes encouraged and even enthused. PEGs in constructive partnerships with their portfolio company have likely instilled some new energy into the company. They've posed questions and ideas they found successful at other companies with different management teams and during previous investment periods. They've identified issues and challenges that are unique to the company and have begun to address them as well. The PEG typically has additional investment capital at the ready, and the entire team begins to envision big and exciting things. This period is marked by embracing priorities to accelerate value and by putting in place the processes to coordinate and manage new initiatives being formed. Together both teams begin to reach consensus regarding what will best drive value during the investment period and what resources will be needed to plan, monitor, and accelerate value creation.

A Bit Overwhelmed (Chapter 6)

This is when things begin to get busy – very busy. At four or five months into the partnership, there are probably 15 to 20 significant initiatives underway. Beyond that, the PEG team is holding management's feet to the fire in terms of meeting goals and fulfilling expectations. There have been update meetings and the PEG is posing difficult questions about milestone dates and why deadlines are slipping and return-on-investment (ROI) commitments not being met. The management team is feeling the accountability-heat for sure. During this period, forward-looking PEGs help portcos address leadership readiness and accountability, initiative team composition, and active program management.

Gaining Momentum (Chapter 7)

About midway through the first year, things truly start to click. By now both teams know each other quite well and are more efficient and effective at getting things done as a joint PEG/portco team. There are numerous worthwhile initiatives underway, and both partners know where they are heading and have the confidence they'll get there. Already some wins have been recorded on the initiative scorecard, and overall both the PEG and portco are energized. But typically around this time, some frustrations emerge as the portco starts to transition to the "next level" of operating performance. This is when hands-on PEGs help the management team increase its efficacy by addressing performance measures and operating cadence and refocus its energies on working together toward a shared vision.

Ringing the Bell (Chapter 8)

Before either PEG or portco know it, the end of the first year of the investment period arrives – one down and somewhere between two and six to go. Together, they evaluate the ground they have covered these past 12 months and then focus on planning for the coming year. They review practical executive feedback and development approaches that are appropriate for lower middle-market private equity and the associated investment period. By this point, the team has "rung the bell" multiple times when successfully completing important initiatives. The ending of the year involves rewards and recognition, formalized reloading of strategic initiatives, and the budgeting process for the coming year. After the first year, routines have been well-established within the company and sentiment has stabilized. That's not to say that there are not new challenges ahead that might pose their own particular challenges and anxieties. The last three chapters look specifically at changes during subsequent years in the investment period and note any particular sentiments that might bubble up as a result of these major events.

Improving Infrastructure (Chapter 9)

By now the team is quite proficient at improvement initiatives and is likely working through a second (or even third or fourth) wave. These often address increased efficiencies, improved infrastructure, and new capabilities. Initiatives may include enhancements to working capital, organizational restructuring efforts, and additional operational improvement work such as technology-enabled process redesigns, new systems implementations, and lean operations. To help fund these improvements, the company likely had initiated earlier initiatives focused on sourcing and working capital as these often result in quicker results with very high ROI.

Expanding Beyond (Chapter 10)

By the third year, the company will have incorporated better information (such as insights into true cost and profitability) to optimize their portfolios of offerings and customers, enable pricing enhancements, and facilitate new customer acquisitions and offerings. At this point, add-on acquisitions often represent an important growth accelerator. Acquisitions bring new challenges to the management team – often challenges not previously encountered – as they must not only run their day-to-day business and continue progress on EBITDA initiatives (perhaps those associated with sales pipeline management and new service offerings) but also now integrate the newly acquired business. Identifying and truly integrating acquisitions is complicated and time-consuming work. With so many balls in the air, management must be particularly attentive to maintaining a positive bottom-line trajectory.

The Exit (Chapter 11)

Inevitably, the PEG in concert with the portco management team will decide the time is right to sell the business and to provide a return to the investors. Maybe they've grown EBITDA nicely, or the market is "frothy," or there's a buyer knocking on the door. Whatever the reasons, the investment period culminates in preparing for and executing a successful sale or "exit." A PEG's exit from its investment requires quite a bit of preparation on behalf of the management team. If the last few years have progressed as expected, the exit also includes financial rewards, personal and team recognition, and new opportunities with new ownership. If executed well, exits are experienced not simply as endings but also as promising new beginnings – particularly if management just enjoyed a successful investment period characterized by opportunity, professional growth, and a genuinely constructive partnership with its PEG.

Key Investment Period Roles

A first and important step in alleviating the anxieties that accompany the consternation phase is by articulating the various roles and responsibilities the PEG will be assuming during the investment period. A constructive partnership relies on everyone knowing not just what to expect but *whom* to expect it from. A constructive partnership will never get off the ground if PEGs do not take the time to articulate specific roles and responsibilities associated with the private equity firm. If they wrongly presume the portfolio company management team is familiar with PEG roles or assume they'll figure it out over time – or worst of all, think it doesn't matter because management doesn't really need to know – the PEG is just sowing the seeds for an unproductive relationship.

Smart PEGs do not leave roles and responsibilities to chance; rather, they work with portco management to define, document, and even adjust responsibilities over time as the company and situation evolve. They understand that the transition to new ownership and a new firm can be confusing, and the roles are not always clear.

They grasp that the PEG/portco relationship will be much better served and indeed become a constructive partnership through role clarity.

The sooner a PEG can help portfolio company management understand the differences and learn to work with the nuances involved in private equity, the quicker the management team can get down to the real business of driving EBITDA growth over the investment period.

PEG Equity Partners: Investing and Operating

The PEG leadership roles working most closely with a portfolio company include those related specifically to investing and operating. These can be filled either by a single equity partner or by two equity partners – an *investing partner* (IP) and an *operating partner* (OP). Regardless of the coverage model, equity partners are often responsible for overseeing several portfolio companies at once. They are the individuals assigned to lead the investment period on behalf of the PEG from purchase through exit. While the IP and OP interact and work with the entire portco executive team, it's the CEO and CFO with whom they'll spend much of their time.

The IP often serves as point person interacting with the PEG investment committee. As shown in Figure 2.3, along with various junior investing team members and supported by banks, lawyers, and accounting firms, the IP has the responsibility to find, evaluate, justify, finance, and ultimately purchase the original platform portfolio company. Similarly, the IP is responsible for working with portfolio company management to identify and complete add-on company acquisitions. At the end of the investment period, it's the IP who takes the lead in facilitating the sale. Responsibilities at exit include engaging a sell-side investment bank, selecting a buyer, coordinating negotiations, and ensuring that relevant legal and financing requirements are covered to finalize the sale transaction.

The role of the PEG OP has historically been much less defined and certainly less standardized among private equity firms. The OP may serve as chairperson of the board for the portfolio company,

Private Equity Phase vs Roles	Investing Responsibilities	Operating Responsibilities
1. Find	• Network in target industries *Lead* • Review numerous offering memorandums • Conduct first company visits and meetings	• Suggest industry and company characteristics best suited to PEG's operating capabilities
2. Purchase	• Complete due diligence *Lead* • Evaluate value creation opportunities • Model financials and expected returns • Convince investing committee of company value	• Participate in diligence (focused on team, capabilities) • Draft preliminary value creation strategies
3. Grow	• Support ensuring right executive team • Support driving strategies and initiatives • Identify, fund and acquire add-on acquisitions • Maintain audit, compliance, legal, lenders	• Ensure and enhance the right executive team *Lead* • Drive strategies and initiatives • Confirm budgets, accountabilities, and incentives • Oversee performance and govern the business
4. Sell	• Retain investment bank *Lead* • Coordinate sale terms and selling decisions • Distribute proceeds to investors and others	• Highlight investment period accomplishments • Articulate remaining opportunities for new owners • Prepare company operations for upcoming sale

Figure 2.3 Private Equity Investing and Operating Responsibilities

as a board director, or serve strictly in a limited advisory capacity. Particularly if operating at the board level, the OP typically has the responsibility to confirm or adjust executive team composition and to work with them to establish portfolio company vision. They help identify and execute strategic initiatives and generally provide operating governance and oversight for business performance throughout the investment period.

The Importance of the PEG Operating Partner

Serving as lead for only a quarter of the private equity phases depicted in Figure 2.3 might make one think the OP has only a quarter of the equity partner workload. Nothing could be further from the truth. PEGs look to their OP to guide the portco management team in growing EBITDA during the entire multiyear investment period. The OP role often has these responsibilities:

Confirm CEO and board participation. The OP is responsible for ensuring that the portco has the right executive leadership and company governance. The OP often has the point relationship with the CEO and each of the board directors and works closely with the CEO during the entire investment period.

Establish vision and strategies. The OP helps establish a clear and well-documented vision for the portfolio company focused on the investment period. He or she further facilitates the development of concise strategies to achieve that vision.

Refine leaders and key roles. The OP assists in defining leadership needs and requirements, evaluating current executives and managers, and developing or replacing them as needed to ensure the right talent is in place.

Execute strategic initiatives and value creation. The OP organizes what we call the Value Creation Program – the set of key initiatives, objectives, milestones, timing, resources, and responsibilities to achieve the strategies and intended EBITDA growth of the investment period.

Establish commercial plans and operational budgets. The OP establishes expectations around requirements and timelines for annual plans and budgets, including key performance indicators and targets. He or she usually works with the CEO and the CFO along with sales and other executives to accomplish this.

Incentivize and manage performance. The OP typically provides the CEO with ongoing and annual performance feedback and developmental support and offers the same with the CEO for the rest of the executive team. He or she should be integral in helping the CEO drive continued improvement in operating performance.

Provide leadership steering support. The OP often assumes a seat on various steering committees for the most important, risky, or otherwise difficult initiatives. The OP will help guide the implementation teams, leveraging his or her experience from other companies. The OP will typically introduce external consultants as needed.

Report to PEG colleagues. The OP has responsibilities to provide periodic reporting and ad-hoc communication back to his or her PEG colleagues. This is both necessary and important to keep the PEG and limited partners informed regarding the status of their investment dollars.

The operating partner plays an important role for both the port-folio company and the PEG. It's a sophisticated and nuanced role, requiring the OP at different times to serve as the CEO's boss or confidant, as an extension of the CEO, or as a utility player who jumps in and helps with guiding the team and executing strategies. The OP needs to pose the right questions at the right time, read the tea leaves of the moment, and problem-solve company needs at any given time. He or she needs to monitor sentiment and man-age the various expectations within the portco and between it and the PEG.

Portco CEO and CFO

Most readers will be familiar with the general roles and responsibil-ities of a CEO and a CFO. But for a private equity portfolio company, the CEO and CFO roles are uniquely circumscribed by the specific time horizons and unique scrutiny of the investment period.

These emerge most clearly when contrasting their role with other CEOs and CFOs outside of the private equity space. For example, public company CEOs and CFOs are focused on quarterly results. No matter how big or small, positive progress quarter over quarter is key. Analysts watch this carefully, as do the stockholders as owners. At the other extreme are closely held or family busi-nesses. Many have been in operation for years, passing through one or more generations. These are typically run for the long-term and focus on cash flow to support the owner's lifestyle. The time horizon for the CEO and CFO of a closely held or family business is therefore essentially a lifetime or several lifetimes.

A portfolio company that has been bought by a PEG sits between those extremes with respect to its time horizon. The finite and relatively short investment periods of private equity necessitate a different mindset for the portco CEO and executive team. While they do need to concern themselves with quarterly performance and keep the distant future in mind, portco executives must focus on driving as much value as they can during the investment period. Their mindset should change linearly as the likely exit date approaches, and investment decisions and risk tolerances are particularly impacted as an expected exit gets closer and closer.

The level of scrutiny is also different for the portfolio company CEO and CFO. For public companies, the stockholders and analysts monitor every single word of every quarterly call and every number of every published financial statement. They scrutinize trading volume and press releases like hawks, but the information they monitor is limited to publicly available information. For family or privately held businesses, the opposite prevails. They have virtually no scrutiny from anyone aside from interested family members who have (or may one day have) a stake in the business. As you can imagine, family dynamics add another level of complexity for these businesses.

For a PEG portfolio company, the CEO, CFO, and executive team can expect a significant amount of scrutiny from the PEG team – not only the IP and the OP but also a variety of junior analysts crunching numbers back at firm headquarters. And this scrutiny (with all the associated real and perceived second-guessing) pertains not only to published figures and commentary but to all the internal intricacies and details of the business.

We've found this continuous contact by the PEG to be one of the most difficult adjustments for executives new to private equity. It is especially hard for a CEO who has often been used to full authority and full control. That CEO may have gone from having virtually no day-to-day oversight outside of quarterly board meetings to weekly and often daily contact from their equity partners. That level of interaction is a hard thing for many first-time portfolio company leaders to get used to.

Additional PEG Roles: Finance Director, Program Manager, and Business Intelligence Analyst

Forward-looking PEGs recognize that while the importance of the IP and OP is indisputable, maximizing the value of middle-market portcos during the investment period requires additional support on the PEG side of the partnership. These PEGs often realize significant value from ensuring the following roles (or at least related responsibilities) are available for their portcos (whether shared across several portfolio companies or housed within a specific one):

Finance director (FD). Because financial reporting and compliance are so critical to the PEG, their investors, and the lenders, the PEG often assigns their own FD to work side-by-side with several portco CFOs. In addition to guiding reporting and compliance, the FD typically supports the development of best practices, including those associated with month-end close, cash modeling and management, bank reporting and covenant compliance, and performance reporting and analytics.

Program manager (PM). The PM is often responsible for working with the OP and the executive team to define, organize, and accelerate the Value Creation Program of key initiatives during the investment period. Beyond simply status reporting, this role should be a value-added one and should include working with executives and team leaders to document scope, quantify ROI, establish work plans, and achieve milestones for all the Value Creation Program initiatives.

Business intelligence (BI) *analyst.* In larger companies, many functional areas often have a business analyst. But in middle-market, particularly lower middle-market, few if any dedicated business analysts exist. Smart equity partners will ensure the presence of the BI skillset in their portfolio companies to provide invaluable analytical support. Their detailed multidimensional analytics inform key decisions around geographies, customers, offerings, pricing, and so forth.

These roles not only benefit the bottom line but help ensure that a genuine constructive partnership emerges between the PEG and portco. Shortsighted PEGs and portcos may respond with eye-rolling when these roles are discussed. *Too expensive,* they might say, or *we're not ready for it.* They're often excessively focused on cost containment rather than broader value creation. But if properly sponsored, scoped, and resourced, each of these three roles can be invaluable in helping portco executive teams improve and accelerate real and significant EBITDA growth – paying for themselves many times over and solidifying the partnership.

IP, OP, and CEO

The connection between the investing partner, operating partner, and CEO is perhaps the most critical relationship within the PEG/portco partnership. We find that supporting and trusting relationships among the IP, OP, and CEO serve as an early indicator of overall investment success. Wise equity partners work hard to nurture these relationships into mutually respectful, supportive, and trusting ones, not only because of their intrinsic value but also because it leads to a rewarding and enjoyable investment period experience for the whole team. Wise CEOs similarly recognize that they can benefit and grow from such a relationship and foster the connection.

Achieving this kind of relationship benefits from frequency in the number of authentic and positive reinforcing interactions among these three leaders. Frequency leads to familiarity, and familiarity is an essential component for trust. The importance of the in-person connection among these three individuals cannot be overemphasized.

Operating Partner Involvement

A key element for the smooth inauguration of a new investment period is to clearly articulate the level of involvement the OP will have in the portfolio company. Without a sense of how the relationship will unfold, CEOs may feel threatened or undermined. A constructive partnership requires the active involvement of both the OP and CEO to make it work.

Some PEGs act imprudently by having little-to-no operating partner involvement or assigning a figurehead providing little if any value. Others maintain contact through an informal cadre of external consultants. But PEGs that want to forge a genuine collaborative relationship carefully assign an OP to each portfolio company, taking into consideration skillset, experience, and specific characteristics of the OP as well as industry and company situation. These PEGs endeavor to find the right fit for each portfolio company and expect the OP will adjust their involvement in the company depending on the specific situation and need at any given time.

Model Alternatives

There is no single best OP business model suitable for all private equity firms. There exist several typical varieties, and we presume that each form has its appropriate home, depending on the culture and organization of the PEG. The range of OP models can be described along several axes, including assigned role, level of specialization, type of deployment, and compensation structure:

Assigned role of the OP. This offers perhaps the most variety, ranging from executive or nonexecutive chairperson of the board, through board director, board advisor, steering committee member, active program manager, PEG-sponsored consultant, and finally to a portco-hired consultant limited to specific efforts. While there are circumstances and reasons for adopting each of the different roles for the OP, in this book we assume the OP serves as chairperson or vice chairperson, with the CEO reporting to him or her.

Level of specialization of the OP. Sometimes the OP role calls for a generalist with broad expertise across several industries and functional areas; other times the role demands specialized skills and experiences. These can take the form of an industry expert or a functional expert, for instance someone particularly adept at sales and marketing or supply chain operations. Another type of assigned expertise could be a solutions expert with subject matter expertise in a specific area, such as pricing or transportation logistics. Depending on PEG and portco circumstances, situations exist for each option. In this book, we assume the OP serves as a generalist.

Type of OP deployment. One type is PEG-sponsored, whereby the PEG specifically employs and assigns the OP to companies within its portfolio, either as a PEG employee or a dedicated contractor. Alternatively, the PEG may choose to require the portfolio company to retain and compensate the OP as approved by the board of directors. In either case, deployment might range from the OP watching over several portfolio companies at once to working full-time or part-time in a single company. While many forms of deployment can work, this book assumes the OP is PEG-sponsored and watches over two to four portfolio companies.

Compensation structure. This represents a fourth variable in the PEG's definition of its OP model. At one extreme, the PEG may provide a combination of base salary, performance bonus, carry in the fund, and an opportunity to co-invest their own money in the fund as well. At the other extreme, the PEG may require the portco to compensate the OP by a simple time-and-expense approach. We believe most PEGs are best served by aligning OP interests both to the portco as well as to the overall fund.

Forward-thinking PEGs tend to prefer models where the operating partner is assigned more authority, covers a few companies, has broad capabilities and experiences, and has a compensation structure that rewards according to the performance of their assigned portcos as well as to the performance of the fund. That said, each PEG should define its specific OP approach that best fits its firm's needs, culture, and portfolio company situations.

Variable Involvement

The operating partner's involvement in a portfolio company will vary over the course of the investment cycle. As shown in Figure 2.4, the OP's involvement starts with due diligence, increasing as the acquisition becomes likely. Once the purchase transaction is complete, the OP will spend the first several weeks working with the executive team for two-way onboarding, defining the Value Creation

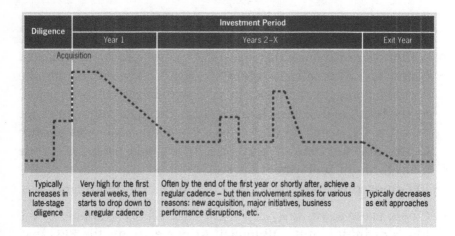

Figure 2.4   Operating Partner Involvement over Time

Plan, and launching of key initiatives. This early scope will likely require significant OP time.

Within a few months, as the operating cadence is effective and value-creating initiatives are underway, the OP will begin to reduce involvement and transition to a more steady-state level of involvement. Often, that means being on-site a couple of days every two or three weeks, helping to steer key initiatives, participating in monthly operating reviews, and leading quarterly board meetings.

Throughout the rest of the investment period, there will be occasion for increased OP involvement. For instance, in the case of an add-on acquisition or a major new initiative such as building a new facility, the OP's time will spike until that change initiative is stable or nearing completion.

Very late in the investment period, the OP role will likely take a back seat as the IP moves to the fore, working with investment banks and the management team to prepare for and market the business for sale.

All that said, sometimes extraordinary things happen: an unexpected downside of the business or an overall shift in market dynamics – even natural disasters that impact the bottom line. In such cases, the OP may become even as involved as the portco CEO to help get things back on track. OP involvement should be fluid and flexible to achieve a genuine constructive partnership with the portco CEO and management team.

Key Characteristics of the Operating Partner

There is no single set of characteristics that serve to produce capable OPs. Successful OPs have emerged from a variety of backgrounds, but many either ran large businesses or served as highly successful operations consulting partners. Their backgrounds often include a progression of career experiences leading to multiple significant transformational results.

But to really understand what makes an effective OP, we need to look at the personality and underlying core characteristics of the successful ones. We find there are at least four key characteristics that serve the role well:

A driven servant-leader. The term *servant-leader* is overused these days, which is unfortunate because the concept is quite appropriate for the operating partner in private equity. We put the word *driven* before it because the OP must be a self-starter who is obsessed with uncovering opportunities to help people flourish and companies grow. Instead of a leadership model that relies on gathering and exercising power, servant-leaders make it their mission to drive growth by tapping into the strengths of those around them. The servant-leader in private equity is not only comfortable with but moreover seeks opportunities to provide active and substantial behind-the-scenes support to portfolio company executives as they grow and flourish in their roles. They model what authentic collaborative relationships look and feel like.

An intuitive creator. The intuitive creator leverages past experiences to generate entirely new ideas for the betterment of a specific portfolio company in a specific situation in time. The OP should have many years of leadership experience at different levels, typically across several industries, companies, management teams, and situations. That experience serves to provide the fodder for intuition as they encounter new situations. They should have the creative initiative to establish new ways to address difficult problems and unique opportunities. In addition, because the OP should be a good sparring partner with the CEO and his or her team, the OP should regularly introduce challenging and provocative questions, creative ideas, and new thinking to keep the executive team focused on problem-solving through effective and often unique answers.

A skilled diplomat. While difficult to define as well as to measure, this is a third critical quality in OP leadership. By virtue of working in side-by-side collaboration with private equity firm leadership, the IP, the portco CEO, their executive team, and all the various professional service providers utilized, the OP by definition needs to be a skilled diplomat. The OP sits at the center of every critical decision, including strategic priorities, organizational restructuring, and initiative priority. At the same time, the OP must be able to at a moment's notice transform from head of the board to coach or mentor, from sparring partner to hands-on helper. They must be skillful at facilitating progress in difficult situations while enabling face-saving for those who need it. Because he or she works with the various interested parties and serves as the glue between them all, the OP must be able to work with and earn the trust of everyone. It requires skilled diplomacy to get everyone to work collaboratively.

A principled individual. Operating partners must separate themselves from portco politics and biases. They bring objectivity and a unique voice that rises above the fray. The OP should not be egotistical but rather have high integrity, consistently conveying an authentic presence and working hard to positively impact outcomes. OPs understand that what they do influences the lives of others. Sometimes an OP needs to make or influence weighty decisions that may be difficult for some people to accept. But OPs must always have empathy and compassion and be respectful in all their dealings. A constructive partnership between portco management and the OP relies critically on OPs being forthright in their interactions.

Core Values

Beginning to establish trusting and collaborative partnerships as the PEG/portco team onboards together gets right to the issue of core values as a foundation for moving forward. Private equity has the reputation of harboring ruthless investors, and certain PEGs perpetuate that reputation by having neither the time nor the patience for articulating and embodying overarching values driving the firm.

In a similar fashion, portco executives do a great disservice to their companies, employees, and customers if they, too, don't have core values guiding their business. They are failing to instill a key ingredient in creating a great and lasting company – particularly in growing lower middle-market companies, where many new faces, few common experiences, and a lack of well-honed processes and documented policies make cultivated values critical.

Nature abhors a vacuum: Like it or not, if PEGs and portcos don't consciously cultivate values they choose, others will show up anyway. We've all seen our fair share of companies rampant with politics, passive-aggressiveness, and punch-the-clock attitudes. But when a company cultivates good values, the opposite occurs: Buy-in means not just management but all employees embrace the company mission and work hard to see it implemented. But values must be habitually practiced if they are truly authentic. If a company says it values integrity but indirectly rewards salespeople for disparaging the competition, then in fact it does not value integrity. Actions certainly speak louder than words.

A company's values represent its fundamental beliefs and standards for all decision-making, directly influencing strategic priorities, value proposition, approach to the market, and business objectives. While a company's strategies, leaders, and employees may change over the years, well-honed core values are resilient. Values therefore not only help explain history but, more importantly, help shape a company's future.

A constructive partnership between PEG and portco requires both teams to embrace shared values if decisions are going to be made together instead of independently or be imposed. That's not to say that there won't be disagreements regarding the expression of those values, but articulating shared values will serve as a foundation for all interactions, discussions, and actions across the company. Together, equity partners and management teams should make a concerted effort to formulate, perpetuate, and demonstrate their core values in all dealings.

Opportunity Gained

Investment periods are short. They need core values from which to effectively guide equity partners and portco executives as they hire new leaders, change out poor performers, set strategies and launch initiatives, negotiate with customers, and select suppliers. Properly nurtured, values are ingrained, consistent, and perceptible – in fact, palpable. They serve to build trust and foster loyalty, providing bedrock from which to judge and act.

Exemplifying core values starts with the CEO, OP, and IP, as well as the portco leadership team. Unless the leaders articulate and live their company's set of core values and challenge decisions and actions that are inconsistent with them, the company will be rudderless and head in the wrong direction. Equity partners and portfolio company executives need to take every available opportunity to do and reinforce the right thing – actions which will be based on their values.

When you read about GrammCo and Patterson Lake Capital, you'll see two companies that share the same values. Each firm is purposeful, practical, and principled, guided by a common commitment to integrity, compassion, and authenticity:

Purposeful. You'll see both companies pledge themselves to specific, meaningful outcomes, embracing ownership, and accountability. You'll see both the CEO and the OP be intentional in their actions, eagerly targeting, tracking, and triaging progress.

Practical. Individuals at both firms sort through complexity quickly, focusing on materiality and needle-movers. Neither the equity partners nor the management team have time for posturing.

The OP and CEO feel no need to be the smartest person in the room but rather to be the objective brokers of great ideas, realistic plans, and hard-to-find talent in order to get things done quickly.

Principled. The leaders of both teams embrace authenticity and are proud to be themselves – real people working to get good stuff done quickly. Integrity is paramount at GrammCo and Patterson Lake Capital, and both companies strive to choose what's right in all situations. Everyone acts in an understated manner to achieve the best outcome with the intent of serving others with compassion.

PEG and portco leadership should start every new investment period together by first defining (or refining) their shared values. Many organizational development firms can help the PEG/portco team explore, craft, and communicate the values that are right for the specific company. They can help the team evaluate their company's history and mission, brainstorm with key personnel, and iterate with the management team.

The hard part – and what comes next in our story – is taking the time to consistently and repeatedly communicate and live those core values every day in the decisions and actions of everyone on the team. Values are only values if they guide decision-making during challenging times, and as we shall see in the next installment of the GrammCo narrative, certainly the consternation felt during the first month of the PEG/portco partnership is among the most anxiety-prone stages of the investment period.

Chapter 3
Month 1: Consternation

"He had already learned there was only one day at a time and that it was always the day you were in. It would be today until it was tonight and tomorrow would be today again. This was the main thing he had learned so far."

Ernest Hemingway, *The Last Good Country*

Chief Engineer David Bedford almost couldn't believe what a whirlwind the last month had been. From the first meeting where the equity partners were introduced to the management team and the one-on-one discussions they had had about Patterson Lake Capital's approach to the investment period to having Shed Cooper shadow him for an entire day – it certainly was one of the most surprising months he had ever spent at the company. The emotional rollercoaster he and other members of the management team had been on had definitely been something else as

(continued)

(continued)

well. Although he had anticipated the onboarding process to feel more like waterboarding, it had turned out to be something entirely different. He hesitated even to admit it to himself, but it looked like Shed Cooper and Ocie Gleason really did want to forge a partnership with GrammCo and dive into the hard work of building a bigger and healthier company.

There was for sure an adjustment period, but David was impressed by how Shed Cooper had worked hard at reassuring everyone starting at that very first meeting. His introduction as the new chairman of the board certainly didn't appear to leave any wiggle-room about who was in charge, but Shed quickly stood up, aware of the potential awkwardness of CEO Dianne Franklin's announcement. He smiled and made eye contact with everyone in the room.

"I'm sure this is a surprise to some of you, and even difficult news to hear for others. Russ Gramm built a magnificent company and has been a trustworthy owner and caretaker of his creation. Indeed, that's why Ocie and I were such advocates for Patterson Lake Capital to invest in your company. And nowhere was Russ's stamp more pronounced than in the people he surrounded himself with."

He paused and leaned forward. "The people of GrammCo are its greatest asset, and we look forward to getting to know you better in the upcoming days and weeks as we embark together on this exciting new chapter for GrammCo."

David had to admit that the excitement Shed had about the future of GrammCo was a minority viewpoint at first. Some managers bristled at the thought of GrammCo no longer being a family company and worried out loud what it would feel like being subject to the business pressures that came with closer scrutiny. Others simply wondered whether the inevitable downsizing that always seemed to accompany a takeover – hostile or not – meant that their days at GrammCo were numbered.

But what struck David and the rest of the management team was how Shed and Ocie really did live up to that initial promise of getting to know them better and their emphasis on authentic teamwork. He had never seen two people work harder at getting to know the inner workings of the company and the people that ran it. Nothing seemed to escape their attention, and no question seemed to go unasked. Nor did they come across as trying to catch anyone out; sure, they wanted to know what you thought about the operations of the company, warts and all, but made it clear that they were interested in the growth and success of the company and not simply getting rid of the proverbial "deadwood."

Yet maybe even more surprising to David was how the questioning was a two-way street: Shed and Ocie were almost aggressive in insisting that everyone at the company have their questions about private equity answered, and they were thorough in their explanations of their respective roles as Operating and Investing Partners.

Yet in the end, David knew that there would be changes afoot at GrammCo. You couldn't accelerate growth without change, and growth was definitely on the horizon. At least they wouldn't be expected to grow without new capital and new thinking. It was clear that Shed and Ocie weren't going to be silent owners but a regular presence at GrammCo, and working closely with Dianne and their CFO Don Crandall.

After a month of this, David could sense that the management team had reached a comfort level with Shed and Ocie. But he knew going forward at GrammCo that things would never return to the way things were either.

Onboarding Together

The equity partner in our narrative, Shed Cooper, is keenly aware of the consternation caused by the sale and purchase of a company like GrammCo. That's why he's particularly careful during his first moments with the management team. What he says and does over the next days and weeks, along with what the management team says and does, will set the stage for the partnership going forward.

Familiarity began during diligence, but under different auspices – that of seller and buyer. Going forward the relationship should be as colleagues working to understand and support each other. Getting there cannot be achieved by decree, and the onus is on both parties to discover the best path forward to creating A constructive partnership early in the investment period, enabling them to jointly build the business – and even enjoy the process while growing the company.

The first month is therefore not the time for either the equity partners or the portco management team to make hasty assumptions, engage in opaque maneuvers, or take hardline stands. Those are the steps a shortsighted PEG would take. If an effort is not made to genuinely begin to get to know one another and start building a constructive partnership, then consternation will linger longer than it normally would because one or both partners failed to invest the time and energy required to reduce anxiety.

Delays in overcoming consternation typically occur in one of two ways. If the OP lacks empathy regarding recent changes or can't walk a mile in their shoes, he or she is likely to drive too fast and focus too much on their own immediate demands for meetings, reports, and numbers. Wiser PEGs realize they've purchased a company that is not simply the sum of its assets and resources but one of individuals having emotions and expectations. They realize people represent the unique and underlying value of their purchase and make it a priority to care for their portco management teams.

Similarly, if portco management digs their heels in and isn't willing to collaborate with the PEG team, they are likely to undermine the best outcome not just for the company but for themselves. They need to realize that the equity partners need their support to do their job. Change is inevitable, and if the portco team wants to create a genuine partnership with their new equity partners, they need to approach the coming investment period with optimism and even enthusiasm instead of hesitation and mistrust.

To create a successful relationship and a genuinely constructive partnership, both teams will need to work hard during these opening weeks to build bridges to the other. To alleviate the understandable initial consternation felt among the management team, the equity partners will carefully explain the transaction process – what everyone has just been through – and then spell out what the private equity ownership period is all about, what the goals are, and what can be expected not only for the company but for management team members as well. The portco team can do their part by listening closely, asking important questions, and offering constructive advice about how to best transition to and through this new chapter.

In the end, the sooner the PEG and portco teams understand each other and learn how to work best with one other, the quicker everyone can focus on building and growing the business together.

Onboarding Activities

Collaborative-minded PEGs take the responsibility of onboarding seriously. They consider it as a two-way street involving getting both the PEG and the portco up to speed simultaneously. They take the time to truly understand the inner workings of the company – to personally "live" the business before attempting to impact it. They also are willing to invest their energies into getting to know the individuals running the portco and help them get to know the roles, expectations, and values of the PEG. This process should not be skipped or rushed if one wants to establish a constructive partnership where information is freely and candidly shared – warts and all.

Figure 3.1 highlights key activities PEGs should consider for the first month of the investment period. Onboarding activities

First Month Post Acquisition	Monday	Tuesday	Wednesday	Thursday	Friday
Prior					Acquisition Completed
Week 1	Kickoff Meetings	Detailed Exchange Meetings (CEO, CFO, PEG)			Touchbases
Week 2		One-on-One Meetings		Normal Routine Monthly Reporting	Touchbases
Week 3	Days-in-the-Life Experiences				Touchbases
Week 4			Diligence Material Reviews	Operational Cadence Review	Touchbases

Note:
■ Gray is observation of normal company routine; ■ Blue is onboarding activity

Figure 3.1   First-Month Onboarding Calendar

typically include various kickoff meetings, one-on-one discussions, and day-in-the-life experiences. These activities set the stage for a strong relationship and prepare the ground for defining what the future operational cadence might look like.

Kickoff Meetings and One-on-One Discussions

As with our GrammCo narrative, the CEO and equity partners typically arrange an initial meeting to formally commence the new investment period. While some executives had already begun to form relationships with their new equity partners during diligence, other executives and many managers and staff have not.

Brief but early kickoff meetings are an important way for the CEO to not only introduce the IP and OP to the full team but also communicate and demonstrate that all is well. Everyone needs to hear that new ownership will begin a new and exciting chapter in the company's history, and having a new financial sponsor means both growth and opportunity for all those who step up to the new challenge.

During the first few days, forward-thinking OPs will schedule one-on-one meetings with each member of the leadership team at the portco (and any other key leaders in the organization). It's usually best to keep these early meetings as simply "get-to-know-you" occasions – informal discussions to begin laying the groundwork for what will become long and fulfilling relationships.

PEGs who don't value creating a partnership likely skip this important step and instead adopt an aggressive stance and begin imposing an intimidating agenda. In such a scenario, portco executives feel like they have to interview for their jobs all over again. They may catch themselves inadvertently boasting of past accomplishments or otherwise ingratiating themselves. With such posturing, honest communication and authentic relationships are delayed – perhaps indefinitely.

This is not to say that smart PEGs don't hit the ground running – they do. But while the investment period isn't a marathon, it isn't a sprint, either. These PEGs embrace a philosophy of "start slow to go fast" during the opening days and weeks to address head-on the feelings of consternation caused by the sale of the company and allow everyone to find their footing.

Detailed Exchanges and Regular Touch-Base Meetings

Collaborative-minded OPs will typically organize several 2- to 3-hour detailed onboarding work sessions with the CEO, as well as for the CFO and PEG finance director (FD) (or team member assigned to that role). The OP and CEO will typically proceed through an agenda of various items continuing from where they left off during diligence. Topics likely will include a review of each functional area (including those of immediate concern), as well as associated key individuals and their capabilities, aspirations, and communication styles. They should discuss continued communications to and from all stakeholders in the business as well as current management reporting and how to begin refinements for near-term PEG needs. And they should begin brainstorming of value creation priorities and how to accelerate efforts.

On the finance side, meeting topics likely will cover current reporting and compliance processes and expectations. The equity partners need to quickly get comfortable with the capabilities of the CFO and establish clear guidelines for candid disclosure and early communication of any possible issues, particularly related to cash, compliance, and covenants.

After these deep dives, conscientious PEGs will suggest scheduling at least three standing weekly touch-base meetings. The first, between the CEO and OP, is to catch up on the past week and to discuss plans for the next. The CFO and FD should also connect weekly, covering current projections for the month and other items as they come up. And the PEG should also schedule an inward-focused third meeting, enabling the IP, OP, FD, and others assigned to the portco to connect, share information, and coordinate their actions to ensure their communication and requests to the portco are consistent and efficient.

Standing touch-base meetings help reduce the frustrations of constant random pinging of the principals via email and phone, as everyone quickly learns to reserve nonurgent requests or discussions for the weekly touch-base. These detailed exchange meetings and subsequent regular touch-base meetings serve as excellent opportunities early in the investment period to continue building constructive partnerships.

Days-in-the-Life Experiences

PEGs interested in an authentic partnership make not only a significant financial investment but also a significant time investment in their portcos. OPs from these organizations look forward to spending hands-on time getting to know the inner workings of their businesses very early in the investment period.

Nothing beats such firsthand knowledge: seeing, doing, and experiencing the core business while conversing informally with those who know the business best. Smart OPs find it invaluable to spend several days riding with and working alongside field reps, sales reps, crane operators, merchandizers, metal stampers, dental assistants, or digital marketers – whatever roles are core to the business. If you've seen the television show *Undercover Boss,* you'll recognize the value of firsthand insight into positioning improvements in a business.

But unlike *Undercover Boss*, collaborative OPs are candid about who's visiting and the reason for the visit – which is simply the OP getting to know the business from those who know the business best. They are not interested in or looking for "Aha! Caught you!" moments. As a caretaker responsible for protecting and improving the business, they will often treat honest insights gathered as deep-background information.

Because onboarding should be a two-way approach, the portco needs to understand the PEG from the inside as well. Better PEGs often insist the CEO visits the PEG offices and meets with the PEG CEO and other key PEG team members. They will provide contact information of other current and past portco CEOs and insist the CEO call several for private and candid discussions about what to expect during the investment period. They will encourage them to ask former portcos about what is it like to work with the PEG and the individual equity partners. These kinds of exchanges help the OP establish an open and frank communication style with the CEO. While some PEGs would likely never suggest such a process for fear of what might be said, collaborative PEGs welcome such conversations because they will provide the CEO with solid advice and insights that will make the next few years successful for everyone.

Diligence Material Reviews

In the course of evaluating a company prior to purchase, the PEG coordinates and conducts endless hours of due diligence investigations across all functional areas: sales, marketing, operations, and so forth. Expensive consultants study and report on the marketplace, industry, competition, and the target company itself, creating many pages of findings, analytics, and recommendations. The IP and deal team then rely on this information as they build their purchase case.

It's a common and unfortunate mistake to waste this valuable detailed diligence information post-transaction. It's typically rarely revisited by PEGs, and it's even rarer for diligence information to be shared with portco management. But forward-thinking PEGs not only share it with management but study it together. They discuss where the diligence provider got it wrong, where they got close to the truth of things, and where the information is spot-on. Together they discuss what they can learn from the findings.

Truly wise PEGs might even invest an entire day or two to jointly review diligence material during an executive offsite session. They might invite the diligence providers themselves to present it and to facilitate discussions to identify opportunities and improvement priorities function by function. Diligence materials and the associated discussions certainly serve as excellent fodder for defining the *Value Creation Plan*: the set of key initiatives, objectives, milestones, timing, resources, and responsibilities to achieve the strategies and intended value creation during the investment period.

As-Is Reporting and Operational Cadence

As noted above, one of the benefits of the onboarding process is to lay the foundation for conversations around financial reporting and operational cadence. One of the earliest and most significant causes of executive consternation relates to questions around how often they need to report to the equity partners. Unsurprisingly, an early parallel concern for the equity partners is how hard will it be to get reports from the management team. Unimaginative PEGs "solve" this tension by immediately demanding all sorts of reports and meetings in specific formats post-close. Their actions ramp up the tension and further act to sow mistrust instead of creating an environment where a collaborative relationship can emerge and grow.

Inquisitive PEGs instead get to know the portco management's current report content and meeting structure and leverages those as much as possible to meet their combined needs. Smart OPs and IPs attend the first monthly financial and operations reviews in the format they have historically been planned and conducted, using the reports and information management has traditionally used. Just like for other functional areas, attentive equity partners want firsthand knowledge of how information has been delivered and processed.

This serves two purposes: On the one hand, the management team has certainly worked hard over the years to develop processes that work best for them. It would be presumptuous on the part of the equity partners to throw away those insights and start from their own perceived needs without thoroughly considering how to blend the old and the new. On the other hand, making a good-faith effort to appreciate the company's perspective is a critical step in forging a practical partnership. Doing so results in a relationship where expectations are shared (and inevitable information availability constraints are openly discussed). The best partnerships work together to discover what information is available and needed for a healthy discourse that enables them to work best as a team.

Toward the end of the first month, the equity partners and executive team have a common foundation from which to begin discussing improvements to financial reporting and operating cadence. These will be addressed in more detail in coming chapters, but the key to remember is that during onboarding, wiser PEGs take the time to get to know what's worked well in the past before trying to "fix it."

Confirming Portco Leadership

Effective partnerships between PEG and portco teams require highly capable leaders helming both organizations. How a PEG goes about determining whether the portco leadership is not only sufficient but best suited for the requirements of the investment period speaks volumes about their core values and the kind of leaders they are.

Shortsighted PEGs take little time to set expectations of their portco leadership team. Instead, they take an "I know what good is when I see it" approach and keep looking and replacing until they think they've found it. They might mouth platitudes like "the numbers speak for themselves" and replace portco leaders in the hopes that the numbers of the next one will sound better. But surprisingly, they typically have never defined for themselves leadership expectations during the investment period. As a result, they don't know what they want from a leader. Their exclusive focus on numbers leads them to ignore taking the time to articulate the requirements and characteristics needed of the right leader to achieve the investment period strategies that enable those results.

Wiser PEGs will set their expectations of leaders early in the process – in fact, starting during due diligence. They illustrate through their words and actions the level of detail and care they put into vetting the company, and that includes the executive team and key leaders in the business.

A Vision of Leadership

For these wise PEGs, leaders are men and women of the highest character, who organize, enable, and motivate their teams to live a shared set of values while achieving a common vision. Unsurprisingly, the core values they see as particularly suited for middle-market private equity firms are the same core values we think the leaders of portco companies should espouse. In order for a genuine partnership to emerge, both PEG and portco leaders should strive to be purposeful, practical, and principled.

By *purposeful,* we mean committing to specific meaningful outcomes and embracing ownership and accountability. Leaders are intentional in their actions, eagerly targeting, tracking, and triaging progress. Their determination is not only evident but also contagious.

By *practical,* we mean sorting through complexity quickly, focusing on the materiality and needle-movers. Leaders do not need to be the smartest person in the room, and in fact relish surrounding themselves with others who have that distinction. They are proud to be the objective brokers of great ideas, realistic plans, and hard-to-find capability.

By *principled,* we mean embracing authenticity and being the best versions of themselves they can be. Leaders are real people working hard to get good stuff done. They believe integrity is paramount and strive to do what's right in all situations, serving others with compassion as understated achievers.

Problem Solvers

In private equity, portco executives should first and foremost be problem solvers. Challenges are inevitable in business, but how executives react to problems and the swiftness of their response is what distinguishes those executives who will be most successful during the investment period. For example, consider three different responses regarding a problem that equity partners might hear from a portco executive.

"We had a problem last month; still trying to figure it out," is one of the worst comments an executive can make to their equity partner. It's clearly something that started a while ago but wasn't brought to equity partner attention. It's impacted a previous month's performance with no chance to recover that impact now. The executive has produced no facts about the root cause and offers no possible solutions. At the same time the equity partner was caught off guard by the problem, has nothing to weigh in on, and maintains no confidence that the current month's performance will be any better.

"We have a new problem; here are the facts and what we're going to do to fix it" is better. Here, the executive is providing early notice that a problem has occurred, has taken a fact-based analytical approach to understanding it, and is being decisive toward resolution. He or she is providing the equity partner the opportunity to weigh in if desired and is not only prepared but intends to proceed with confidence to fix things. The equity partner in this situation feels much more confident the problem will be resolved.

As good as the second comment is, a third reply is even better: "We anticipate a possible problem; here's how we'll avoid it," clearly indicates the executive is looking ahead to evaluate options and to avoid issues through insight, discourse, and decisiveness. The executive is providing *early warning* about what *could* happen – not what did happen or what is happening. Early warning enables the equity partner to participate if desired, but this time proactively versus reactively.

Equity partners expect strong problem-solving skills coupled with decisiveness in portco executives – leaders who think and act like owners. Portco leaders must have the capability and competence to get the work done, as well as possess a partnering attitude in how they approach their equity partners and a willingness to work within the private equity model. Timely solutions are crucial, and particularly so in middle-market portfolio companies. Every month a problem perpetuates is one less month in the investment period not focused on growth.

Executive Capabilities and Competencies

Role expertise and experience. This is perhaps the first and most obvious expectation regarding capabilities – to already have demonstrated that one is excellent at what the role requires. Private equity firms do not want to hire "firsts" – they want someone who's "been-there-done-that" and whose executive capacities have already been well-tested.

Middle-market mindset. As noted in the opening chapter, middle-market companies have certain peculiarities. They are like teenagers in being both grown up and yet still immature. They have evolved to have defined processes, but what they have might be inconsistently and manually executed and still clunky. They have infrastructure, but likely cobbled together and suboptimized. They have talent, but it's scattered and inconsistent. Like an adolescent, middle-market companies have tons of potential but are still awkward and unsure. Successfully steering them requires executives with the right blend of delegation and hands-on skills.

Private equity familiarity. Equity partners realize they have unique expectations that differ from those in the corporate or private company world. Private equity has certain expectations regarding their oversight and involvement in the portco as well as their intended time horizon for owning the portco. Portco CEOs and the CFOs should be at least familiar (if not well-versed) in the expectations and idiosyncrasies of private equity and comfortable with the extra level of PEG oversight.

Demonstrated speed of success. Time is measured differently in a portfolio company than in public or private companies. Instead of multiple unending quarters or multiple lifetimes, private equity operates in specific individual investment periods of typically only a few years, with a specific starting point and an end (if not in sight) at least in mind. Portfolio company executives must operate with an intensity of speed, driving all success for an endgame that corresponds to the exit from the investment period.

Calibrate to the horizon. The time horizon for executives working in private equity portfolio companies must correspond specifically to the investment period timeline. Decisions during the investment period will be influenced by the remaining time available until exit. While early in the investment period there is less differentiation from non-portfolio companies, as the exit approaches the timeline must shorten accordingly. This should not imply shortsightedness, as both the equity partners and portco management team embrace the fact that increases in company value are based largely upon long-term value creation.

Executive Attitude

Accept oversight. Because PEGs do lots of monitoring, they request lots of reporting – both standard reports and ad-hoc analyses as well as standing meetings and impromptu conversations. PEGs expect reporting ranging from industry analyses to operations and financials. Successful portco executives accept and welcome this high-level oversight because they understand that a constructive partnership requires the equity partners to be fully informed in order to be fully involved. They recognize that OPs and IPs are not only obligated by their fiduciary responsibility to their investors but are genuinely interested in helping the company grow.

Embrace collaboration. Successful portco executives not only expect involvement from their equity partners but embrace a collaborative mindset. For PEGs who want to be a constructive partner in the portfolio business, it's difficult and inefficient when a portco executive is excessively defensive or unduly or continuously pushes back against PEG practices or the equity partners themselves. Although the OP will likely have final say as chairperson or board director and can certainly play a trump card when necessary, portco executives should genuinely want to collaborate and offer their constructive input – not a "yes-man" but not "Dr. No" either.

Pursue good-of-the-investment. The goal of the investment period should be to exit having maximized the company value, and all actions by all parties should be directed toward that end. To ensure this outcome, portco executives must have both "skin in the game" where their futures and even fortunes are linked to the company's success by making them an investor and a "burn the ships" outlook where the management team sees a shared destiny and opportunity in always moving forward to reach this goal.

Operate decisively but open-mindedly. The investment period is short, and therefore decisions need to be made expeditiously. There simply isn't time for months and months of dithering over the correct course of action. The portfolio company executive needs to analyze quickly and make decisions with incomplete and inexact information. A few months may very well be 10 percent or even 20 percent of the total investment period. Portco executives need to be willing to act thoughtfully but decisively and then react as necessary (including an ability to let go and change course if needed, regardless of the sunk costs).

Of course, portco executives aren't the only ones that need to be decisive problem solvers. In middle-market private equity, equity partners also need to be decisive and address the question of whether individuals in the various executive leadership roles of the portfolio company are suitably assigned. Considering the investment time horizons and the importance of each executive role, equity partners may need to make changes to the CEO role or work with their CEOs to make personnel changes to other executive roles. That does not always mean terminating an individual or eliminating a role. Equity partners are interested in keeping excellent executives with high capability and great attitudes within the company and changing their roles as needed to optimize the team and the likelihood of success at the exit.

Executive Performance

Forward-looking PEGs begin evaluating portco leadership before the acquisition during diligence. They follow a specific method among several available and update their thinking as diligence progresses. These PEGs then work with their portco CEOs to continuously update leadership evaluations throughout the investment period and work together to address shortcomings through a combination of performance improvement plans, professional development plans, reassignments, added support, and individual replacements.

Figure 3.2 provides an illustration contrasting a typical scalar evaluation system in place at many lower middle-market firms with a more sophisticated and nuanced 9-Box evaluation technique.

In the typical approach leaders and staff alike are evaluated on a simple 1–5 scale – excellent, very good, good, fair, and poor. Inevitably, we find profiles like what we show in the illustration – a few outstanding individuals, three-quarters doing just great, and a handful of plain old "goods." This one-dimensional approach often leads to "grade inflation" and a lack of differentiation, rendering it relatively useless as an effective evaluation tool. The picture it delivers is not unlike that of Lake Wobegon, the fictional town in Garrison Keillor's *A Prairie Home Companion* where "all the women are strong, all the men are good-looking, and all the children are above average."

With the 9-Box approach, the OP and CEO can have specific and candid conversations about each executive and key leader. For each, the conversation covers both their specific performance against expectations as well as their future potential during the

Typical Evaluation			9-Box Evaluation Performance vs. Potential				
Score	Frequency	Total	3x3 Score	Lower	Performance	Higher	Total
5: Excellent		4/20 20%	Higher	High–Potential Team Member ● ●	High–Potential Performer ○ ○	○ Star ○	6/20 30%
4: Very Good		14/20 70%					
3: Good		2/20 10%	Potential	Under- Performer ○ ○	Core Team Member ● ● ●	High Performer ○	7/20 35%
2: Fair		0	Lower				
1: Poor		0		Poor Fit ○	Effective but Limited ● ●	Capable Performer ● ● ●	7/20 35%
Total		20/20 100%	Total	5/20 25%	8/20 40%	7/20 35%	20/20 100%

Note:
● Dots represent an individual – executive, senior leader and key roles
■ Green is high;   ■ Yellow is medium;   ■ Red is low

Figure 3.2 Performance Evaluation Models

remaining investment period. A relative grading scale for each results in individuals being uniquely categorized within one of the nine boxes. The 9-Box enables specific actionable conversations about each individual's progress, development plans, and upcoming assignments.

For instance, consider the upper-left box, High-Potential Team Member, having high potential but lower current performance. Conversations concerning this individual would likely focus on his or her need for active coaching. Progressing down the Potential column, the Under-Performer would likely be placed on a short-term performance improvement program; and the Poor Fit individual would likely be transitioned out quickly. In the right-hand column, the Capable Performer is excellent at what he or she does but will likely not progress beyond the current role. They might be willing to take on more workload but of the same kind. The High Performer might appreciate being challenged with increased responsibility or with mentoring others. And the Star speaks for itself.

Observant readers will note the absence of an attitude evaluation in the 9-Box approach. We believe effective PEGs should adopt

GE's Jack Welch's philosophy with respect to values and attitude. In GE's *Annual Report 2000,* he explained how he differentiated leaders into four types. The first type shares the company's core values and gets results – the "sky's the limit" with them. Another type – the other extreme – neither embraces company values nor gets results. These should be transitioned out of the company. For the type who embraces company values but misses their numbers, Welch advocates giving them "another chance, or two" because they have the right character and attitude and the right energy.

The fourth type represents a difficult but important decision. They get results but do not embrace company values. As Welch puts it, they deliver great numbers but "on the backs of people, often 'kissing up and kissing down' during the process." Welsh admits letting these high achievers go is an "unnatural act," but because this fourth type has "the power, by themselves, to destroy the open, informal, trust-based culture" that is so important to the company, they, too, need to be transitioned out.

That philosophy – the philosophy of values and character first, even above results – is critical for responsive PEGs. Equity partners prize integrity, embrace strong values, and emulate a can-do attitude, and they surround themselves with portco leadership that does the same. In fact, they view an individual's lack of these positive traits as a "knockout" factor in that person's participation on the team.

Teaming Authentically

Effective and well-functioning management teams working seamlessly together is critical for the performance of any company, but considering the short investment period in private equity, it's doubly true for portco management teams. Yet not all management teams are smoothly integrated groups working in concert. Some are well-honed, effective and efficient, trusting each other, engaging in spirited debate, and making and keeping commitments. Others are quite ineffective – perhaps with everyone appearing pleasant, but in the end, few decisions are made and even less follow-up is completed.

When PEGs begin working with a new portco, it quickly becomes clear where the portco falls on the management teamwork effectiveness continuum. While some PEGs might consider the topic of teamwork as soft, collaborative PEGs work hard to improve the functionality of the teams they work with to improve the capabilities of the executives within their portfolio companies, even as they onboard and integrate themselves into the team. Smart OPs constructively call out dysfunction when they see it and promptly help address the reasons for and potential remedies of executive team dysfunction within their portfolio companies. Addressing portco team dysfunction can be one of the most value-added early activities the OP and portco CEO can begin to do together.

In a perfect world, that might involve pausing to intentionally design and construct teams that practice regularly to generate high levels of effectiveness. But the nature of private equity doesn't allow for building the rhythms and actions of the portco team from the ground up. Because PEGs enter the picture in the way they do, with portco management teams usually already in place, they need to work together to improve *how* they work together.

Elements of Effective Teaming

Teaming is a mindset that embraces the practices of teamwork – coming together to work as a team – either as scheduled or on the fly. Understanding that it's not feasible to start from the beginning, responsive PEGs instead seek to implement practices and habits that lead to effective outcomes with their existing teams in-flight. Teaming still requires all the elements of good teamwork – coordination, trust, and interdependence – but it recognizes that those skills need to be practiced continually at the moment in dynamic and unexpected configurations.

For many of those on the management team, the consternation experienced during the first month counts as one of those moments.

Functional v. Dysfunctional Executive Teaming		Executive Teaming Process				
		1 Mindset	2 Exchange	3 Decisions	4 Follow–Through	5 Results
Executive Teaming Attributes	Functional Teams	Trust Authenticity	Embrace Conflict	Make Commitments	Demand Accountability	Experience Success
	Dysfunctional Teams	Hide Vulnerabilities	Appear Harmonious	Avoid Commitments	Accept Mediocrity	Suffer Disappointments

Note:
Source: Authors adaptation of Patrick Lencioni's book "Five Dysfunctions of a Team"

Figure 3.3   Effective Teaming Attributes

During that time both the frequency of executive team meetings and the length of participant lists tend to ramp up considerably. It's important therefore for OPs and their executive teams to understand what it takes to achieve effective teaming. Using Patrick Lencioni's excellent and comprehensive "The Five Dysfunctions of a Team" as a starting point, Figure 3.3 is our interpretation of the five elements needed for high-functioning, successful teaming – not only for the core portco management team but for the broader PEG and portco partnership as well.

Mindset refers to the underlying character and current wiring of individual team members – their state-of-mind as they participate as part of the team. Teams need authentic members who are genuine and who trust that others will accept them unconditionally. Similarly, team members need to be willing and able to support and value others on the team where and when needed. Team members must be able to trust each other and feel safe to express their thoughts and opinions to the rest of their team.

Exchange involves how team members approach talking and listening to one another. In order to be both genuinely respectful and productive, effective teaming requires both active listening and candid responses, including constructive disagreement when necessary. Conflict within functional teams is inevitable. It's also a healthy part of teaming, so long as it's focused on ideas and not personalities and values facts over opinions. Without candid and respectful discourse, teams may feign harmony only to later experience ruinous passive-aggressiveness.

Decisions in the middle-market are often based on sparse or imperfect information. Uncertainty is commonplace. After good leaders make their best decisions based upon *available* information and input from their team, team members need to then make relevant commitments and proceed accordingly. Dysfunctional teams avoid commitments and keep revisiting and re-legislating decisions, paralyzed by the lack of perfect information. Effective teaming happens when leaders are decisive and team members make and embrace commitments to execute what's been decided.

Follow-through is essential for putting decisions into action, and the critical element of it is accountability. Effective team members demand accountability of themselves and each other. Where ineffective teams accept mediocracy and delays, effective team members raise their hands as soon as they need help and seek raised hands to provide help. Much of this book is dedicated to exploring the commitments the PEG and portco make to implement specific initiatives and reach associated milestones, deliverables, and due dates. Accountable follow-through on commitments is essential to meeting those goals and requires effective teaming by those involved.

Results are the ultimate endgame and measure of a team. Are they achieving the results they promised to get within certain costs and completed on-time? Effective teaming involves measuring progress continuously to ensure success. Key performance indicators (KPIs) are a core part of the vernacular of effective teaming because results-achieving teams talk facts and respond to numbers. They know where they stand and where they are going and have the confidence to get there. If they veer off course, they pull it back in; if their original source of value and benefits falter, they replace it with another source, enabling them to achieve the numbers to which they committed and for which they feel accountable.

Reducing Dysfunction

Functional executive teaming does not occur overnight, particularly if the starting point is far along the dysfunctional side of the continuum, but reducing dysfunction should start Day 1. There's no single recipe for effective teaming, but there is a primary ingredient, and that is leadership's dedication to it.

Effective OPs and portco CEOs are consciously present and in close proximity to the team. They continuously reinforce the need for authenticity and trust among everyone. They nurture candid discourse and respectful conflict that leads to effective and actionable decisions. They make and require commitments, and then hold themselves – each other and each team member – accountable for those commitments. In doing so, effective teams relentlessly target, track, and triage results to the bottom line.

Unsurprisingly, the best teaming is a reflection of core values. Effective leaders and effective teams are purposeful in achieving specific outcomes, practical in the way they achieve their results, and principled in all personal and business dealings – emulating authenticity, integrity, and compassion. Happily, success is the ultimate team motivator, and once a team gets a taste of success, it wants another bite. When the PEG and portco experience successful teaming as a result of their constructive partnerships, they eagerly pursue new goals and set out once again to achieve them.

Overcoming Resistance

Of course, dysfunctional teaming isn't the only way the opening days and weeks can go off the rails. While there might be systematic reasons for why teamwork is ineffective, oftentimes the success of the partnership between the PEG and the portco management team boils down to individuals. The consternation felt by members of the executive team can quickly lead to resistance to new or unfamiliar ideas, practices, or expectations of the PEG if not addressed head-on.

Attentive PEGs not only recognize the contributions of their portco management colleagues but empathize with them as well. They understand the expectations and demands of private equity are at times overwhelming. Because the amount and pace of change during investment periods is so high and the periods so short, a certain level of management resistance is not only a possibility but likely a certainty. Because it's not a matter of if but when, these PEGs work to overcome the natural resistance to change in portcos associated with the investment period.

Resistance to Change

The investment period is fundamentally a multiyear change program. The change, of course, is the execution of strategies and initiatives to achieve the growth objectives during the investment period and thereby delivering the investors' expectations of sufficient returns. Yet if achieving company objectives involved only systems, facilities, products, and services, success would be straightforward and relatively easy.

But strategy execution is mostly about people, and people dislike disruption. They like consistency, normalcy, and control, and when that's disrupted, they tend to resist. It's not necessarily the new that concerns them but leaving behind the tried and true. And as a result, most resistance isn't overt rebellion so much as concealed and even unconscious foot-dragging. Nevertheless, because covert resistance is hidden and behind the scenes, it has the potential to be longer-lasting and more damaging as a result.

The first step then to overcoming resistance is to make the covert overt. To do that, responsive equity partners and CEOs first find and even anticipate it. Anticipating resistance is enabled through an understanding of people's biases and natural inclinations that serve as barriers to change. We often encounter the following biases in middle-market private equity:

Status quo bias represents the persistent pull of a previous commitment. It's like inertia for the past. Once an individual commits to a specific practice, allegiance, or belief, it's difficult to uncommit – particularly if that commitment was publicly made or has been long embedded. When a PEG buys a company, the previous management team often retains significant status quo biases that must be addressed.

Loss aversion bias emerges when the perceived pain of a loss is more intense than the expected joy of a corresponding gain. People tend to weight the cost of failure more heavily than the benefit of success, and the more costly the failure, the more powerfully the bias is felt. Loss aversion bias is the reason people might hold a dissatisfactory job longer than they should, or why they might not implement a process improvement initiative for a functioning process despite the process being inefficient or costly.

Sunk cost bias might occur when confronted with a better approach moving forward after having committed considerable time and resources on a current approach. It's difficult to abandon large previous investments in systems and processes despite the existence of better alternatives. Yet OPs need to help management make the best decisions at any given time regardless of the water under the bridge.

Ambiguity bias or fear of the unknown is particularly present in middle-market private equity. We've all experienced ambiguity bias at one point or another. Often, the anxiety we experience prior to change is worse than the actual concern we experience once change is underway. It's helpful in these situations to take FDR's advice from his first inaugural address: "The only thing we have to fear is fear itself."

Diagnostic bias comes about because in private equity there is a tendency to quickly diagnose (even with few facts) and then experience hesitation about changing our position when presented with compelling new facts. It's a bias against changing our minds because doing so involves admitting you were either wrong or hasty (or both). It's seemingly human nature to dig in further to avoid admitting a poor decision, and yet it's essential for overcoming resistance to tackle diagnostic bias directly.

All these different forms of bias particularly emerge when individuals are feeling overloaded. There is a natural and healthy resistance to change because of a perceived or real lack of capacity to effectively undergo it. Too much change all at once is not only difficult but often counterproductive, and management needs to be constantly vigilant about putting too much on the plate. Central to that philosophy is moving deliberately during the opening days and weeks to address the feelings of consternation brought on by the change in ownership.

But once those feelings have been addressed, it is time for change in order to grow the portco. Resistance to change – whether in the form of passive-aggressiveness or one or more of the biases noted above – needs to be overcome, and being cognizant of when it emerges is critical to overcoming it.

Pathway for Positive Change

The best way to minimize resistance to change is to try to avoid resistance in the first place. That means understanding and planning for the process of change itself, which is inherent in the investment period in the various strategies and initiatives a portco implements during the investment period. Figure 3.4 spells out a pathway for achieving positive change through identifying the four primary phases of agreement, preparation, progress, and results.

Agreement for needed change involves two elements – identifying a shared destiny and making the case for change. Agreement requires coordinated leadership, partnership, and teaming to identify the current state as being unacceptable and the future vision being desirable. Getting to "yes" can involve recognition of a "burning platform" for change that reinforces the immediacy and importance of moving from one state to the next, or it can

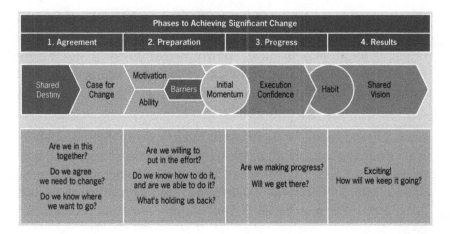

Figure 3.4   Change Management Phases and Components

involve dispassionate analysis that persuades through rational argument. In either case, the pain of doing nothing must be viewed as greater than the anticipated pain of the change process itself, and the team must have confidence that they are willingly embarking on the path rather than it being forced on them.

Preparation for change focuses on targeting motivation and ability to overcome barriers. Motivation for change stems from numerous sources and often involves more than one. It can be financial incentives, the necessity of the moment, the opportunity change presents, and even the sheer joy of engaging in something new and exciting. But preparation is not just motivational – unless you identify the capacities and capabilities needed to achieve change, you'll be unable to change, whether you're willing to or not. Preparation requires specifying the skills, resources, and time needed to achieve the change you want. It involves addressing both explicit and implicit barriers to change; if barriers aren't overcome, change does not happen, or it happens with difficulty and does not last.

Progress occurs when initial momentum feeds confidence. Nothing reinforces positive change more than does progress toward the result, which in turn spurs confidence and more momentum. Early successes lead to momentum and the ability to sustain that momentum drives progress. For most portfolio company change efforts, progress manifests itself in noticeably improved organizational effectiveness, newly streamlined and efficient operations, optimized commercial offerings, interactions, and arrangements, completed integrations of add-on acquisitions, or any other resulting business improvement.

Results might speak for themselves, but achieving them is no small feat. Results are dependent on developing good habits that sustain a shared vision. They speak to a job well done, and the sense of accomplishment in the result is the ultimate motivator. Results also become the new baseline from which even more progress can be made.

We like to think of the primary change cycle in private equity as initiatives-based: establish the right Value Creation Plan, line up and complete the highest priority initiatives, then "rinse-and-repeat."

PEG and portco leadership should therefore work together to overcome resistance and put the company on a change path for value creation. The changes they pursue through future initiatives will be intentional and purposeful, and addressing the resistance they will encounter needs to be so as well. Doing so is an essential part of what effective PEGs do to embrace their core values and shows a sincere and genuine commitment on the part of leadership to cooperative partnering.

As change is continuous over the investment period, addressing concerns about change is never a one-time event. As Chief Engineer David Bedford recognizes in our GrammCo narrative, change was going to be a constant companion for the foreseeable future. PEG and portco leadership must take the time to recognize apprehension to change as it occurs and seek to overcome resistance through teamwork instead of imposing a solution – just like Shed Cooper and Ocie Gleason did at GrammCo. And collaborative-minded PEGs recognize that doing so isn't just the right thing to do – it's also the surest pathway to maximizing value creation during the investment period.

Chapter 4
Month 2: This Might Be Okay

"Then the sun came up and shook the night chill out of the air the way you'd shake a rug."

John Steinbeck, *Cannery Row*

Across the table from Dianne Franklin, GrammCo CFO Don Crandall set his Hefeweizen down and sighed. "Things are starting to feel almost normal again."

It was late and she was tired, but Dianne raised her glass, smiling, "Yes, I think things will be okay."

Since Patterson Lake purchased GrammCo only a few short weeks ago, things had been busy. Very busy. *The new normal,* everyone was saying. Back to running the business, but now with the added expectations and the proverbial "care and feeding" of new owners.

(*continued*)

(*continued*)

Having had multiple daily discussions and several meals together, Dianne had a good sense of Shed. During each discussion, they'd covered a variety of topics to help each other get up to speed – one with the company and the other with the firm, and both with how they'll best work together. They quickly agreed on an operating cadence, starting each week with a standing touch-base call and monthly updates between her, Don, Shed, and Ocie.

Shed had been in town for three days each week since the purchase and was scheduled to be back again the next week. Not only had he found the time to traipse around oil fields last week with the regional sales rep and join the engineering team on an all-day ASV test-drive 15 miles into those sweltering desert mountains, but he worked elbow-to-elbow with Diane going over the numbers from the "digital data room" they had set up when they first decided to sell the company.

Although Diane had a good sense of what was in the trove of documents Don had deposited in the diligence archive, she was impressed with how Patterson Lake's deal team had transformed that data into usable information. What she found harder to swallow was the suggestion that GrammCo needed a new analyst to support operational reporting and initiate a business intelligence capability (or "BI" as they called it). But Shed made a strong case and Dianne deferred to his judgment. It was undeniable that many of their decisions had always been based on intuition, and that upping their game on facts and analytics would be a welcomed improvement.

Don was equally impressed by how Ocie had approached the issue of reporting monthly financials. Instead of barging in with her own forms and upsetting the applecart, she had watched a full cycle to see the systems they had in place operate. It was clear she was going to advocate for changes – and Don didn't disagree that their financials were short on both clarity and details – but it was nice to be involved in the process of building the materials instead of having it imposed from above.

"Tomorrow we're talking about the Value Creation Program. It sounds like Shed and Ocie don't see the need for going through an entire strategic planning process but want to launch right into defining and accelerating the initial priorities for growing the company even faster," Dianne observed.

"That's right," Don chimed in. "These guys don't want to lose any momentum coming out of the diligence review and the conversations they've had with us. I know Shed and Ocie are brimming with ideas about how we can start tomorrow to explore some new things. They don't ever lose sight of EBITDA; in fact, I'm not sure either could go an hour without mentioning the word."

Dianne turned that idea over in her head. She certainly knew about EBITDA and knew a thing or two herself about optimizing value – after all, she had grown the company quite nicely in the three years she had been at the helm. She also knew that Shed and Ocie weren't just going to propose more of the same, but help the team investigate new and additional ways to accelerate growth at GrammCo. And she knew it wasn't going to come in drips and drabs – there would be a full-court press to make a significant impact, particularly during the coming months. It was going to be an exciting new pace for sure. Exciting and tiring.

"Time to head home, then. Tomorrow's going to be another full day," Dianne quipped.

"You're not kidding. And it's only been two months!" Don said as they headed to the door.

Baselining the Investment Period

In our narrative, Dianne and her executive team have just finished the first few weeks of working with their equity partners. They're now experiencing similar sentiments to most portco management teams at this point: a level of acceptance and a sense of the new normal. As a result, the teams at GrammCo and Patterson Lake Capital are starting to settle into a new relationship.

And what's true for them is true for portcos and PEGs in general. After the first month or so, if both parties have adopted a collaborative partnership approach, the portco executive team should start feeling comfortable with its PEG and vice versa. Both portco and PEG will have gotten to know the individuals on each team and the process of beginning to trust one another will be well underway. The next step to forging a constructive partnership and settling into a rhythm involves putting into place several fundamental building block activities. These involve achieving a common understanding of the starting point for the investment period, putting in place initial reporting, and preparing for an early and quick start on the heavy lifting of accelerating value creation.

Leveraging Diligence to Memorialize the Start

The first of these is baselining the investment period by returning to and thoroughly reviewing the diligence materials that led to the purchase of the company in the first place. During diligence, the portco team pulled together reams of data regarding suppliers, purchases, costs, customers, products, services, and countless other topics. Assembling this material required many hours and days of effort by the finance team and various other individuals across the company. They placed all requested data into a virtual (online) data room, which quickly became chock-full of various Excel files, PDF documents, and PowerPoint pages – each in response to a specific inquiry from a potential buyer, lender, diligence provider, or another interested party.

That effort was well worth it as the material served to support a successful sale at an acceptable if not impressive company valuation. But the half-life of all that raw data is extremely short, and it will become obsolete very quickly post-transaction. Nor is it useful in its raw state for moving forward: a random bunch of miscellaneous files, facts, and figures, each unreconciled and perhaps even inconsistent with each other, that someone at some point requested for some now unknown reason.

Some PEGs unfortunately squander away the opportunity to continue to leverage the materials the portco team painstakingly accumulated and provided during diligence, leaving these valuable diligence files unused. But having a baseline early in the investment period turns out to be incredibly helpful to generate efficient ongoing analyses. Forward-looking PEGs take advantage of the wealth of data that's been accumulated and memorialize a full suite of baseline information.

What is needed moving forward is a concise repository of key information representing the company from the start of the new investment period. Information is different from data in that the former is a structured, reconciled, and concise set of intelligible facts and figures usable for analytics and decision-making (typically simple but complete files in Excel data form for future use). They can serve as the baseline information for the investment period: succinct and organized digital files containing a comprehensive yet manageable picture of company details at the time of acquisition.

Smart PEGs will organize at least five groupings of concise usable files capturing a snapshot of the company at the beginning of the new investment period: financials, employee, physical assets, suppliers, and commercial. Figure 4.1 illustrates the kind of information these PEGs include in the baseline.

Applicability and Resources

Creating baseline information is particularly applicable in the lower middle-market, where integrated systems are largely unavailable

Financials	Employees	Physical Assets	Suppliers	Commercial
3-Year History Budget & actual, detailed P&L, BS, CF by month	**Org Charts** Full set, reporting relationships	**Facility** Type, location, size, contract details	**Supplier/Vendor** Master name, category, locations	**Offerings Master** Products, services, categories, $, units, histories
Expenses Lowest available level; by location, dept, category	**Employee** Name, title, department, dates	**Fleet** Type, lease, mileage, records	**Contracts** Terms, dates, document filing location	**Customer Master** Location, segmentation, spend history
Banking & Debt Terms, covenants	**Performance** Historical, current	**Equipment** Type, lease, mileage, records	**Historical Spend** By vendor by item, $, units, pricing, DPO	**Purchasing History** by customer by offering, $, units, pricing, DSO
Working Capital Data and trends for inventory, A/P, A/R	**Compensation** History by person, salary, commission, bonus, target & actual	**IT Systems** Systems architecture maps & flow, contracts	**Performance** Service-level requirements and statistics	**Customer Scorecard** Cost-to-serve, service records, returns, complaints

Figure 4.1   Baseline Information Starting an Investment Period

and easy to get data turns out to be not so easy to get. Unlike larger companies, lower middle-market companies often do not have integrated enterprise resource planning (ERP), data warehouse, and business intelligent systems and applications at the ready to answer any desired query regarding current or historical information. Smaller companies likely do not have a business analytics team to efficiently re-pull the data that had been manually assembled during diligence.

Rather, smaller companies typically find they need to cobble together data from various disparate systems – a tedious and time-consuming effort that rarely results in a consistent set of facts and figures. Baseline information represents a concise source of Day-1 facts and figures that's easy to use and all in one place. It provides not just a common ground from which to start, but a basis of comparison in the weeks, months, and years ahead. It helps management avoid redundant data work – energy that instead can be redirected toward growing the business. If done well, baseline information will likely be consulted and used often.

Aggregating a rich and accurate but succinct set of baseline information will not be onerous as the hardest step is already complete. The raw data had been accumulated during diligence, so all that is now necessary is guidance and templates. Yet performance-oriented PEGs will not merely settle for a set of neatly organized spreadsheets but rather urge their portcos to consider investing in two complementary areas:

Business intelligence tool. Smart OPs know that a multidimensional database and analytics application is worth its weight in gold in terms of managing the information created by the baseline (and all the future information that will be compared to it). Thankfully, these days such tools don't cost a king's ransom – they are both readily available and very affordable. If the portco chooses to delay what is likely an inevitable investment, Excel files will suffice, but the volume and complexity of the information the portco soon will be handling will outstrip their ability to successfully manipulate these files.

Business intelligence analyst. Hiring one will undoubtedly be a harder sell than just getting the management team to purchase a piece of software, but here is an instance where the OP may well consider putting their thumb on the scales. Onboarding a skilled analyst at the outset when they have the opportunity to truly examine all corners of the diligence data room makes a great deal of sense. This, too, is a case where many portcos don't know what they are missing – namely access to top-quality business analytics drives unique insights and better decisions.

Applications for Baseline Information

Particularly over the first several months of a new investment period, baseline information will be highly useful in the context of both onboarding and analyses.

Resourceful onboarding. The wealth of concise company data is perfect for onboarding activities. The equity partners, consultants, and other providers coming onboard will certainly find it useful, but perhaps most telling is how useful baseline information will prove to be for management team members. Though they may have known and lived in the company for years, this is often the first time they've seen such a clear and succinct set of all the critical details of their business – a plethora of information now at their fingertips for new insights and analyses.

Consistent analyses. From a single source of baseline files, any user will have the data they need for efficient analytics in customer segmentation and pricing improvement opportunities, product rationalization ideas and end-of-life reviews, and supplier and vendor consolidation opportunities and purchase price discrepancies. They will be able to look at cost of sales and gross margin trends for improvement opportunities, identify areas for refined investment, and even target immediate short-term opportunities for cost-takeout to fund other investments.

From this one set of baseline information, opportunities will be evaluated, ROIs will be determined, initiatives will be justified, targets will be set, and progress and results measured. It's nothing short of essential, and wise PEGs and portcos, particularly those with poor systems and limited analytical capabilities, will leap at the opportunity to codify diligence information before it's out of date.

Reporting Monthly Financials

Within the first few weeks, equity partners will start to want to see reporting. They need something to begin monitoring the business they just bought, and they'll have their own expectations for what that reporting might look like. Portfolio companies should therefore expect some disruption in standard reporting early in the investment period.

Overly aggressive PEGs typically require one extreme or the other: reams of reporting requiring many hours to compile or limited reporting requiring little time but providing scant insight for governance and oversight. Pragmatic PEGs work with their portco teams to iterate to a balanced approach that generates insightful and actionable detail but isn't onerous to compile.

There are as many variations of reporting expectations as there are companies in the world. Everyone seems to want his or her specific report, at a certain frequency, in a prescribed format. After seeing a cycle of "as-is" reporting, there will likely be a meeting of minds to refine reports to include new information moving forward. Some changes to the previous format will undoubtedly be enhancements, and some will simply be differences. The key is to focus on blending the best of both PEG and portco expectations in generating the new standard reporting approach.

Concise but Informative

In private equity, monthly reporting should be operationally informative, succinct, and standardized. It should be routine and relatively easy to pull together. It should facilitate a common vernacular and a consistent cadence illuminating what's important to the business and what levers drive results. Unsurprisingly, it should therefore have a heavy focus on EBITDA, including variance details for actual performance against last year's actuals and current year budgets and forecasts. And it should have an eye toward expectations for full-year performance.

The right reporting is something the equity partners and the management team should have at their fingertips at all times. They will then know the numbers and know what they are focused on in the coming month to improve results and grow the business. With the right reporting, the PEG and portco alike can spend more time developing insights and exploring implications of the numbers and less time generating reports and interpreting formats.

Getting this report package right so that it's useful for both the PEG and portco is crucial for navigating the Value Creation Program during the investment period. Arriving at the right content, level of detail, and reporting format will be an iterative process, but it's worth the effort, as the monthly package and review is the primary component of a productive operating cadence. The OP, CEO, FD, and CFO should spend the time necessary to find a system that works for them and their teams.

Figure 4.2 represents one example of a high-level profit and loss (P&L) report that includes many elements that both PEGs and portcos find important to have in their monthly package.

High Level P&L	Year-to-Date					Current Month					Full-Year Forecast				
	LY	B	F	A	%B	LY	B	F	A	%B	LY	B	F	A/F	%B
Revenue	$0	$0	$0	$0	0%	$0	$0	$0	$0	0%	$0	$0	$0	$0	0%
Cost of Sales	$0	$0	$0	$0	0%	$0	$0	$0	$0	0%	$0	$0	$0	$0	0%
COS %	0%	0%	0%	0%	–	0%	0%	0%	0%	–	0%	0%	0%	0%	–
Gross Margin	$0	$0	$0	$0	0%	$0	$0	$0	$0	0%	$0	$0	$0	$0	0%
Gross Margin %	0%	0%	0%	0%	–	0%	0%	0%	0%	–	0%	0%	0%	0%	–
SG&A	$0	$0	$0	$0	0%	$0	$0	$0	$0	0%	$0	$0	$0	$0	0%
Adjustments	$0	$0	$0	$0	0%	$0	$0	$0	$0	0%	$0	$0	$0	$0	0%
Adjusted EBITDA	$0	$0	$0	$0	0%	$0	$0	$0	$0	0%	$0	$0	$0	$0	0%
Adjusted EBITDA %	0%	0%	0%	0%	–	0%	0%	0%	0%	–	0%	0%	0%	0%	–

Note:
LY = Last Year; B = Budget; F = Last Forecast; A = Current Actual; %B = Actual as a Percent of Budget
■ Green is favorable; ▨ Yellow is slightly unfavorable; ■ Red is unfavorable

Figure 4.2   High-Level Monthly Financial Reporting

Key Reporting Attributes

Standardized summary level. Many PEGs have a way they like to look at financials across *all* their portfolio companies, with both specified content as well as a consistent format. In such cases, the portco will need to provide it. But that can be separate from the reporting that works best for the partners in the business. The OP and CEO along with the PEG finance director and portco CFO, should collaborate to find the right summary report that provides everyone the financial as well as operational story of their business at any given time, with the content and format as they prefer. We tend to recommend a two to three-page summary so that everyone is literally on the same page seeing and using the same numbers.

Operationally focused detail. For the summary monthly report we suggest not only key financial information, but also primary financial ratios, leading and lagging KPIs and operational statistics, as well as key commercial information such as customer sales pipeline. The reporting package, as well as monthly review meetings, should be operationally focused, blending financial dollars with commercial and operational facts and figures. Naturally, supporting this high-level report requires detailed schedules for each major line item.

Basis for comparison and highlighted areas of concern. Middle-market companies inevitably report actual performance each month and most report variance to budget at least for primary P&L categories. Many portfolio companies stop there. We suggest going well beyond and reporting performance against other comparables: last year's performance, multiyear trends, common size comparisons, analyses on a per unit of cost-driver basis, and components of price/volume/mix. Intracompany comparisons (e.g., by geography, business unit, etc.) and relevant industry benchmarks are often useful. Multiple yardsticks help highlight concern as well as opportunity areas. Like many PEGs, we favor coding reports in the standard red, yellow, and green indicators based on materiality and variation from target.

Starting with Momentum

After the first month has elapsed the management team and equity partners have onboarded together, efficiently baselined the new investment period, and initiated refined monthly reporting. That's a good start, but more still needs to happen early in the investment period to start the portco on the Value Creation Program.

Following the purchase of a new platform portco, management teams often tell their new equity partners "we've just been through a lot; allow us to take a breather and get back to simply running the business for a while." While that certainly sounds reasonable, the "take a breather" approach will come at a significant cost to everyone. Some PEGs will acquiesce as a result of either being swamped in reports or possessing scant information on which to act. They, too, waste several months before using (or gathering) information to help drive the business, resulting not only in a significant reduction in the eventual exit value but also in a reduction in the value of management options.

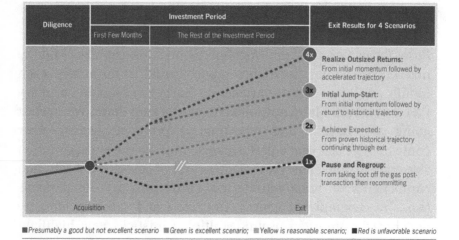

■Presumably a good but not excellent scenario ■Green is excellent scenario; ■Yellow is reasonable scenario; ■Red is unfavorable scenario

Figure 4.3   Outcome Scenarios Based on Initial Momentum

Quick-acting PEGs spare no time in helping the portco management team accelerate and augment high-value growth initiatives in an organized way – prioritizing opportunities and profiling initiatives. They use reporting to help identify opportunities for improving efficiency and areas for development and growth. And having jointly identified those opportunities, they don't wait for folks to catch their breath but move quickly to capitalize on them, recognizing that initial momentum is particularly important given the investment period is limited in its duration.

Figure 4.3 shows several illustrative scenarios based on a new investment period's starting effort. We've called them Pause and Regroup, Achieve Expected, Initial Jump Start, and Realize Outsized Returns.

Pause and Regroup

The seemingly reasonable and innocuous request on the part of portco management or PEGs to "pause and regroup" is akin to momentarily taking their collective foot off the gas pedal. Here, the management team convinces their equity partners (or the equity partners passively acquiesce) to briefly relax expectations and, if not pausing their involvement, then merely engaging in months-long passive observation of portco activity.

Yet losing even a few months of accelerated progress can make all the difference to an investment period. As shown in Figure 4.3, a delay could lead to marginal returns over the investment period or even a zero percent return; and if investors make no return, portco executives lose their financial incentives as well. Taking a breather may result in years of hard work just to get back to the investment period starting point.

Clear-minded PEGs appreciate the financial incentives at stake for themselves and their portco teams, and also recognize the fiduciary duty they owe to their investors. They likely just paid a lot for the business, based on a combination of management's past and projected performance as well as their conviction that they could maintain and in fact accelerate trajectory. Laying off a bit at first is simply not in the best interests of anyone involved.

Achieve Expected

This scenario involves the portco team continuing as they have been to maintain the historical growth trajectory of the company. In this scenario, the executive team and PEG merely meet previously proven expectations and achieve consistent (if unremarkable) growth targets aligned with the previous trajectory. Unlike in the Pause and Regroup scenario, the results may lead to growth, but staying the course is not typically a convincing justification for buying a portco. It's perhaps even arguable that these returns would have been achieved without the intervention of the PEG, which raises the question of what value the PEG is adding through their involvement.

Initial Jump Start

The Initial Jump Start scenario involves the PEG and portco teams working together immediately from the get-go. Instead of taking a breather post-transaction, they identify and launch a series of initiatives focused on quickly – but not necessarily structurally – improving EBITDA. These quick wins might include immediate price changes, consolidations, or cost reductions. After the Initial Jump Start of near-term EBITDA improvements, the management team in this scenario then reverts to its historical trajectory of growing the business. It's the difference between planting some fruit trees then letting them grow on their own versus tending to them – staking, weeding, and pruning as necessary – in order to maximize what's produced.

In the Initial Jump Start scenario, the company still exited with a healthy return, but one based primarily on a handful of initial efforts. The PEG's initial interventions yielded real value, but after that initial period, the PEG/portco partnership failed to continue to produce new significant benefits.

Realize Outsized Returns

To realize outsized returns, the PEG/portco team needs an accelerated kickoff early in the investment period. Quick wins certainly help, as in the Initial Jump Start scenario. But even more important than quick wins is creating content as well as a consistent a lasting and sustainable team that continually generates momentum. Outsized returns emerge because the team promptly identifies and prioritizes value creation opportunities aimed at improving infrastructure and capabilities, driving operational efficiencies, and initiating new sustainable EBITDA growth. Working in concert, they must then launch and execute the early highest-priority initiatives of their new Value Creation Program. A focused and positive investment in initial momentum will serve to put the portco on a pathway toward continuous trajectory improvement over the course of the investment period. But achieving outsized returns necessitates the team reinforcing their collaborative performance-based culture focused on both day-to-day excellence and value creation efforts.

Identifying Value Sources

The quick-start momentum we're talking about includes launching immediately post-purchase into an exercise of prioritizing and initiating a new set of key strategies and initiatives – ones that make sense to get started on right away. Quick-acting PEGs want to accelerate value creation and achieve early wins to get the momentum started on the portco's new trajectory.

Before jumping into discussing prioritizing opportunities, profiling key initiatives, and launching a broad Value Creation Program, let's begin with a discussion of value sources outlined in Figure 4.4. We've previously offered high-level descriptions of the big three – increasing EBITDA, enhancing the balance sheet, and the less tangible "improve exit multiple." It's time to get a bit more granular regarding each major category and describe actions that forward-thinking PEGs can take, and over the course of the remainder of the book we will dive deeply into these topics.

Some PEGs tend to focus mostly on EBITDA but typically primarily on the cost side. They squeeze value from their companies by excessively trimming and disproportionately managing costs

Figure 4.4 Value Creation Sources

while underinvesting and continuously demanding more from less. Such an approach is unsustainable and fails to create true, lasting, long-term value. But performance-oriented PEGs work side-by-side with their executive teams to optimize value across all three primary value categories. They start by evaluating the full range of applicable value sources before jointly narrowing the list and establishing priorities.

Increase EBITDA

As we discussed previously, EBITDA is the kingpin of investment-period value drivers. EBITDA tends to offer a larger stand-alone impact on value than the other two categories and serves to positively impact the others as well (for example, operating cash flow is used to pay down balance sheet debt, while consistent, predicable, and likely future EBITDA growth serves to improve the sales multiple).

Unsurprisingly, the majority of the OP and CEO's time is then focused on influencing the growth drivers of EBITDA. There are three fundamental ways to grow EBITDA: grow profitable revenue, control direct and channel costs, and right-size overhead.

Grow Profitable Revenue. At the heart of growing EBITDA is revenue growth. One of the attractions of the middle-market are companies with reliable growth rates above industry averages. If the OP and CEO can achieve operational leverage by generating revenue and EBITDA growth rates, well above overhead growth rates all the better. At the end of the investment period, buyers will pay up for industry-leading leveraged growth.

Equally important yet often overlooked in this equation is what constitutes *profitable* revenue. By definition, all products and services sold contribute to revenue, but not all revenue is good revenue. Selling certain complex or low-price products and services may not contribute to the bottom line at all or may even detract from the bottom line. Revenue for revenue's sake at the expense of profits is usually a problem that one way or another will not last long.

Profitable revenue opportunities cover a range of possibilities, from incorporating innovative pricing focused on customer's assessment of value, to implementing customer relationship management (CRM) and sales pipeline reporting, or launching marketing automation and marketing campaigns. Opportunities also might include rationalizing unprofitable products, services, geographies, and customers or piloting an inside selling function, remote sales support, or customer engagement efforts. All of these and more focus on generating sustainable revenue streams that are profit-driven.

Control Direct Costs. Historically across many industries direct costs represented the lion's share of the company's overall cost structure. Although it varied by industry, oftentimes 60–75 percent of costs were tied up in these areas. Over time, companies learned how to control material and labor costs, and today those same costs may represent 40–50 percent of a company's cost structure. This is a marked improvement, but still represents half of the overall cost structure and still plenty of opportunity.

Standard costing methodologies are one of the best ways for many companies to not only control but reduce material, labor, and other direct costs – not only for manufacturing but also for service-based companies. Even a full century after they were introduced, we still find companies not employing such methodologies or with wildly inaccurate bills of materials, standard processing rates, and operational routings. Without accurate standards from which to base and compare actual performance, these companies are operating with one hand tied behind their backs. They know actual cost but don't have anything to compare those to. Without the ability to identify and analyze variances from expectations, management teams are less able to control and improve cost structure.

Prudent PEGs and portco teams understand they need appropriate, available, and accurate costing information to run their businesses. While costing methodology is no panacea, it does impact the ability for companies to target, track, and triage improvements. Opportunities for companies to reduce direct costs include those associated with labor efficiencies, processing and service times, and purchased items. Opportunities also typically include reducing waste, such as material scrap and overusage, and wasted service activity. Companies should be looking to improve or rationalize the supplier base, enhancing partnerships, and negotiating supply contracts. Other areas for cost reduction include improving fleet and equipment utilization and efficiencies while optimizing distribution networks and transportation time and costs. And of course, any company – regardless of industry, size, or health – should always be working to continuously improve safety and quality.

Right-Size Overhead. While direct cost structures have generally declined over the years, overhead cost structures have increased. As a percentage of revenue, overhead has steadily increased from perhaps 20 percent or so early in the twentieth century to often over 50 percent today. By nature, both manufacturing and service overhead as well as selling, general, and administrative (SG&A) are more difficult to associate directly with products and services, and therefore are often harder to understand and manage systematically.

One reason why overhead is so difficult to wrestle with is that it does not move in a straight line with sales, but rather, in chunks. Maintenance, engineering, customer service, product development, and marketing are all essential elements of a business, and yet none is directly proportional to unit sales. Overhead increases according to batches of activities and outputs – the number of market segments served, how many product and service offerings you have, or the number of orders, returns, field visits, service calls, customizations, and so on.

Overhead improvement efforts undertaken by the new PEG/portco team tend to be two-fold: better understanding, controlling, and reducing of unneccessary overhead, while at the same time investing in new infrastructure and capabilities. Opportunities run the gamut from reducing overhead to increasing overhead. For instance, companies may find opportunities in consolidating facilities or investing in new operations, improving asset utilization or purchasing more efficient equipment, and reducing organizational structures or adding new team resources. Other opportunities may include implementing spending controls in some areas or increasing ROI-justified spending in others, or outsourcing noncore corporate functions or taking critical functions back in-house.

EBITDA improvement efforts will flow to the bottom line in various degrees based on their starting value and location on the P&L. Take, for instance, a $100 million revenue business as shown in Figure 4.5. Improving pricing by 5 percent delivers the entire amount directly to the bottom line, in our example increasing EBITDA $5 million (a 33 percent improvement). If we increase unit volume by 5 percent, cost of sales also increases 5 percent, so only a portion falls to the bottom line ($2 million, or a 13 percent

EBITDA Impact of 5% P&L Change Scenarios	Original P&L	New P&L by Scenario			
		Price Increase 5%	Volume Increase 5%	Cost of Sales Decrease 5%	Operating Expense Decrease 5%
Average Unit Price	$100 per	$105 per	$100 per	$100 per	$100 per
Unit Volume	1.000m	1.000m	1.050m	1.000m	1.000m
Revenue (R)	$100m	$105m	$105m	$100m	$100m
Cost of Sales, %R	$60m, 60%	$60m, 57%	$63m, 60%	$57m, 57%	$60m, 60%
Gross Margin, %R	$40m, 40%	$45m, 43%	$42m, 40%	$43m, 43%	$40m, 40%
Operating Exp, %R	$25m, 25%	$25m, 24%	$25m, 24%	$25m, 25%	$23.75m, 24%
EBITDA, %R	$15m, 15%	$20m, 19%	$17m, 16%	$18m, 18%	$16.25m, 16%
Impact ($, %)	–	$5m (+33%)	$2m (+13%)	$3m (+20%)	$1.25m (+8%)

Note:
■ Blue highlighted boxes in scenario columns refer to the primary changed field to reflect relative impact

Figure 4.5   Relative P&L Impact by Source

improvement). Five percent improvements in cost of sales and operating expense results in 20 percent and 8 percent bottom-line improvement, respectively.

Enhance Balance Sheet

A second source of value comes from enhancing the balance sheet. When companies have a healthy balance sheet, they have more money to invest in growth, they have more satisfied customers and suppliers, and they have banks that are happy and nonintrusive. They can use three different levers to achieve these ends: improving working capital, leveraging physical assets, and paying down debt. Not only can targeting the balance sheet generate value at the beginning of the investment period, but upon exit, a healthy balance sheet results in higher returns for investors and management teams.

Improving Working Capital. Net working capital is the difference between a company's current assets and its current liabilities. Accounting 101 says assets are good and liabilities are bad, so more working capital is better. But that's not always true.

Assets are generally good, but there are exceptions. Having too large of an accounts receivable balance, for instance, can be unhealthy (particularly if many accounts have aged receivables). Inventory is generally good, too – after all, you can't sell what you don't have. But too much inventory is risky because inventory tends to get old, lost, stolen, damaged, or obsolete if it sits around for long. And while many say it's good to "stretch payables," doing so runs the risk of angry vendors and supply stoppages. Even simply stretching payables a single day beyond preferred terms may preclude the opportunity for a nice purchased discount.

Sustainable opportunities to improve working capital abound and include taking advantage of discount terms, rationalizing stock-keeping units (SKU), improving purchased lead times, adjusting commercial terms, and enhancing other business practices associated with cash, receivables, payables, and inventory.

Leverage Physical Assets. The second balance sheet factor involves getting more productivity out of the asset base you already have. On the face of it, it doesn't seem that leveraging physical assets would matter much in private equity where the focus is so much on EBITDA (where asset depreciation is excluded). Unlike a public company that focuses on net income or return on assets, why should a portfolio company care about how much they spend on assets?

The reasons PEGs and their portcos do care about leveraging assets is because assets are both significant and high drivers of value. If they spend cash on new assets, they have less to invest in other (EBITDA generating) areas of the business or to pay down debt. And when a company borrows money for additional asset purchases, they're becoming more leveraged and therefore a riskier business. These businesses result in a higher cost of capital as well as lower exit multiples in general. Additionally, if the portco becomes even more asset-intensive, it will likely incur even more maintenance and operating costs along with those new assets, which impacts EBITDA. Asset-intensive businesses often command a lower sales multiple.

Portfolio company management should certainly invest when and where it's properly justified, whether it's for improving efficiencies or enabling growth. But first they should continuously strive to optimize the use of the assets already on their books. That can involve anything from reducing setup times and implementing preventive maintenance programs to increasing machine uptime, equipment utilization, and processing speeds.

Paying Down Debt. Reducing debt burden is the third balance sheet lever. Debt is expensive, and many an executive has lamented each month the cash impact of having to service their expensive debt through high-interest payments. Just like an individual with a large mortgage, multiple car and student loans, and several maxed-out credit cards, being saddled with debt is limiting and stressful to any business as well.

Some debt can be good, like when it provides (reasonable) leverage to equity. Debt can serve to accelerate expensive high-value initiatives that require more investment than could be funded through free cash flow. But too much debt can limit a company's ability to grow. Interest payments reduce cash flow that otherwise could be used to drive normal business growth and new initiatives.

Debt reduces enterprise value dollar for dollar. That's why strategic PEGs look for opportunities to reign in portfolio company debt, including implementing bank revolver management practices, refinancing, and of course paying down any debt as soon as is possible and practical.

Improve Exit Multiple

The impact of increasing the sales multiple experienced at the end of an investment period is enormous. Even small changes implemented during the investment period can have a lasting impact on the multiple and therefore dramatically impact the sale price of the company.

As we've discussed, portfolio company valuation is calculated by multiplying EBITDA by an appropriate multiple (and then accounting for debt and working capital). For example, if a $50 million EBITDA company is sold for a multiple of 12×, it goes for $600 million (excluding balance sheet considerations). If one more "turn" could be justified and the company sold for 13×, that's worth an incremental $50 million.

Some executives believe they ultimately have little impact on the eventual sales multiple of their business. They believe the multiple is determined much less in reference to the actual company but independently based on the merits of the industry, such as growth trends, seasonality, cyclicality, market attractiveness, predicted future growth rates, asset intensity, competition, disrupting technologies, and so forth. Yet although exit multiples are most certainly impacted by external dynamics, the internal dynamics and the specific merits of the company play an important role and are factors that can be influenced. There are specific ways portfolio company management can positively impact the eventual sales multiple of their companies. Let's consider three of them.

Overhire Leadership. The quality of portco management teams represents a significant reason to purchase a company. Building the right leadership team during the investment period is essential – not only must they be well suited for the here and now, but they must be the kind of team that can run a business three times as big. Some PEGs cut corners when it comes to assembling the best possible portco management team, but forward-looking PEGs create excellent teams that are both nimble and built for the long haul.

This is particularly important as PEGs do not want to (nor are particularly well suited to) run their portfolio companies. They instead want the right teams to run their companies the best way, creating the most value during the investment period and generating the highest value at the end of the investment period. When buyers find an opportunity to purchase a company with an exceptional team, they pay up. That's why attentive PEGs look for opportunities to invest in leadership through developing their capabilities regarding insightful analytics, effective teaming, and project management, while not hesitating to invest in new talent where needed. They also offer career growth opportunities and enhanced long-term financial incentives while planning for succession in key executive roles.

Build Infrastructure. Businesses in the lower middle-market have often been underinvested. The previous owner may have run the business for cash, or a PEG may have refrained from important spending to momentarily prop up EBITDA in hopes of increasing the purchase price. But better PEGs do what's right and invest properly to create a sustainable business with the right processes, technologies, and organizations to see it grow. That's because when there's an opportunity to purchase a company that has a deep sustainable infrastructure already built, investors are willing to pay extra on the multiple.

These PEGs and their portcos therefore ought to consider investing in new systems that will support future growth and expanding capacity (including the capability to diversify offerings over time). Other opportunities for building better infrastructure also offer similar sufficient justification, including building new facilities, adding new and better equipment, improving the fleet, and enhancing customer-facing showrooms.

Create Future Strategic Options. The third consideration for increasing the exit multiple is admittedly more nebulous and harder to pin down, but it's equally important as the other two. In short, the buyer of the portco wants to see remaining "runway." They need to be able to conceptualize some interesting and exciting options for growth during their own investment period. As we already noted, a steady-as-she-goes approach of achieving historic returns is often not what forward-thinking PEGs are after when purchasing a portco. They want to see a path for them to realize sufficient and preferably outsized returns for their own investors and the associated rewards for the management team during their time with the company.

Because PEGs and portcos are going to be busy with immediate value creation initiatives – creating the infrastructure they should have had, enhancing immediate capabilities, and aiming for monthly, quarterly and yearly growth targets – they must be both strategic and selective about developing future options. The management team has neither the bandwidth nor the capability to pursue every possible shiny new thing, and can neither afford the time nor the cost of pursuing all options.

Future strategic opportunities might include leveraging current offerings into new markets or initiating additional channels (recognizing that multichannel businesses offer unique opportunities). Or they might involve entering new geographies and enlarging the company's footprint or building partnerships with the intent to explore creative new opportunities a few years out.

Whether these larger forward-looking strategic options are better implemented in the current investment period or during a future one is a challenging question to answer. Thoughtful PEGs and their portcos put in place a stage-gate process to help them manage the numerous new ideas that could germinate into future opportunities. By establishing a governing approach to manage the flow of opportunities based on idea and marketplace viability as well as management capacity to explore them, the stage-gate process serves to shepherd the holding pen of ideas through a formal evaluation and prioritization process. This facilitates a culture of restraint and a willingness to funnel and launch opportunities at the right time and place (even if that is well into the future).

Working together as a new PEG/portco team to identify and consider all possible sources of investment period value – including immediate introspective opportunities as well as far-out-there future ones – is all part of the early excitement of a new investment period. Having properly onboarded together with diligence reviews, baseline information, and new reporting, and having initiated the beginnings of long and collaborative partnership enables opportunity to become a reality.

Starting with momentum accelerates that reality. Forward-thinking PEG/portco teams understand that organizing and prioritizing a Value Creation Plan that incorporates all the key levers – increasing EBITDA, enhancing the balance sheet, and improving exit multiples – is the best way to accomplish their goals of optimizing portfolio company performance and management team returns. The principals at GrammCo – Dianne and Don – both know that creating the baseline and refining the reporting system are just the first steps to capturing the momentum needed to create a truly successful Value Creation Plan. It's time we take a close look at what a Value Creation Plan looks like and how one gets constructed.

Chapter 5
Month 3: Guarded Enthusiasm

"... the great artist when he comes, uses everything that has been discovered or known about his art up to that point ... goes beyond what has been done or known and makes something of his own."
Ernest Hemingway, *Death in the Afternoon*

Dave Bedford barged in late again and fell into his chair just as the wrench fell from his pocket. Leaning down to retrieve it with one hand, GrammCo's chief engineer waved a ratty old manila folder with the other. Only then did he realize the staff meeting was already underway and CEO Dianne Franklin had been talking. "Oh, am I interrupting?"

Without waiting for an answer, his big-Dave hand shot up, holding a long and oil-stained handwritten page of notes. "I've got my list!"

(continued)

(*continued*)

"We got it, Dave," Dianne smiled. "We're now talking about how we'll prioritize the items from everyone's list."

Returning her gaze to the screen, Dianne resumed her explanation. "Shed and I pulled all the items from everyone's list," she said, glancing at the room. "We then eliminated redundancies, combined some ideas and, well, here's where we are." She hit the down arrow and paused while the team took in the slide.

A 2 × 2 matrix covered the entire screen, and on the matrix a couple dozen labeled dots were plotted.

"The Y-axis on the left represents relative benefits. The X-axis across the bottom represents relative implementation cost and effort. And these dots here represent the relative rough-cut cost and benefit of each opportunity."

"Is my new test-lab up there?" Dave was the first to take in the matrix, list still in hand.

Others soon spoke up. "Where's my CRM system?" "Is the Salt Lake depot there?" "What do you mean by 'right-size'?" "I don't see the new call system." The commentary came fast, following a split-second delay as 12 other brains simultaneously registered what was and wasn't on the screen.

"Okay, okay, hold on. It's all there." Shed was smiling, both hands up to settle down the group. After absorbing the chart, over the next two and a half hours the team discussed and debated the relative merits of each opportunity. Dianne and Shed guided the conversation to focus on benefits and costs using the criteria scorecards they developed for each. Shed was particularly emphatic that the scorecard was a starting point for a discussion – the scores weren't final, nor would they be the final say. But Dianne was quick to chime in: "There are no sacred cows here, either. Everything is on the table, including initiatives that have already been underway. It's not personal if the initiative you're most enthused about gets moved for the time being to the back burner."

The conversation flowed easily, with just a few heated moments. Shed and Dianne facilitated and took note of everyone's perspectives. Time passed quickly, and people either didn't notice or didn't care they were missing lunch.

"Great meeting, everyone," Dianne said as they were wrapping up. "Tomorrow, we'll start profiling our highest-priority initiatives." Only stomachs grumbled as people packed up their things and cleared out quickly. Dianne flipped off the projector and smiled at Shed. The team was enthused and energized, and Dianne was, too. She was impressed at just how many opportunities her team was able to articulate, and how easily the ideas fell into logical "strategic" buckets. Both Dianne and Shed's intuition proved right – there was neither the time nor the need to pause months of progress to undergo a formal drawn-out strategic planning effort. What was undeniable was the sense of urgency she felt from Shed in getting the initiatives underway, and this first set of initiatives everyone agreed were the right ones to start with.

But in her many conversations with Shed, Dianne knew the team only had an inkling of the work that lay before them. Talking about and agreeing to an exciting set of initiatives is one thing, but getting them done would be something

(continued)

(*continued*)

else entirely. There would be extensive initiative profiles to generate for each that included targeted impacts and milestones. There would be dozens of small initiative teams to assemble and the all-important team leaders to settle on. And then there would be finalizing and communicating the Value Creation Program. Dianne wondered if any of them knew how much they'd be living and breathing the VCP for the next several years.

Generating and Aggregating Ideas

The executive team at GrammCo has become hesitantly enthused. In their roles as OP and IP, Shed Cooper and Ocie Gleason have instilled new energy into the company and have posed questions and initiated discussions that have led to dreaming big about their future. Everyone is ready not to just identify high-value initiatives but also organize and accelerate their implementation by putting in place the processes and capabilities to coordinate and manage them.

But there is a right way to do this and a wrong way. Some PEGs will demand EBITDA growth from everywhere and all at once, or push hard for growth from nebulous or unrealistic sources. Others will take a different route, concentrating on hacking out costs to a point that is either unsustainable or precludes the ability to grow. The way these PEGs go about this is also unbalanced: Some are largely hands-off while others are excessively hands-on. But one thing is assured: Neither their demand nor their approach leads to long-term sustainable value creation.

Collaborative PEGs waste no time in working with management to identify all relevant potential opportunities for EBITDA growth, but they are also smart and don't expect everything to be pursued at once. Rather, they put in place a process to explore the relative viability of each opportunity and to prioritize the best avenues to achieve sustainable EBITDA growth during the investment period. Experienced equity partners are cognizant of when their expertise is needed or helpful and when they should take a back seat. Their level of interaction is dictated by circumstances and opportunities, not personalities.

The Opportunity List Facilitator

In the previous chapter we discussed general sources of value creation, mentioning a handful of typical ideas within each general source. But the specific opportunities worthy of consideration for a given portfolio company depends on its current situation, including the availability of leadership and other resources to implement such courses of action.

Before deciding which opportunities to jump right into at the beginning of the investment period, the equity partners and management team should start with aggregating a substantial list of possible and relevant EBITDA growth ideas to consider – an opportunity list.

Who gets assigned the task of facilitating the opportunity list is an important question to answer. Often, the perfect fit is the OP. Generating the list of opportunities is a great way for him or her to meet individually with each executive and manager, to get to know them better, and to work one-on-one brainstorming and exploring ideas – what's been tried before, what's currently being considered, and what else might be contemplated. This work helps the operating partner to get further engrained in the business.

But sometimes it makes sense for others to participate in pulling the list together in addition to or instead of the OP. The CEO might have a trusted lieutenant in mind or want to do it themself. Other times, it's a consultant hired to facilitate the process on behalf of the team if the OP is not available. The right person varies with the situation, but regardless of who it is, that person needs to have relevant experiences and a strong character to accomplish the task positively and productively. We suggest evaluating potential opportunity list facilitators against the following criteria:

Experiences. Are they senior enough to have had a wide variety of accumulated experiences, and therefore to have the instinct to sniff out opportunities? Do they have enough broad-based experiences across functional areas to establish their own hypotheses, but be inquisitive enough and open-minded enough to adjust their thinking continuously throughout the process?

Character. Are they approachable but confident? Are they tactful and savvy enough to ask provocative questions in the right way to tease out challenging or even controversial ideas without offending or creating defensiveness? Are they discreet regarding information and information sources, and do they maintain confidences?

Objectivity. Have they learned enough about the company and industry to offer a point of view, but not so much that they have long-held preconceived notions? Are they unbiased and eager to expand ideas and see linkages throughout the business? Do they have impartiality and credibility in the eyes of the management team?

Sources for Opportunity Ideas

Opportunities come in all shapes and sizes, which is why it is important to get the right person in place to uncover what these might be. Once the opportunity list facilitator is selected, it shouldn't take long to generate an initial exciting list. There is a range of familiar sources for opportunity ideas:

Diligence ideas. The equity partners have recently completed due diligence, and in the course of diligence they'd gathered many hypotheses and ideas for investment period growth. That's a logical starting place to begin generating the list of opportunity ideas, some of which the portco team has recognized as well from having conducted the baselining.

In-flight efforts. The company will have various formal and informal efforts already underway, and these should be included on the list of opportunity ideas. While many if not most will make it to the eventual prioritized shorter list, some may not. What's important here is that in-flight initiatives should be put through the same screening process and receive the same level of scrutiny as the new ideas.

New contemplations. Executives and managers will have planned or contemplated initiatives that haven't yet been started or even suggested. They may have ideas that haven't received support or ideas that got squashed. And they'll likely come up with ideas they haven't thought of until being asked. All these – to the list they go.

External practices. Not only do we want to include ideas that team members come up with (including from their past working lives) but we want to look outward to better practice ideas and benchmark performance levels found within and across industries and functions. Some research will likely be required here, and there exists a variety of relevant associations, published whitepapers, and private sources for fodder.

Suggestions from customers and suppliers. Diligence may have included input from customers – often called the "voice of the customer" (VOC) – and input from suppliers. But sometimes diligence did not include VOC, or the diligence input in these areas was sparse or excessively backward-looking. Improvement ideas from customers and suppliers can be invaluable for generating loyalty in the future and forging a genuine partnership with them that can sustain a portco during difficult times.

Objective fresh-eyes assessments. This source is often overlooked. While many ideas come from those closest to the company, fresh and unexpected ideas often come from those outside the company and the private equity firm. The opportunity list facilitator may choose to bring in trusted outsiders for their observations and insights. If the equity partners have already appointed outside board directors, this is a perfect opportunity for their initial input.

Approaches to Assembling the Opportunity List

There are generally two broad approaches for assembling the opportunity list: one-on-one meetings and group brainstorming meetings. Rather than starting with a large room full of people and a clean sheet of paper, we prefer a sequenced blend of the two. We like to start with the informality and candor of one-on-one conversations followed by larger meetings where broader idea clarifications and extensions occur and consensus starts to build for the best course of action.

What we do not recommend is conducting a single large cross-functional brainstorming session to initially draft the opportunity list, as such meetings at the beginning in fact stifles its creation. Such meetings typically include executives and managers of various levels from across the organization, and as a result, they risk excessive influence by those more senior and bring to the fore internal politics, personal agendas, and extremes of personalities. Some participants will dominate airtime while others will not speak much at all. The resulting opportunity list will be lopsided and will lack the kind of 360-degree perspective that we want.

Instead, the opportunity list facilitator should start with individual face-to-face conversations to gather a comprehensive range of perspectives that identify emerging themes sourced from multiple discussions. People are simply more comfortable and more willing to share in private settings. To encourage creative thinking during each one-on-one discussion, the facilitator should employ elements of the appreciative inquiry model (AI), which we learned from David Cooperrider at Case Western University (this approach applies to group settings as well).

The overarching idea behind AI is that more and better ideas come from positive engagement. How that translates to idea generation is that rather than basing discussions on problems or weaknesses, AI starts from first understanding and appreciating an organization's past successes and current strengths. Instead of asking, "What's the problem here?" or "How can we fix our current situation?" AI begins by framing questions in the positive, such as, "Remember a time when we were at our absolute best? What was the company doing well during that time?" or "What strengths are we most proud of, and how can we leverage those going forward?" The questions are engaging and positive, fostering creativity and optimism for the future – all important factors in assembling the opportunity list.

Once the facilitator gathers all the ideas from previous materials and new inputs and discussions, they sort, consolidate, clarify, and categorize them into a single preliminary opportunity list. But rather than taking that list directly into large-setting reviews and brainstorming sessions, we've found it useful to first refine the list through small working sessions with the IP, OP, CEO, and the CFO. In so doing, they can eliminate various ideas they deem to be non-starters, inconsistent with investment period strategies or timing, or otherwise simply off the table for cost or other reasons. They can clarify, narrow, combine, or expand certain ideas, and can add late-coming ideas that may not have made the list. The intermediate vetting process saves valuable time and avoids unnecessary discussions later on.

Armed with a couple dozen exciting and viable ideas – ranging from easy small wins to incremental breakthroughs and large systematic overhauls – PEG and portco leadership will be ready to engage in a widely inclusive management team discussion to review the merits and risks of each opportunity and to add preliminary thoughts regarding details such as benefits, costs, and implementation approach. The opportunity list facilitator uses this time to work diplomatically and discreetly with the CEO and others to push, poke, and prod the management team toward finalizing a Value Creation Plan.

This process for assembling, ranking, and ultimately initiating ideas on the opportunity list is outlined in Figure 5.1. It illustrates how to gather these ideas and work through a step-by-step analysis to arrive at the prioritized opportunities that will be implemented to launch the Value Creation Program.

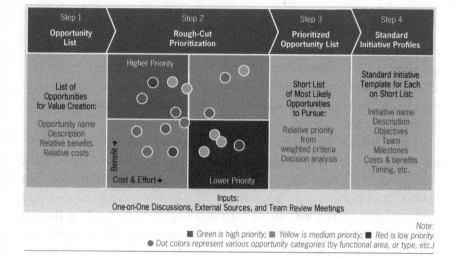

Figure 5.1 Progressing from Opportunities to Initiatives

Evaluating and Prioritizing Opportunities

Overly aggressive and unfocused PEGs push portfolio companies to do everything at once, often repeatedly redirecting attention from previously agreed opportunities to others. This results in "priorities" changing randomly from week to week or month to month. Lack of focus leads to disappointing results, followed by unrealistic increased pressure to launch even more improvement efforts in a never-ending to-do loop.

Starting from all the possible opportunities that might be pursued, strategic PEGs work with portco management to prioritize and focus on the best-fit opportunities first and avoid "boiling the ocean." Instead of being tempted by aimless redirection, they work as a team to successfully sequence and complete opportunities, constantly reloading at the right pace to maintain the accelerated trajectory we talked about in Chapter 4.

Evaluating Criteria for Opportunities

Loaded with valuable input from the opportunity list creation process, the equity partners and portco management work together to formulate a prioritization matrix to help select the preliminary set of opportunities from which to plan and launch the initial set of key initiatives. In so doing, they evaluate each opportunity, comparing the degree each benefits the portco against the cost and effort of implementing them.

Central to evaluating the benefit of an opportunity is its strategic fit for the investment period. Alongside questions of fit are ones regarding impact – how much, where, and how long of an impact the opportunity will make. Does the opportunity generate an annualized recurring EBITDA impact, or is it a one-time positive cash impact? Is it directed at operating performance, infrastructure, and capabilities-building, or new commercial growth? Is it designed to have an impact now or does it enable future opportunities?

The variety of benefits that opportunities can deliver need to be weighed against cost and effort. These involve not just the one-time implementation cost but a range of additional factors: time requirements for implementation, personnel demands, cross-functional coordination required, and other resources that need to be tapped for the opportunity to be a success. The degree of complexity and level of systems-intensive effort is a major consideration, as is expected implementation risk.

At this point, precision is elusive, so we instead recommend making relative rough-cut comparisons between opportunities. We often just use ranges for categorizing each opportunity's annualized EBITDA impact ($0–100k, $100–250k, $250–500k, $500k–1,000k, etc.).

The fancy name for the method of evaluating alternatives against multiple variables of various relative importance is "weighted criteria decision analysis." It's a way to create a single relative score for each alternative to assist in prioritizing them. For evaluating our list of opportunities, we give each criterion an importance weighting (1–10) and each opportunity a score for each criterion (1–5).

Figure 5.2 shows an example of a weighted criteria scorecard, comparing three opportunities and their relative benefits and costs and efforts. It illustrates how three generic opportunities – a commercial expansion opportunity, a local quick-win opportunity, and

Weighted Criteria Scorecard	Weight 10=High	Opportunity #1 Large Expansion		Opportunity #2 Local Quick Win		Opportunity #3 Large System	
		Score	Total	Score	Total	Score	Total
Strategic Fit	10	5	50	2	20	5	50
Net Annualized EBITDA Impact	10	5	50	2	20	4	40
One-Time Positive Cash Impact	5	0	0	0	0	0	0
Other (Capabilities, Enabler...)	4	5	20	2	0	5	20
Relative Benefits			**120**		**40**		**110**
One-Time Implementation Costs	8	4	32	0	0	5	40
Implementation Duration	6	3	18	1	6	4	24
Systems Intensity and Complexity	6	2	12	0	0	5	30
Other (Cross-Functional Effort, Risk)	2	2	4	0	0	3	6
−Relative Cost & Effort			**66**		**6**		**100**
= Net Relative Benefits			**54**		**34**		**10**

Note:
■ Green is favorable; ■ Yellow is slightly unfavorable; ■ Red is unfavorable

Figure 5.2   Multifactor Decision-Making

a larger systems implementation opportunity – might get evaluated using such an approach.

In this example, while Opportunity 3 has high relative benefits, its cost and effort score particularly high as well, so it is the least attractive of the three opportunities. Once we calculate relative weighted scores for all opportunities, we plot each opportunity on the benefits versus cost and effort matrix.

There are three important caveats to mention at this juncture:

Score is not the final say. The score is not the ultimate arbiter in the decision-making process. The weighted criteria scorecard is simply a single input – a useful and focusing one – to guide further executive discussion and subsequent decisions. With the grid in hand, it's useful to then reconvene the executive team to fine-tune priorities. Inevitably, there will be opportunities in the high-benefit, low-cost quadrant that after further discussion are not pursued in the first set of efforts. Similarly, certain lower-value and lower-cost opportunities may receive higher priority in the end, perhaps to accelerate lower-risk quick-wins to help the team gain initial momentum. Opportunities for which there is high and broad employee enthusiasm or opportunities that unlock and enable other high-value opportunities might be prioritized higher than the black-and-white scoring would have us do.

No in-flight passes. In-flight initiatives need to be evaluated with the same rigor against the same criteria as all other opportunities. At any given time, companies have dozens of efforts underway. Particularly in the middle-market, these projects often have happenstance origins, were not rigorously vetted (or vetted in a vacuum), or are "one-off" efforts that were not compared and evaluated against an entire suite of options. Hard as it may be, in-flight initiatives and associated costs incurred and progress made to date should be considered as sunk costs. Just because the team spent a million dollars so far on building a system that they now know provides insufficient benefits compared to newly illuminated opportunities is no reason to continue putting money into it. Sunk-cost bias should not prevent PEG and portco leadership from deprioritizing, pausing, or even canceling lesser value in-flight initiatives.

Nothing personal. Undoubtedly, various individuals, executives, managers, and staff alike have put a lot of personal capital – commitment, time, and effort – into in-flight initiatives or in proposed new opportunities. When "their" project is deprioritized, paused, or canceled, they naturally might take it personally. Others may see it as a personal condemnation that "their" new opportunity got pushed to the back burner. Significant personal commitment and enthusiasm for an effort – to the point that the effort seems fully associated with an individual or team – is admirable. But smart OPs and CEOs will have built a teaming environment such that it's clear that individuals (and their opportunities) have not "won" or "lost" a place on the priority list. It's all about limited resources, relative costs and merits of opportunities, and hard choices. The surest route to channeling the strengths of an individual or team whose "initiative" did not make it through the first round of vetting is to assign them one of the new high-priority opportunities to shepherd, enabling them to continue to grow and excel.

Number of Opportunities

How many is the right number of opportunities to pursue at once? The starting point for this discussion typically begins by observing that too many simultaneous initiatives mean lots of resources spread thin. When project budgets and people's time are spread too thin, project quality deteriorates, project timelines lengthen, and project outcomes disappoint.

As a result (and for reasons that are hard to pinpoint), we see lots of leaders gravitate to a seemingly inevitable answer of three to five opportunities. It's as if years ago some business guru uttered the statement in a specific context that now has become a baked-in law of business.

The three-to-five range does have merit, but it depends a great deal on the scale and scope of the opportunities you're considering and the organization that's implementing them. For a large multinational company, simply hiring a divisional controller, piloting a preventive maintenance program, and implementing the annual US price increase would be underloading the number and kind of improvement efforts it could handle. On the other hand, a small local business would be aiming too high if their opportunities included becoming the international market leader, converting from manual to lights-out automated production lines, and restructuring the organization top-to-bottom. Some companies have four independent business units, where others rely on a single small executive team. The rule of three to five is therefore pretty useless decontextualized, but since opportunity lists that have been thoroughly evaluated are always contextualized, a much better and more organic answer of how many priorities a portco can adopt will emerge upon consideration.

The right number of opportunities a portfolio company can pursue simultaneously depends on a variety of situation-specific considerations. The size and structure of the company and the general health and current performance of the business are important starting points. Also important are the availability of financial, systems, and particularly personnel resources (both internal and external), as well as program and project management skills and processes. The capabilities, bandwidth, and experience the management team has in organizing and driving focused efforts matters a great deal, as do intangible factors like the degree of "can-do" mindset present in the CEO and leadership team and the general culture of accomplishment and accountability.

So let's imagine a hypothetical portco: a healthy small-to-midsized single site, single P&L company led by a long-proven CEO, a well-oiled leadership team, and a capable management team that possesses all the necessary experiences and resources to drive focused improvement efforts. In a scenario like that, we suspect it could in fact pursue a few broad strategies during the investment period, each of which could have several initiatives associated with it at any given time. The number of *simultaneous* opportunities that such a company could successfully tackle at any given time might in truth be in the vicinity of a dozen or two.

Regardless of the number of opportunities pursued, the team needs to make sure that each one is doable within an appropriate time horizon, valuable with respect to at least one of the primary value levers (EBITDA, balance sheet, multiple), and sustainable for the long-term benefit to the company and the investors.

Profiling and Planning Initiatives

The initial key to success in turning opportunities into initiatives is planning and support. Forward-looking OPs and CEOs ensure all initiatives are properly resourced, and they work with the executive team to create a plan to drive accountability for timing and ROI commitments. Initiatives fall short when PEGs have not worked to create a genuine partnership with their portcos, and therefore have created neither an initiatives-based nor accountability-based culture. If PEGs do specify objectives, they're often out of reach by way of scope or timing or lack support and buy-in from the team. Strong PEG/portco teams set clear expectations through a well-defined initiative planning process.

Defining Initiatives

By an initiative, we mean an opportunity that is instrumental for a company to accomplish in order to achieve a major strategy during the investment period. At exit, a well-positioned portco can point to a half-dozen major strategies that it accomplished through the myriad initiatives that were implemented and that drove value.

Let's take a concrete example to illustrate the point (temporarily setting aside the question of how strategies were identified). A major strategy for a middle-market portco might be to "Expand into Europe" with the related objective of achieving an incremental $20 million annualized EBITDA within five years. To accomplish this strategy and reach their objective, the PEG and portco may decide to undertake four initial initiatives in the next 12–18 months, and then reload with new initiatives as they accomplish initiatives from the first set. That first set of initiatives could include developing the EU market-entry plan, hire EU leader and core team, establish EU corporate office, and partner with country distributors.

Completing an individual initiative typically requires somewhere between two and eight months (give or take a month). Initiatives are impactful, with tangible and preferably quantifiable benefits – either from a P&L, balance sheet, or (admittedly less quantifiable) exit multiple perspective. They are often cross-functional (but don't have to be).

Together, these initiatives and strategies will add up to the accomplishments of the investment period. The team will have only a few years to get a handful of strategies accomplished to make hopefully 3× return or more for their investors and to optimize the outcomes for the management team.

Profiling Initiatives

Particularly in the middle-market, we find executives and managers have various levels of experience in the science of project management and therefore various degrees of skill at efficiently and effectively scoping and planning initiatives. Managers who are new to lining up and driving initiatives require some training and support in profiling them. The OP might get tasked with assisting these managers, or forward-looking portcos might decide to formalize this new support by bringing on a specific full-time (albeit temporary) program manager to support the initiative profiling effort and then to coordinate and drive the set of initiatives.

The initiative profile (also sometimes called a project charter) should follow a standard format because the management team and OP will be reviewing many profiles for final prioritization and will be repeatedly referring back to them over time. Each profile should be complete with a common set of components to facilitate ease of understanding, comparison, and prioritization. With clear initiative profiles, everyone knows who is signing up to complete what, achieve what, and in what sequence. It enables both PEGs and portcos to hold each other accountable for how a particular initiative will achieve value creation expectations. Figure 5.3 offers an example of an initiative profile.

Initiative	Initiative Name	Initiative Description: Insert Description, Objective, Scope		
Responsibilities	Executive Sponsor: Name	Initiative Leader: Name	Team Members: Name, Time Rqts.	External Support: Name of Firms
Benefits & Costs	KPI Impact: Description	Annualized EBITDA: $420k (See Detail)	One-Time: –$100k (See Detail)	ROI (NPV, Payback): $1,200k, 3 Months

Timing and Impact ($000) by Month by Milestone	Jan	Feb	Mar	Apr	May	Jun	Jul	Aug	Sep	Oct	Nov	Dec
Analyze: Describe milestones	0	–5										
Design: Describe milestones		–5	–10	–10								
Develop: Describe milestones				–5	–20	–20	–20					
Implement: Describe milestones							–5	0	35	35	35	35
Total Cash Flow	0	–10	–10	–15	–20	–20	–25	0	35	35	35	35

Note:
Annualized EBITDA is net ongoing post-implementation
■ Green is favorable; ■ Yellow is investment

Figure 5.3 Initiative Profile

Initiative Name and Description

Every initiative needs a name and a description. While that might seem obvious, choosing and writing these are both important and informative.

Initiative name. We've found that properly naming the initiative serves to continuously reinforce its objective. The name assigned to an initiative should clearly communicate initiative intent. For instance, "Establish Inside Sales Team," "Reorganize Inside Sales," "Develop Inside Sales Playbook," or "Double Outbound Calls" is much clearer than "Inside Sales."

Description. Each initiative profile should include a section for a clear definition or description. The definition should expand upon the name, clarify details of scope and objectives, and articulate in simple terms why the initiative is important and what it will bring to the company. From the description alone, anyone in the company should easily understand what the initiative is and why it's being pursued. For instance, an initiative "Consolidate Warehouses" might be described as "Consolidate Smith Street warehouse into Maple Street warehouse within six months to eliminate double handling, reducing combined operating expense by $1 million (25 percent) and improving shipping lead time by one day."

Team Responsibilities

For each initiative, we like to specify four primary roles – executive sponsor, team leader, team members, and external support. Assigned names should be specific, and typically only a single point person named in the executive sponsor and team leader boxes.

Executive Sponsor. The executive sponsor is a single member on the executive team (sometimes the CEO but more often one of his or her direct reports) that is responsible to help finalize initiative scope and objectives. He or she should secure the right resources to see the initiative through. The executive sponsor is responsible to help remove roadblocks and resolve issues, especially those that are significant and cross-functional. They should serve as an ongoing coach to the initiative team leader, continuously challenging and assisting to generate better and faster results.

Team Leader. An initiative team leader has the primary responsibility to plan and accomplish the initiative. The team leader is the point person through which the initiative flows and is the single person responsible to identify and resolve issues and execute the plan. The team leader organizes and guides team members as well as external support when needed. While he or she does not need to personally accomplish every task, the team leader does need to ensure every task is properly accomplished.

The right team leader will have an excellent blend of knowledge, capability, and character. Because the team leader role is often a part-time one (particularly in smaller companies), he or she should have the dedication and drive to go the extra mile to accomplish initiatives in addition to doing their day-to-day roles. Great team leaders get great stuff done for the business and create future opportunities for themselves, their team members, and the rest of the organization. Being selected as a team leader should certainly be viewed as both an opportunity and an honor. Needless to say, selecting the right team leader for an initiative is perhaps the single most important factor in whether or not an initiative will succeed.

Team Members. Particularly in the middle-market, initiative team members often serve part-time on one or more initiatives. They include subject matter experts (SMEs) and the taskmasters that together drive the initiative forward. The team should also include process owners – those people responsible for the areas being impacted by the initiative. A good team, working well together, will likely meet regularly (typically weekly) to report accomplishments and assign new tasks.

External Support. Many initiatives require a temporary skillset not otherwise available within the company, and in these cases we typically look to external support. These are the independent contractors and boutique or larger consulting firms that provide necessary skills when and as needed. They are resources that the company needs to execute the initiative, but not necessarily full-time beyond the initiative end-date. Examples here include system programmers for an ERP initiative, expert equipment installers for a new manufacturing plant, or a brand strategist that can help a company reset their messaging.

Benefits and Costs

As described earlier in the opportunities list prioritization discussion, the initiative leader will want to consider the range of likely benefits associated with their initiatives, including impact on KPIs, net annualized EBITDA impact, one-time costs or benefits, and ROI.

Initiative profiling is more detailed than what the team did as part of opportunity prioritization. It's at this point that we move from rough-cut relative impact calculations to more accurate assessments of costs and benefits, and the associated expected monthly impacts of those figures. In calculating costs, benefits, and ROIs, the focus here should be on accuracy over precision. We recommend focusing time and energy on sensitivity analyses on the various assumptions over calculating a single number to an implied precision, which will never be perfectly proven. The first two digits for a $1.2m initiative need to be right; after that, whether it's calculated as $1.232m or $1.245m is inconsequential.

KPI impacts. Many initiatives will serve to improve KPI results, which in turn impact the bottom line. For instance, the initiative "Implement Customer Ordering Portal" might eliminate a full day from processing times as orders will no longer be queued up and then manually entered by customer service reps. The KPI order lead time should be reduced by one day, say from three to two days, or a 33 percent improvement from this initiative alone. While they can plan for and track that KPI, it will be more difficult to track the bottom-line impact of the presumedly happier customer getting their stuff faster. But because customer service will no longer enter orders, which took say 20 percent of their time, the team leader may commit to reducing 15 percent of the associated costs (while aiming for 20 percent).

In this example, the team leader will commit to achieving one-day lead time improvement and 15–20 percent cost reduction, which results in a high enough ROI to justify the initiative, with the revenue impact from more satisfied customers as icing on the cake.

Annualized EBITDA impact. Many if not most initiatives will result in a net positive impact on the bottom line. While some initiatives may require new, ongoing expenses to achieve, their benefits more than offset those expenses, resulting in net benefits perpetuating each month post-implementation. There are many examples of net positive EBITDA initiatives, such as opening a new service facility, launching an internal sales team, improving service or production quality, or developing new products or services.

There are also plenty of examples of important initiatives having a net negative direct impact on future EBITDA. For instance, a company may decide to undertake a sale-leaseback of its property. In this case, it might find more value in the large near-term one-time favorable cash impact than in the ongoing negative EBITDA impact. Maybe the company will sell a building for $10 million, then lease back office space for $500k per year and apply the cash influx to various other high-value opportunities.

Like the example above, most initiatives will have a mix of positive and negative operating expense impacts. Implementing new systems to generate efficiencies down the line will undoubtedly have one-time cost outlays such as system configuration expenses and negative ongoing expenses, such as system lease expense, but these are intended to be offset by operational benefits going forward.

One-time impact. One-time impacts can be favorable or unfavorable. Some initiatives result in a one-time benefit – a favorable one-time impact. Examples here may include selling equipment for a one-time cash pickup, reducing product offerings and associated SKUs and their inventories, reducing lead times and therefore the need for extra capacity, or implementing better commercial policies and practices that might favorably impact accounts receivable balances.

Unfavorable one-time costs are often thought of as implementation costs – those required to support the analysis, design, development, and implementation of the initiative. These costs have a definitive start and stop, typically at the end of a certain milestone or by the end of the project. Examples of unfavorable one-time costs might include consultants to help analyze the situation, travel expenses for team members to work together, programmers to develop a new tool or system, and implementation training before rollout. Companies will often exclude normal internal costs from attribution to specific initiatives. For instance, the internal cost of personnel working part-time on an initiative might not be included in the one-time costs associated with an initiative because presumably they are not incremental costs.

ROI and payback. Each PEG and portco will have its own preference for how to combine quantified costs and benefits into an initiative's targeted return-on-investment, including internal rate of return (IRR), net present value NPV – with or without terminal value – or a simple payback calculation in terms of months or years. Financially savvy PEGs typically prefer a combination of methods.

It's worth noting that in light of the relative brevity of the investment period, private equity tends to be more conservative in high-cost project approvals, expecting shorter payback periods than what large public companies or small closely held private companies might expect. Worthy initiatives having less than a one-year payback are usually highly likely to be pursued, whereas initiatives with paybacks longer than three or so years usually require particularly convincing justification.

ROIs ffor initiatives also tend to tighten as portcos approach the exit. For instance, a PEG looks even harder at an initiative showing a three-year payback during the last year of an investment period than it would early in the period. That's not to say paybacks extending beyond expected sell-dates should not be considered, as progressing on but not yet completing valuable initiatives should be viewed positively and indirectly rewarded through attracting better buyers and higher bids.

Milestones and Cash Flow

It is at the milestone level that people outside of the direct initiative team can best understand and track progress. This is the level for which those outside the core initiative team – the executives, board of directors, equity team, and others associated with the portfolio company – can clearly grasp what must be done by when. Initiative leaders sometimes incorrectly assume more detail is better, but for VCP steering, less – but concise, clear, and informative – is better.

Milestones. We define milestones as the most significant events during an initiative. For most initiatives, half a dozen or so milestones typically suffice. Milestones sometimes represent the completion of major deliverables such as current state reviews, future state plans, or newly signed contracts. Other times, milestones represent the completion of major initiative phases such as analysis, design, development, and implementation. Or milestones may instead relate more to outcomes – such as obtain approval, secure funding, and achieve first production. If the initiative is "Relocate Corporate Office," the milestones might include selecting a commercial real estate firm, defining requirements for a new office, identifying new space and obtaining a lease, building-out office space changes, moving into the new building, and subletting the old building.

Assuming an initiative may require anywhere from a few weeks to several months to complete, initiative milestones would tend to occur every two to four weeks, with each milestone having a completion date associated with it. It's therefore logical to target a total of four to eight milestones – any more than that tends to cloud and confuse those not intimate with the daily details of the initiative.

The use of milestones does not negate the need for detailed work plans for the initiative team's use. While milestones are useful as a status communication tool for steering members as well as a focusing tool for the initiative team itself, it is usually insufficient for planning and accomplishing task-level activities. Team leaders need to use whatever is necessary to plan their initiatives and guide their teams – detailed work plans, individual task lists, and sometimes formal project management systems.

Cash flow. Each initiative has associated costs and benefits as described, and therefore associated monthly cash flows as well. We like to include cash flow projections in initiative profiles. Having monthly cash flows planned up front enables tracking of actual inflows and outflows against that plan as the initiative progresses. With that, the team can be confident that the financial impacts are occurring at the expected levels and can make adjustments mid-project if they are not. For instance, if consultants are engaged to support the initiative and their monthly burn rate exceeds expectations, the team leader and sponsor can intervene – either to reduce spending or to confirm the additional consulting time and spending is providing more than offsetting incremental value.

The alternative to planning for and then tracking monthly cash flows – both ins and outs against the plan – is to wait for the end of the initiative to do the final accounting. By that time, it's too late to impact initiative economics.

Suspending Strategic Planning Formalities

We've articulated our rationale for specifying core values and explained at length the process for arriving at the initial suite of initiatives, but have not spoken much about formal strategic planning. There's a reason for that: As counterintuitive as it sounds, we believe performance-oriented PEGs begin investment periods leveraging materials already in hand (sell-side I-bank presentations, diligence market studies) and in-head (management team and equity partner insight) to get a jump start on new momentum. They do not delay value creation to plan, organize, and complete an elaborate and somewhat redundant formal strategic planning exercise.

The benefits of unbounded strategic planning are plentiful, not the least of which is an informative and exhaustive review of all possible future options available to a company. But at the risk of offending proponents of the process, the problem with traditional strategic planning is that it often takes a lot of time, costs a lot of money, consumes scarce leadership mindshare, and at times produces disappointing results or binders that just get shelved. Middle-market private equity does not have the time, money, or energy to spare, and can often get better results through a different route.

To be sure, the reason strategic planning has not delivered consistent "bang for the buck" cannot be placed entirely on the process. We've certainly seen instances of precise analytics and intellectual frameworks undercut by leaders simply reverting to their intuitions. Still, we've also seen our fair share of too many meetings accompanied by too many slide decks loaded with painstaking data and coupled with academic frameworks that in the end either fail to compel concrete and actionable next steps or simply serve to confirm an already-known path forward. In fact, there's a strong case that can be made against engaging in broad-based strategic planning at the outset of the investment period.

Not Wanting to Delay

Traditional strategic planning takes time. Time to decide to do it, time to find, hire, and scope a consultant to help, and time to get organized, research, document, facilitate, workshop, and iterate. It simply takes a lot of time. At the beginning of a new investment period, we don't want to wait to start gaining momentum. Months of diligence and subsequent onboarding have revealed many actionable things to do that can add value right away. Opportunistic PEGs and their portco partners prefer to get started with the Value Creation Program and initial execution as soon as possible, then tweak it later.

Didn't Want to Get Distracted

Early in the investment period there are so many new things at play – new relationships, additional reporting, and a fresh operating cadence. Adding a new strategic planning process on top of everything else is liable to topple the delicate balance that is just beginning to emerge. Just getting on the same page regarding what strategic planning will entail and how to go about it is a distraction. Better to focus on the here and now with what is known to be necessary and immediately beneficial than to pause progress to ponder several years out. That can be done later, when the PEG/portco team have some joint experience under belts. Nor is the traditional approach of a 10-year vision for the company suitable for the investment period time horizon.

Weren't Prepared Yet

The PEG team and portco team all just onboarded together and barely know one another. At this early point in the investment period, they've likely not yet identified or onboarded outside board directors, which are often selected based on their deep industry experiences and strategic insight. Those board directors should be part of any formal strategic planning process.

At the same time, while the equity partners know the business from diligence, they do not yet know the lived reality of the business – the team, the individuals and their strengths and capabilities, the customers, the unique things that make the company unique. The portco leadership team is similarly not yet familiar with their PEG partners, likely having little understanding of the private equity industry and the goals and constraints of a typical investment period. All these are important inputs to an effective and efficient strategic planning process in a private equity portfolio company, and all of them are unknowns at this stage.

Pretty Much Already Did It

It's worth also taking a deeper look at what the strategic planning process promises to deliver. The details vary, depending on whom you speak with, but they all typically involve three main components: external situation assessment, internal situation assessment, and company objectives and priorities definition. A closer look at diligence and VCP opportunity gathering reveals that conscientious PEGs and their partner portcos have already completed 90 percent of the strategic planning process by this time anyway:

External situation assessment includes analyses of the industry, marketplace, customers, and suppliers – the trends, opportunities, and threats, the customers' current and evolving needs, the competition, suppliers, and overall industry dynamics. At this point, the PEG and portco already have that: The portco team just worked for weeks and months with their sell-side investment bank to create the situation assessment inputs for the confidential investment memorandum (CIM). They likely retained an investment banker and painstakingly documented the business – unique company capabilities, future opportunities, and rational justifications for why a potential buyer would be so excited about buying the business. Similarly on the buy-side, the PEG just commissioned hundreds of thousands of dollars of due diligence analyses, including a plethora of market and industry studies, industry expert interviews, and voice of the customer research, and then spent weeks and months studying all that. And as part of the onboarding process, the PEG/portco team has spent a good deal of time debriefing using precisely those materials.

Internal situation assessment is the second element to strategic planning, including analyses of portfolio company core capabilities, critical success factors, processes, systems, and organizations – their strengths and relative weaknesses. Better PEGs and their portco partners already have that, too: The management team knows the intricacies of their company and the PEG team just spent weeks and months studying the details of the company during diligence, with management interviews and tons and tons of company data. The equity partners have been expanding insights from diligence as they onboarded, completed days-in-the-lives, worked through monthly reporting and operating cadence, and partnered with management on developing a set of KPIs with important cause-and-effect logic of what drives the business. Plus, the PEG/portco team just finished onboarding together and working through baseline information.

Company objectives and action priorities typically comprise the third component to strategic planning, including understanding the internal and external situation and the associated strengths, weaknesses, opportunity, and threats, and coming up with the highest expected-value initiatives for creating value in that environment. If the point is to achieve an understanding of overall business and financial objectives, those have been clear since day one: Optimize enterprise value during the investment period to achieve an attractive cash-on-cash return for the investors. Accomplishing that involves organizing initiatives into logical (i.e., strategic) buckets and prioritizing and planning them out from a time, scope, cost, and benefits perspective. It also involves succinctly documenting those initiatives and the organization and sequencing of those initiatives and communicating those clearly across the company. But the PEG/portco team has already done this as well as they developed the Value Creation Program.

		Traditional Strategic Planning		Pragmatic Strategic Planning	
Preacquisition	–		–	Leverage	Leverage I-Bank CIM (strategic analysis), due diligence, VOC
First Year	Pause & Prepare	Decide how to do strategy; find consultant; scope work		Quick Start	Onboard, develop Value Creation Plan, & initiate execution
	Analyze	Discovery, analysis, voice-of-customer (VOC), slide-ware		Execute	–
	Workshops	Off-site meetings, update deck of presentations, revise & edit		Execute	–
	Finalize	Incorporate new strategies into budget, refine for feasibility		Execute	Reconfirm strategies, integrate into budget (while execution continues)
Second Year	Execute	After 6–9 months and $100k–$300k, implement strategies		Execute	Achieve 2–3 more quarters of focused execution at fraction of cost

Note:
Pragmatic Strategic Planning starts with initial Value Creation Program followed by reconfirmation
■ Green is highly productive; ■ Yellow is partially productive

Figure 5.4   Traditional versus Pragmatic Strategic Planning

Figure 5.4 sums up the timelines for the two alternative strategic planning approaches – traditional and pragmatic – and illustrates the delays involved in a traditional approach versus the benefits of focusing on the VCP right out of the gates.

Finalizing the Value Creation Plan

At a fundamental level, slow-to-act PEGs don't understand the importance of focus and clarity. They don't appreciate the importance and benefits of rowing in the same direction all together – in the same boat, in unison, and across a reasonably sized lake. They don't take the time to be succinct and clear regarding the intended objective and direction for the company to take.

Better PEGs take the time to document and communicate a concise vision for the direction of the portfolio company, summarizing portco objectives, value proposition, strategies, initiatives, and core values. They realize it's important for the entire team to understand and literally be able to personally articulate where the company intends to go and how it will get there.

The One-Page VCP Summary

As it turns out, the components of the strategic planning process have all been largely addressed. The only thing that's missing is putting that succinctly all into a single document – an extremely clear and concise Value Creation Plan. Over the days and weeks of generating ideas, prioritizing opportunities, and profiling initiatives, the OP and CEO will simultaneously be spending time organizing all that thinking and work product into a crisp, overarching plan for what's most important for the company.

The resulting document, similar to the illustration shown in Figure 5.5, includes the first pass at a one-page summary of the Value Creation Plan. Think of it as the cover sheet or executive summary for the individual initiative profiles the team has been developing together.

Investment Objective	Achieve $X EBITDA (X% margin) on $X revenue by 20XX up $X from the investment period starting point of $X (X% margin) on $X in 20XX			
Value Proposition	Be the preeminent ... for customers in the ... through ...			
Strategies & EBITDA Impact	Strategy A ($0–0m)	Strategy B ($0–0m)	Strategy C ($0–0m)	Strategy D ($0–0m)
Key Initiatives (Next 6–12 Months)	Initiative A1	Initiative B1	Initiative C1	Initiative D1
	Initiative A2	Initiative B2	Initiative C2	Initiative D2
	Initiative A3	Initiative B3	Initiative C3	Initiative D3
Core Values	Value 1 | Value 2 | Value 3			

Figure 5.5 Value Creation Program Summary

Investment objective. The investment objective will be quite clear, as the equity partners developed that to obtain approval from their investment committee to purchase the company. They will have an investment model showing a reasonable scenario for the outcome of the investment period, often largely predicated on what the portco executive team said during the recent sale process (through management presentations and diligence meetings) regarding what they could deliver during the investment period. Prudent PEGs will hedge that "management case" a bit if possible.

For the VCP, it makes sense for the OP and CEO to summarize the objective into a simple statement focused on EBITDA growth – for instance, "Achieve $60m EBITDA (15% margin) on $400m revenue by 20XX (up $30m from the investment period starting point of $30m (10% margin) on $300m revenue in 20YY)." There's no ambiguity that the objective is to grow this business – both revenue and margin – to achieve a healthy return for the investors.

Value proposition. The value proposition (at least initially) will also be fairly clear. This early in the investment period, the equity partners will likely choose to simply continue the company's course with how they've been addressing a specific need in the marketplace. Once the PEG team becomes more familiar with the business, they may choose to expand, tighten, or even change their value proposition. (The same is true for the Value Creation Plan – it, too, will evolve throughout the investment period as more initiatives on-board while others are completed).

As with the investment objective, we recommend keeping things focused and clear – for instance, "To be North America's preeminent provider of heavy-duty advanced all-terrain field service vehicles for rugged and remote pipeline, transmission, and forestry industry deployments."

Strategies and EBITDA impacts. As explained above, the strategies emerge as a product of leveraging the collective wisdom of the equity partners and portco management coupled with diligence and baseline materials already in hand. Using a top-down and bottom-up process driven by both investment objectives and initiative profiles, the CEO and the OP will nurture and articulate a refined set of a half-dozen strategies to get started with. Through an intuitive process of manipulating, enhancing, clarifying, and grouping of initiatives in light of investment objectives, a practical and cohesive set of main strategies emerges.

For instance, despite top-down claims of the ability to expand into all of Latin America, the bottom-up process (at least for now) has focused on only enlarging the company's footprint in Mexico and using that as a launching point into Costa Rica and Panama. So the CEO and OP bucket the five related VCP initiatives under the strategic heading "Expand into Central America" and note a targeted incremental $2m for that first set of initiatives.

Key initiatives. We've spoken at length about generating ideas, prioritizing opportunities, and profiling initiatives for the VCP. As shown in Figure 5.5, the VCP will have just the *first* set of key initiatives, maybe covering the initial 6–12 months. These represent the most impactful, important, or high-risk initiatives that need careful steering attention. Smaller, less risky projects and intra-functional efforts will not necessarily be tracked formally in the VCP.

The VCP is and should be a living and breathing instrument monitoring the most important things going on in the business, periodically refined to reflect new thinking and new initiatives to further pursue the value proposition and investment objectives.

Core values. Earlier in the book we spoke about core values at length. The VCP must reflect a clear set of company core values to help steer decisions and guide behavior on an everyday basis. Core values are critical to a well-run and fast-growing middle-market portco. We believe it is important to always keep core values front and center, including displayed as the foundation of the VCP.

Kickoff. Once the Value Creation Program is set, there's only one more thing that needs to be done: hosting the VCP kickoff meeting. The kickoff represents the opportunity for the CEO to gather the entire management team and professional staff together to clearly communicate the Value Creation Program for the investment period – the objectives, value proposition, strategies, initial initiatives, and the related timelines, ROI expectations, and importantly, team assignments. This meeting serves to get everyone on the same page regarding the vision and specific priorities for the next year or so. It sets the stage for a new set of vernaculars that will serve to reinforce the VCP each day.

Living and Breathing the Value Creation Program

To be certain, assembling a succinct and clear approach to achieve targeted value during the investment period requires work. As the vignette from GrammCo illustrates, it takes time and discussion and many iterations to decide and articulate the definitive initial VCP summary. There's also the understanding that the VCP is not written in stone. Over the coming months and years, GrammCo's VCP will morph in many ways – initiatives finishing and moving off the page while new ones come on, while new insights and market changes arise and so new strategies are identified or emerge. But with the Value Creation Program in hand, everyone at the company knows where they are going and how they will get there – both qualitatively and quantitatively – which will help GrammCo weather its first storms and bumps in the road.

Chapter 6
Quarter 2: A Bit Overwhelmed

"He had only one thing to do and that was what he should think about and he must think it out clearly and take everything as it came along, and not worry. To worry was as bad as to be afraid. It simply made things more difficult."

Ernest Hemingway, *For Whom the Bell Tolls*

"Don't they... realize we're... trying to run... a business here?" Kathleen Easton huffed as she speed-walked across the shop floor alongside colleague and Chief Engineer David Bedford. Kathleen was GrammCo's VP of Supply Chain, but as of late felt she was training to be a sprinter given the uptick in meetings she was involved in.

"Evidently not," David added, keeping pace with Kathleen while striving to maintain his own oxygen level.

(continued)

(*continued*)

"This will be the fourth meeting I've attended this week!" he exclaimed, now habitually but needlessly glancing at his watch in reference to the week. The watch was a new addition to his wardrobe, as Dianne and Shed had let him know it was no longer okay to amble into meetings late as he always had before.

Making a mental note to tease him later about his watch-checking, Kathleen let her thoughts turn to their new regimen as they hustled through the building to the conference room ...

It was true they'd been meeting quite a bit. During the last few weeks, all executives and most managers had participated in a variety of meetings and activities to develop, organize, and initiate the Value Creation Program. The new program manager Sam Fredericks was definitely keeping the trains running on time. Sam fit right in and Kathleen knew his dedication would be instrumental to the VCP process becoming fully engrained. GrammCo was a pretty tight-knit team, but Sam proved his value right out of the gates when he saved a couple of potentially costly mistakes from happening and accelerated the timeline for the *Relocate Vegas Facility* initiative by four weeks.

Despite the extra hours devoted to meetings, the team found they'd enjoyed the exercises, appreciated the process, and were subsequently thrilled to see their priorities documented so clearly. Russ had never taken an interest in – and Dianne never had time for – succinctly documenting GrammCo's full set of objectives and strategies, as well as initiatives, accountabilities, milestones, and targets for the next 18 months or so.

They'd been especially pleased to finally all be on the same page regarding company direction, quite literally with the one-page summary VCP. Each GrammCo leader could pretty much re-create that single strategy page from memory on their whiteboards to share with their own teams. It felt good to be so focused and to be able to keep the whole team focused as well.

And Kathleen liked the teams she was working with on her initiatives. But the momentum was overwhelming at times. She was no longer just responsible for day-to-day execution of Supply Chain activity; she was involved in much more and was being held personally accountable in ways she had never felt back when Russ owned the company. It was both daunting and invigorating.

Rushing together now past the break room, David interrupted those upbeat thoughts with others. "Between driving these new initiatives and attending the new meetings and babysitting those new consultants and still trying to get all my normal design work done, I'm bustin' my tail!" he said, adding, "Seems I've been working late every day since PLC bought us."

"It is a bit overwhelming," Kathleen commiserated as they approached the conference room door, becoming distracted now with concerns of her own. She sensed she was about to get a clear demonstration of the difference between being responsible and being accountable.

It wasn't five minutes later when Kathleen was wrapping up her three-minute summary of the *Redesign Receiving Processes* initiative. Dianne was squinting, focused, "It shows Green, but what you just said sounded like we're not on track. In fact, it sounds like we're significantly off track, not only in timing but with the benefits you'd signed up for."

(continued)

(*continued*)

"Well, I'm hoping to ... "

"Stop. Kathleen. We need to be candid here, remember? We're a team, and when one of us needs help – and we all do from time to time – we huddle up. We want to support you; what can we do?" Dianne glanced only briefly at Shed Cooper and Sam Fredericks. They'd anticipated this conversation and were ready.

The next 10 minutes were productive. Kathleen acknowledged she needed help, and the team banded together to do just that. Dave Bedford suggested he could help Kathleen work through some adjustments in the morning and Shed offered to join as well. The VP of Sales offered up his analyst, who'd expressed interest in supply chain operations and had some good ideas, too. Reenergized by her colleagues' support, Kathleen concluded, "Thanks all! With your help, I'm confident we can get back on track."

"Excellent, thank you, Kathleen, and thank you everyone. We're counting on these process enhancements to help achieve next quarter's revenue plans. No one likes meetings, but we have them for exactly this purpose – to ensure these initiatives get done on-time and as planned."

"Okay let's move on to the next initiative." Dianne turned to David, smiling, "You're up."

Ensuring Leadership Coverage

Things continue to get even busier at GrammCo. There are probably 15 or 20 initiatives underway covering a multitude of avenues for EBITDA growth and other improvements, organized into strategies to form their Value Creation Program. But making a plan and holding people accountable for implementing it are two different things. Shed has attended update meetings and asked all sorts of questions about milestone dates slipping and benefit commitments being broken, which naturally leads to questions of commitment and accountability. Lurking in the wings are feelings of being overwhelmed.

A hallmark of inattentive PEGs is the abdication of responsibility, and since responsibility starts at the top, that leads back to a failure of leadership. PEGs like these do not take enough time to evaluate leadership requirements needed to implement intended value creation strategies. Some assume that merely dangling a large enough potential bonus or a lucrative option package will simply do the trick – that portco leadership would suddenly now have both the capabilities in addition to the motivation they didn't have before, or think that if portco leadership wasn't trying before they'll "buckle down" and work harder to get it all done.

Performance-oriented PEGs realize that lining up and knocking down initiatives to support investment period objectives – and then lining up the next round – is quite different from the common day-to-day of running the business. They realize that while many business leaders and managers are capable of doing the latter, they haven't had the experience of simultaneously driving the multiple initiatives that make up the Value Creation Program. Forward-thinking OPs and CEOs therefore work to shore up the team – with skillsets, bandwidth, and processes – setting them up for success.

Ensuring proper leadership coverage is perhaps the single most important thing for private equity partners to get right once they've purchased a new portfolio company. This is particularly true in the middle-market, where the leadership bench is small. For the most part, these companies have grown up lean and underinvested, with their leaders spinning many plates simultaneously. But during the investment period, each leader is critical to maximizing returns, and the right or wrong selections and reinforcements will have a tremendous impact on value creation. That's why the operating partner and CEO need to work together to identify leadership coverage gaps by strategy early in the Value Creation Program process and to close those gaps through various leadership changes and reinforcement.

Leadership Enhancements and Reinforcements

When a private equity firm purchases a portfolio company, it is purchasing much more than assets and offerings. It's purchasing the management team and their capabilities. Yet like any management team, those found in portcos are rarely if ever perfect and can almost always be improved. Forward-thinking PEGs are not hesitant to make changes to the leadership team, replacing and "top-grading" as necessary. That said, these PEGs are not trigger-happy. Replacing an executive or manager is expensive from several perspectives, not the least of which is the human costs. Collaborative OP and CEO partnerships evaluate the team and adjust or reinforce as necessary – and certainly carefully and respectfully.

Central to those adjustments is analyzing the fit relative to the overarching strategy and its related initiatives, as seen in Figure 6.1. That analysis falls into three steps: evaluation, adjustment, and reinforcement.

Leadership Coverage by Strategy					
Strategy Leader	Strategy 1 (Initiatives 1–3)	Strategy 2 (Initiatives 4–5)	Strategy 3 (Initiatives 6–12)	Strategy 4 (Initiatives 13–20)	Overall for VCP
CEO	High	High	n/a	n/a	High
CFO	n/a	n/a	Medium	High	High
COO	High	n/a	Low	Medium	Medium
VP Sales	Low	Medium	Medium	n/a	Medium
Planned Support	Hire new LATAM leader reporting to CEO	Add external CRM implementation support	Retain consultant for outsourcing work	Monitor 3–4 months; possibly hire new director of operational excellence	1–2 new hires plus selective use of consultants for temporary support

Note:
Each cell has separate supporting detail
■ *Green is high capability;* ■ *Yellow is medium capability;* ■ *Red is low capability*

Figure 6.1   Leadership Coverage Matrix

Evaluation

As described in Chapter 3, executive evaluations look at both their general capabilities and attitudes largely in the abstract, but once the VCP is on the table it's time to also specifically examine their ability to lead and execute the strategies and initiatives with which they're associated.

Not all strategies and initiatives require deep involvement from all executives. As the Value Creation Program is materializing, the OP and CEO should be continuously reviewing leadership coverage, plotting who needs to be involved where and in what way. They need to be identifying coverage gaps where current capabilities and attitudes may be insufficient to ensure strategic success and close those gaps through planned leadership support, adjustments, and reinforcements.

Adjustment

Clear-minded OPs and portco CEOs work together to adjust their leadership teams. They will have instilled such a teaming can-do culture that a periodic moving of chairs and responsibilities as needed is expected if not embraced. Responsibility assignments in execution-oriented businesses should be fluid, evolving as new business requirements are uncovered, individuals' capacities change, and new interests and talents emerge.

Strong OP and CEOs will have the pulse of their team and can make adjustments without offending (and in fact enable face-saving). Sometimes capable managers will need to be reallocated or reassigned to either more demanding or less demanding roles as needed. Part of this is figuring out the right organizational roles (including which need to be created and others that need to be eliminated), and another part of this is monitoring individuals and how they fulfill the demands of the roles they are assigned to.

Reinforcement

The strong partnership between the OP and CEO will lead them to be regularly measuring the capacity and capability of their leaders in order to provide reinforcement as needed. This may involve incorporating additional team members, introducing new reporting or monitoring to ensure progress within guide rails, or introducing external consultants for focused assistance at specific times.

Day-to-day management and project leadership involve different wirings, and there's no shame in bringing in assistance to help with one side or the other. Indeed, the OP does the same when they turn to the expertise of their investing partner, finance director, or anyone else at the PEG. This awareness and candid assessment (including self-assessment) is crucial for successfully executing value creation initiatives on top of running the normal day-to-day business.

Leveraging Consultants

Particularly in middle-market private equity, portfolio companies are saddled with several hurdles related to the use of external resources. The first is simply a recognition of need; they may never have had to manage day-to-day operations while driving a Value Creation Program, and so may not be savvy at scoping their needs and assessing their available talent. And often there is insufficient high-level in-house talent to achieve the intended initiatives at the intended pace. These companies were often built conservatively, and unsurprisingly tend to be under-resourced as a result. These portcos would likely benefit from consultants but rarely register the need.

Then there's the price of consultants – even when portco leadership does recognize the need and their inability to fill the gap in-house, they usually see themselves as being unable to afford big, expensive consulting firms or find affordable consulting talent. Lingering memories of bootstrapping a small, growing, cash-strapped business can make even the most aggressive portco CEO shy away from leveraging consultants.

There's also the perceived level of "care and feeding" required of consultants new to the company – the time and attention they require onboarding to the industry, the company, and the issue at hand. The pushback heard is that consultants in the end slow the company down.

But maybe the biggest sticking point is a misplaced sense of pride. Whether the stated pushback is that there's no real need for a consultant or the price is unaffordable, or the care and feeding is a distraction, implicit in those words is often a fear of being judged as inadequate, as if bringing on a consultant is an admission of failure or lack of trust.

Yet the truth is just the opposite. Mature, capable, and confident portco executives appreciate any justifiable support that will help them achieve their objectives within the few short years of the investment period. Fortunately, in private equity, the use of consultants for specific implementation work may be treated as an "add-back" to EBITDA, meaning that while their use has a negative cash impact, it would not have an unfavorable impact to adjusted EBITDA when compared to budget.

Practical PEGs appreciate executives who assemble the right resources from wherever they can to achieve results. The decision to hire a consultant should simply be about value creation and ROI. Scoped, onboarded, and managed properly, the right consultant with the requisite experience can significantly accelerate an initiative. Their hiring is well justified if it results in a sufficient reduction of implementation timing or risk or drives more benefits to the bottom line.

There are many varieties of consultants: industry, function, or solution specific; large firms, boutiques, or independent contractors; project-mode or by the hour. Used properly, consultants can help accelerate and augment results. They can help during any or all phases of an initiative – analyzing, planning, designing, developing, testing, and implementing. We can summarize what consultants can bring to the table along three dimensions: capability, capacity, and catalyst.

Capability. Portcos can leverage consultants for specific expertise, skills, or knowledge that the company does not have resident in-house. Perhaps it's marketplace insight, new ideas, or technical solutions. Examples are numerous, relating to everything from new six-sigma processes to tax solutions.

Capacity. Middle-market portcos have too much to do and too little time to do it. Each leader wears many hats, supported by too few staff and inefficient systems. Their day-to-days are consumed and consultants can help them to simply get more done. While these leaders could probably do it all if they had more time, they simply haven't the capacity to do it all.

Catalyst. People get stuck in their ways, and in the middle-market, we often see a heads-down focused mentality on the day-to-day getting product out or services done. Consultants can bring an independent review and a fresh perspective to an issue, providing an objective and safe sounding board. Without the baggage of office politics, they can serve as roadblock-breaker or new idea catalyst. Such support is often just the ticket needed to move forward on a course of action.

Consider the assessment in Figure 6.1 that Strategy 2 would benefit from a CRM system implementor to assist related initiatives. That provider will likely bring all three benefits of an external provider: new system capability, development capacity for system customizations, and will serve as a catalyst to migrate the organization to an entirely new platform.

Leveraging consulting help is not and should not be viewed as failure. In fact, we find the more capable and mature executives are the ones who not only willingly accept but actively pursue external support where it can be helpful. The measure of a leader's success is not what they accomplish personally, but what they accomplish through and with their teams, including both internal and external resources. The yardstick is success and possessing the leadership qualities and self-awareness to achieve it regardless of who is eventually responsible.

Responsibility, Accountability, and Ownership

Value creation strategies require accountable leaders who are responsible. Leaders with assigned responsibility get things done, but leaders holding accountability ensure things get done. Accountable leaders assign responsibility but remain on the hook for team results. Because the accountable leader maintains ownership for results – good or bad – he or she works hard to ensure team members accomplish their assigned responsibilities.

An accountable leader has the moral courage to protect team members from the repercussions of well-intentioned mistakes, accepting the consequences on behalf of their team. He or she accepts blame for missed targets, insulating team members so they can focus positively on getting things back on track. That same leader enthusiastically and publicly acknowledges and celebrates the successes of their responsible team members, taking pride in their accomplishments.

While responsibilities can be assigned, accountability is more of an ownership mentality. When leaders act like owners they ensure things get done. They establish a high-performing learning environment and continuously enhance and augment their team's attitude and capabilities whenever they can. They're continuously triaging to achieve the results they committed to and don't let ego get in the way because they're focused on positive outcomes.

When accountability is not embraced, finger-pointing and blame ensue. Accountable leaders know exactly where the blame lies – with themselves. So they do all they can to ensure that no blame is necessary.

Recruiting Executives

Executive recruiting in any company is usually a very important capability – be that for adding to the team, creating new roles, top-grading existing roles, or simply replacing underperformers. Unfortunately in the middle-market, the mindset around executive recruiting is sometimes shortsighted. Many portcos employ an informal process when it comes to recruiting for key roles. Once the company decides a role is needed, it asks around the community or posts the role on job boards, then someone glances through the resumes that arrive, chooses a few people to speak with, and then picks a candidate who seems good. The results are hit-and-miss because the process relies on happenstance.

Process-oriented OPs will instill a formal recruiting approach that includes specifying requirements and likely utilizing a professional search firm. It will involve previewing and prescreening candidates against specific criteria (including the strategies and initiatives they'll need to execute), completing multi-person, in-person interviews with multiple candidates, ensuring a solid comparison, implementing leadership and personality profile testing, completing a detailed comparison scorecard, and facilitating a decision session to pick the candidate most likely to succeed. Like other critical decisions, it's best if executive recruiting is completed by a team made up of the OP and CEO as well as others, with the CEO making the final decision for who he or she brings on the team (typically pending OP or board approval).

Oftentimes, recruiting decisions are made with compensation as the primary consideration. While such a mindset is impressively frugal, it is ultimately shortsighted. It is far wiser to "pay up" for the right leader who will be instrumental in leading an investment period with outsized returns. That involves a flexible mindset when it comes to envisioning what the compensation package looks like as a whole. Different people have different priorities, and getting it right for the specific candidate is what's important: base compensation, annual bonus, guaranteed bonus, sign-on bonus, relocation, options, exit bonus, role assignment, team selection, housing allowance, and no-required relocation should all be up for consideration to help the OP and CEO land the right leader.

The alternative is truly costly. The cost of a mistaken executive hire (or a delayed but necessary replacement) is much more than simply ill-spent dollars on their compensation package. The time impact is even more troubling. To get that new leader on board and delivering at full potential may well take up to a full year when you factor in recruiting time, getting up to speed, and ultimately taking charge and impacting change, which is a significant chunk of the investment period. Having to fill the role again midstream represents a huge opportunity cost, considering what that leader could have been achieving during that time.

Organizing the Value Creation Team

Some PEGs play lip service to teaming and structure in the support of initiatives. They fail to properly organize, train, and resource initiative teams, and instead tend to simply demand more from the existing pool of resources and their current levels of capacity and talent. By expecting more with less (or at least more with the same), they give little thought to how the portco team will squeeze it all in. These PEGs provide little-to-no support by way of the means to execution, including helping their companies think through and organize highly capable initiative teams.

Strategically minded PEGs help their portfolio companies understand the difference between excellent day-to-day management teams and excellent initiative-based teams – and the structures that support both. They realize that initiative-based execution is not always in the existing DNA or muscle memory of their portfolio company, and they work to organize the right executive steering, program management, and initiative team structures to ensure Value Creation Program success.

Team Structure and Responsibilities

The Value Creation Program of strategies and initiatives to optimize outcomes during the investment period is separate from day-to-day business execution. It requires a supporting structure separate from the normal organization chart. OPs should work with their CEOs

VCP Executive Steering Group	VCP Program Management	Value Creation Program Initiative Teams		
		Initiative 1	Initiative 2	Initiative 3
CEO & Executive Team	Active Program Manager	Executive Sponsor	Executive Sponsor	Executive Sponsor
		Team Leader	Team Leader	Team Leader
Operating Partner		Core Team Members	Core Team Members	Core Team Members
		External Consultants (if Beneficial)	External Consultants (if Beneficial)	External Consultants (if Beneficial)
PEG Support as Necessary	Support Staff as Required (IT, HR, Etc.)	Subject Matter Experts	Subject Matter Experts	Subject Matter Experts

Note:
Bold is VCP Executive Team; ■ is VCP Leadership Team; Entire is VCP Full Team

Figure 6.2 Value Creation Program Team Structure

to help define and organize the VCP teams, as the OP has likely organized VCP efforts across many portcos before and understands the requirements of each role and the typical demands and hurdles those roles will face. The OP and CEO should then collaborate in assigning team leaders and executive sponsors to each initiative. As shown in Figure 6.2, an effective and efficient VCP teaming structure includes three primary levels.

Executive Steering Group

This top-most level is typically led by the CEO and includes most if not all his or her direct reports (i.e., the executive team) as well as the OP. This group of half a dozen executives establishes the Value Creation Program vision, guides the program, sets priorities, provides resources, and clears roadblocks. They are ultimately accountable for the success of the VCP, and therefore help hold the program manager and initiative teams leaders responsible for results. The VCP executive team (including the OP) typically meets with the program manager biweekly to review VCP status and issues and to provide guidance to the program manager. The VCP leadership team – executive steering group, program management, and initiative team sponsors and leaders – will typically meet monthly to review the entire Value Creation Program, focusing attention on initiatives that are off course (or heading that way).

Program Manager

Leading the day-to-day oversight of the VCP is a very active program manager – a talented hands-on servant-leader who is well-respected throughout the organization. Unfortunately, this role is sometimes mistaken for an administrative one, whereas the right program manager can and should play an active and integral role in the success of the VCP. An external consultant is often a good choice for program manager. Selected wisely, this person will come with deep and wide experience in organizing and driving broad company-wide EBITDA improvement programs. They'll have a specific toolkit they've used in the past and which they've continuously refined. Importantly, they'll be able to commit full time to leading the program and haven't any internal company baggage or responsibilities that will get in the way.

The key function of the program manager is to work with and support initiative team leaders and executive sponsors to direct the implementation and completion of VCP initiatives. Available resources for the program manager can include part-time representation from finance, IT, HR, and other cross-initiative support functions. The program manager typically meets with each initiative team leader (or each entire team of leaders) each week, providing tools and techniques as well as guidance and support. The program manager maintains close contact with the executive steering group and the OP, making them aware of any potential hitches in the execution of any aspect of the VCP.

Initiative Teams

As explained in Chapter 5, these are led by a team leader and are sponsored by a company executive. The initiative leader is an important role and needs to be carefully assigned. This role may be full or part-time, depending on initiative requirements.

Each team also typically has a few core team members that devote part of their time to driving the initiative, and various subject matter experts and external consultants can contribute to the team depending on the task at hand. Each team is responsible for implementing the initiative within the planned timeline and for successfully reaching their objectives.

Initiative leaders are also responsible for updating the program manager on the prescribed basis and updating whatever tracking tools might be in place. Initiative leads usually meet weekly with their team, and perhaps even daily with certain team members as necessary. They reach out to their executive sponsor as needed for guidance and support.

Managing the Value Creation Program

Active program management is essential for the success of the Value Creation Program. It's a little-known fact that over 50 percent of large transformations or other large-scale programs fail to deliver as planned, and addressing the reasons why is one way attentive PEGs distinguish themselves from their inattentive counterparts.

Conscientious PEGs support their executive teams not just by establishing their VCP but also by guiding them in how to best accomplish its intended results. Their OPs invest time and resources in preparing, training, and facilitating program management capabilities within their portfolio companies. They invest in, and are vested in, maximizing the benefits of the investment period by concentrating their energies on the VCP, and together with their CEOs embrace the mantra that "if it's not in the VCP, we shouldn't be talking about it."

Unsupportive PEGs by comparison demand program success but provide little support to their portfolio companies regarding executing Value Creation Programs. They leave it to their executives to figure out on their own how to organize an accelerated approach to drive more initiatives at once and faster than they've ever successfully demonstrated before. They rarely designate a program manager, and if they do, view it largely as an administrative position. Needless to say, their conception of what active program management constitutes is miles apart from the steps a performance-oriented PEG takes.

Four Levels of Program Management

Traditional program management has received a bad reputation, and for good reason. Often referred to as the PMO or program management office, PMOs have often served as an overhead function, keeping score without adding value. It is reminiscent of the proverbial "give me your watch and I'll tell you what time it is." These PMOs will ask all the initiative leaders what their status is and pull together fancy PowerPoints to communicate the same. By contrast, smart PEGs will instill a more active and high-value-added program management approach. Figure 6.3 shows four different levels of competency in program management with respect to scope and excellence:

	Level 1	Level 2	Level 3	Level 4
	Rudimentary	Basic	Standard	Active
Description	Aggregate and report initiative status	Plus... Provide standard and repeatable methodology across all initiatives	Plus... Facilitate team meetings and steering approach for the entire program of initiatives	Plus... Support teams to augment & accelerate benefits beyond what teams might do on their own
Activities	• Status Reporting	• Methodology • Status Reporting	• Process Facilitation • Methodology • Status Reporting	• Active Triage • Leverage Consultants • Process Facilitation • Methodology • Status Reporting

Figure 6.3 Program Management Levels

Rudimentary program management simply provides status tracking and basic variance reporting of planned versus actual cost, benefits, and timing across the key initiatives. This is simple scorekeeping. With it, projects will likely move along at first, albeit slowly, with ever-waning enthusiasm, and eventualy fizzle out for lack of meaningful oversight.

Basic program management provides standard, repeatable methodologies to initiative leaders in addition to rudimentary status tracking and variance reporting. Methodologies might include standardized initiative charters, work planning tools, and reporting templates. Consistency in nomenclature and report structure enables efficient executive steering reviews across all initiatives, enabling managers to quickly evaluate initiative status and resource requirements. With basic PM, the company begins to experience improved consistency across initiatives but still fails to generate anywhere near the potential of active program management.

Standard program management moves portfolio companies past passive scorekeeping and methodologies. In addition, the program manager now facilitates regular updates for steering groups and across all initiatives. They assist initiative leaders where and when needed, providing support to help drive results. With standard PM, the program manager is always available "on-call" and is able to jump in to support a specific meeting or to continue weekly progress in the event the team leader is out of the office or otherwise unavailable. Program managers help drive all VCP initiatives forward and help resolve roadblocks when they occur.

Active program management does not just report status, provide methodologies, facilitate the process, and assist initiative leaders. The program manager now works side by side with team leaders and their executive sponsors, attending team meetings and serving as an ongoing coach while offering their unique perspective, experience, and knowledge. Wired properly, the relationship between the program manager and team leader becomes trusting and collegial. The active program manager manages initiative inter-dependencies and secures consultants as needed to support the teams. Active PM perpetuates a performance culture where skills are transferred and cross-functional collaboration is promoted. The active program manager augments and accelerates results beyond what the teams might otherwise achieve on its own.

The program manager role is often assigned during the planning stages of the VCP. He or she ramps up quickly once the first set of initiatives have been selected, the necessary resources have been assigned, and the formal VCP kickoff meeting has been scheduled. At that point, a strong and skilled active program manager will begin using all their available talents to help shepherd the VCP through a continuous process of targeting, tracking, and triaging results.

Targeting, Tracking, and Triaging Value Creation

Virtually all PEGs apply some level of pressure upon portco management to deliver on financial performance commitments for each month, quarter and year of the investment period. While stressful at times, that's both expected and appropriate. But overly aggressive PEGs inflict undue pressure and unilaterally impose financial and operational demands over unrealistic timelines. They expect impressively detailed board presentations showing good things being done but fail to instill an execution regimen enabling those good things. They become inflamed at imperfect results but provide nothing constructive to improve outcomes. Without knowing it, they've created a culture of pretenses where good news is excessively played up and the occasional and sometimes unavoidable bad is minimized or even veiled.

Conscientious PEGs expect the same performance-to-commitments, but also bring relevant skills to the table so their portfolio companies can successfully achieve their VCP. They expect clear and consistent communication, including the good, the bad, and the ugly. When things go wrong, equity partners expect and require candor from their management teams. And because of previously established collaborative partnerships and effective teaming, they usually receive it. Management provides early warnings, and equity partners have the opportunity to participate in remediation plans.

Targeting Details

In Chapter 5, we covered at length the process of aggregating improvement and EBITDA growth ideas, prioritizing opportunities, profiling initiatives, and finalizing the Value Creation Program. That all represents "targeting" where the entire team now has concrete plans in place, including overall investment period objective, value proposition, strategies, initiatives, and milestones as well as associated sponsor and leader accountabilities and team member assignments. Each team has specific quantified targets for their initiatives and milestones – they've committed to start and end dates, costs, and benefits as outlined in the VCP initiative profiles.

Effective program management of the VCP does not necessarily require consistency in detailed planning and execution approach between initiatives. Each team leader will leverage work planning tools and techniques that reflect the complexity of the initiative and work best for them and their initiative team. An initiative like *Build a New Factory* may require sophisticated relational database project software, while *Launch an Inside Sales Team* might simply require a spreadsheet for planning and tracking purposes. For these reasons, the VCP program manager will typically not specify the tool or approach for project work but will simply specify frequency and approach for reporting milestone progress into the VCP.

Whichever way the team leader organizes project management for the initiative, having a basic standard process and regular and frequent communication among team members is what is most important. A typical expectation is for initiative team members to make daily progress on tasks and convene weekly as a team to debrief status and triage next steps. A skilled and active program manager will be a valuable support for many team leaders, not only providing tools and techniques but helping to facilitate program management and accelerate progress. Team leaders will want to work with their program manager to close any gaps they may have in their project management and team facilitation skills.

Tracking Status

As soon as initiative plans are set and the teams begin, tracking progress-to-plan should begin. Like the original planning effort, we find it best to organize a standard initiative tracking approach and template for each initiative team leader to use for purposes of communicating at the program and steering levels.

Value Creation Program tracking and reporting to the PEG, board, and portco executive steering group is at a significantly higher level than the detailed work plans the initiative teams rely on for initiative execution. With VCP tracking, teams provide consistent and concise visibility reporting on major milestone progress. As reflected in Figure 6.4, the program manager and executive steering group will want to see the following three primary tracking components in a VCP Status Update Report:

Original plan. This spells out the approved initiative as it appears in the VCP in thumbnail fashion. The most important plan components for each strategy and initiative are individual accountabilities, planned timelines (including both start and end dates), planned net EBITDA impacts, and planned one-time impacts. Sometimes other planned performance measures and targets will be included. Not shown in Figure 6.4 but important as well are planned milestones and associated timing.

Forecasted figures. These usually include at minimum the forecasted end-date, forecasted EBITDA impact, and forecasted one-time impact. The report should highlight variance to plan in some way. Often, the report shows quantified variance amounts and percentages, color-coded red, yellow, or green for variances

Strategies & Initiatives	Lead	Value Creation Program							Forecast			Status and Action		
		Q1	Q2	Q3	Q4	End	EBITA	1X	End	EBITA	1X	Code	Comments	Next 2 Wks
Strategy A			Today											
Initiative A1	MM	*	*	*		0/0/0	$0	$0	0/0/0	$0	$0	G	Highlights	Highlights
Initiative A2	BT		*	*	*	0/0/0	$0	$0	0/0/0	$0	$0	Y	Highlights	Highlights
Initiative A3	BT				*	0/0/0	$0	$0	0/0/0	$0	$0	R	Highlights	Highlights
Strategy B														
Initiative B1	MM	*	*	*		0/0/0	$0	$0	0/0/0	$0	$0	R	Highlights	Highlights
Initiative B2	BT	*	*			0/0/0	$0	$0	0/0/0	$0	$0	G	Highlights	Highlights
Etc.	BT		*	*	*	0/0/0	$0	$0	0/0/0	$0	$0	G	Highlights	Highlights

Note:
*1X is one-time impact; End is initiative end date; ■ is planned timing; * is forecasted timing*
■ Green is favorable; ■ Yellow is slightly unfavorable; ■ Red is unfavorable

Figure 6.4   Value Creation Program Tracking

outside certain thresholds. The steering group may want to have visibility into forecasted milestone timing for off-track initiatives as well.

Status and action. Initiative status reporting usually starts with the common and useful conventional status codes of red, yellow, or green, indicating whether the initiative is significantly off-track, off-track but recoverable, or on track. The report will provide status comments to (if only briefly) clarify status codes, for instance, "Delayed two-weeks for new equipment" or "Leveraging diligence data to accelerate." We also recommend leaders highlight recent accomplishments and near-term plans to accomplish before the next meeting.

Ongoing tracking of VCP progress should be a simple activity, requiring only a few minutes each week by the initiative leader to update. We recommend status reporting be electronic, cloud-based, and always available for the PEG, board, and executive team to review. Some reporting tools offer auto-notification, a useful feature that sends an electronic update to users when an initiative status is updated or when the status code is modified. Yet despite their simplicity, equity partners and portco leadership should require status reports be updated accurately, provided in a timely fashion, and most of all reflect the spirit of candor and transparency that a true partnership entails.

Triaging Results

Triaging results means actively monitoring and managing the entire Value Creation Program. Triage focuses attention and resources on at-risk initiatives, getting them back on track as soon as possible. Active triaging helps executive sponsors and team leaders improve and accelerate benefits, thereby improving the expected outcomes.

To that end, the OP, CEO, and steering group need full visibility into the status of each initiative so that they can support team leaders to help them achieve their commitments. Steering and sponsor support may include any number of activities, including brainstorming solutions, prioritizing work, augmenting the team, providing new funding, recommending consulting support, and so on.

In addition to status reporting, formal initiative status meetings and informal touch-bases are important inputs to the triage process. As before, candor and full transparency are essential for all parties to successfully guide initiatives.

VCP Initiative Status Meetings

The OP and CEO should institute a standing schedule of VCP Initiative Status Meetings starting immediately after the planning efforts. Typically facilitated by the program manager, these meetings should become a regular part of the normal operating cadence for each portfolio company. For the middle-market, chaired by the CEO and facilitated by the program manager, the meeting typically starts with an overview of the entire Value Creation Program status. Each initiative team leader (with support from their executive sponsor) provides a brief status update for each of their initiatives, with the focus on the off-track initiatives.

Early in the process, we typically recommend full-VCP team status meetings (including the executive steering group, program manager, VCP support staff and all team leaders) every two weeks.

After the process is wired, the cadence of these meetings can usually move to monthly, supported with a biweekly meeting between the executive steering group and program manager.

Yellow and Red Touch-Base Meetings

Triaging initiatives and accelerating EBITDA growth should not be limited to periodic reports and meetings. Effective triaging of initiatives that have "gone" yellow or red requires attention by the executive sponsor and program manager beyond basic reports and status meetings. They should be huddling up with initiative leaders in between meetings, offering support and guidance to reinforce commitment and accountability to fully enable their success. When an initiative is at-risk, it is up to the initiative leader not only to advise of current and potential issues but also to provide recommendations or at least options for how to avoid or recover from "going yellow" or "going red."

Initiative leaders need to be candid regarding true initiative status. If an initiative is not on track, the initiative leader needs to say as much and solicit help to get it back on track. Executive sponsors and steering group members need to be supportive and focus on ideas and solutions and not individuals. There's nothing to be gained from blame. If an initiative is off track, it's off track, and the only thing accountable leaders need to do now is to get it back on track the best way the collective team knows how. It goes back to the notion of teaming authentically and living a culture of trust, candor, and honest professional discourse.

If getting back on track is deemed unachievable, it's up to the accountable sponsor and initiative leader to replace or add a new initiative enabling them to achieve the benefit commitments they made. The VCP is best thought of as a zero-sum game: The management team should be committed to achieving the benefits they signed up for, and not achieving them should not be an option. If an initiative fails or falls short, the team should look to replace or augment with new initiatives to achieve total benefits committed. That's part of accountability.

A Team Sport

As important as the organizing and planning of the Value Creation Program are that we spoke of in Chapter 5, it's the execution of the plan that makes the difference. A great plan poorly executed is a failure; a decent plan well-executed is a success.

VCP execution success will come from having the right leadership in place with the right support, an enthusiastic VCP team fully committed to achieving their plans, an active program manager and dedicated executive steering group to guide and facilitate the program, and a regular cadence of candid reporting, authentic teaming, collegial support, and continuous triaging of results.

As the GrammCo vignette illustrates, with the Value Creation Program underway there is no rest for the weary. Fortunately, with the right structures and supports in place, the burden is shared not only among portco leadership but with their PEG partners as well. Executing the Value Creation Program is a team sport – and as with any successful team, achieving the desired result is a product of endless hours of demanding and exhausting teamwork directed at a common goal. It requires everyone to be committed to the team and the outcome. And as the team at GrammCo will start to experience as the VCP gains momentum, winning – as exhausting as it is – is more than worth it in the end.

Chapter 7
Quarter 3: Gaining Momentum

"That's why I'm talking to you. You are one of the rare people who can separate your observation from your perception. You see what is, where most people see what they expect."

John Steinbeck, *East of Eden*

"Did you hear?"

"Hear what?"

"About Ronnie?"

And so it continued, the conversation about Ronnie being let go. GrammCo CFO Don Crandall and VP Supply Chain Kathleen Easton were walking to their cars at the end of a very long day. It was dark outside and getting colder now but they continued their filling in of one another with

(continued)

(*continued*)

details and speculations. It had only been an hour since encountering this bump in the GrammCo road.

Dianne had terminated Ronnie – respectfully and with empathy – but letting someone go is never easy. Dianne and Patterson Lake's OP Shed Cooper had commiserated over the necessity of the change for several weeks now. They'd certainly given Ronnie ample opportunity to change his attitude and step it up. But Ronnie chose not to step it up, and so Dianne chose to step him out.

Early next morning, Dianne called an impromptu leadership team meeting. She wanted to explain why it became necessary to make a change with Ronnie and to give her team a chance to ask questions. "We certainly appreciate Ronnie, his role on the team, and his many contributions over the past four years. As many of you had noticed, despite Ronnie always watching the KPIs and usually making his numbers on the Weekly Signal Report, he never became comfortable with our new operating cadence and the pace of change.

"I know our new operational reporting has been an adjustment. But there's good reason for why we're paying more attention to measurement than ever before. Tracking leading indicators this way allows us to better deliver on our value proposition. There's real cause and effect behind these numbers, directly resulting in EBITDA – our prime target.

"With our heightened focus has come a new operational cadence I know you've all felt. Having the leadership team, as well as our equity partners, on the same page helps us continuously clarify responsibilities, make informed commitments, and hold each other accountable. We have more meetings because we have more going on. Team meetings as well as one-on-ones help to ensure we each are giving and receiving immediate feedback and support. That's the new reality, and it's helping."

Various team members then asked questions and made some points, and the team conversation was open and candid. Each in their own way showed their embrace of GrammCo company values. After each had a chance to comment, Dianne continued.

"We've ratcheted up our game considerably and we each need to have enthusiasm for the changes underway. We need to be *energized* – to embrace our new momentum while inspiring our teams to feel the same and achieve exciting things. I know I'm energized, despite some difficult decisions. And I know you are as well."

The meeting tone had changed perceptibly since it began. Dianne had reactivated the room's energy as she refocused their thinking on achievement. She offered this observation: "We need to continue honing our edge as leaders – the self-confidence to make difficult but necessary decisions without second-guessing ourselves. And we need to keep making commitments, holding ourselves accountable and executing our Value Creation Program."

It was Chief Engineer David Bedford who finalized the transition back to their normal informal, spirited and can-do mood, "Hey, is Elizabeth still visiting today? I can't wait to show our new Board Director the new caterpillar tracks for Bighill Mining – she'll think we're as cool as we think we are!"

Elizabeth Garrison was one of the three new board members Shed and Ocie had brought to GrammCo. She had a wealth of knowledge about the national parks system, came with the fresh perspective of having been a liaison between industry and government, and most of all was whip-smart,

(continued)

(*continued*)

asking truly probing questions that no one else in the room had thought of. After attending her first quarterly business review, Shed and Dianne both knew Elizabeth was going to be a valuable voice in the room.

Elizabeth did visit that day, checked out the new caterpillar tracks, and thought they were in fact "cool." More importantly, Elizabeth thought the energy and enthusiasm throughout GrammCo was *very* cool.

Managing with Performance Indicators

By the third quarter, things are moving quickly and everyone is settling into their new pace. Those who haven't demonstrated the right attitudes have one way or another left the business, making way for those with the right capabilities and attitudes to flourish as an enthusiastic and effective team and continue to grow the company.

The equity partners and management team have so far focused their efforts on the necessary basics of onboarding and financial reporting, and importantly on wasting no time in establishing, initiating, and actively managing their Value Creation Program. This is all excellent work focused on initial momentum to achieve accelerated growth for which the team should be proud.

Still, there's more work to be done around the normal operating cadence of the business. Over the past few months, the team has been making enhancements to its monthly and quarterly routines, and now is the time to lock that down. If they haven't done so already, they should soon be settling into a new standard of monthly and quarterly reporting and reviews to monitor and influence all aspects of the business – VCP initiatives as well as the day-to-day.

Importance of Indicators

Shortsighted PEGs sometimes myopically focus on financials to the exclusion of everything else, and demand ever-improving numbers without getting their hands dirty in the underlying metrics that cause those numbers. Other times they may go to the other extreme and demand every possible metric that comes to mind, grasping in hopes that the next one proves to be the silver bullet.

Better PEGs know there will be no silver bullet and no free lunch. They work with the portco leadership to define a manageable and finite set of insightful and actionable KPIs, then over time continue to enhance everyone's understanding of underlying cause-and-effect logic. This enables the systematic improvement of core operations that ultimately leads to sustainable EBITDA growth.

The team needs to establish a dashboard – a succinct set of KPIs working seamlessly together to tell the full operational story of results, including the impacts of day-to-day management as well as specific VCP initiatives. Instilling the right set of targeted KPIs enables portcos to do the following:

Clarify vision. Quantitative targets transform a qualitative generalized image of the future into a specific, clear, and tangible one, and enable consistency of interpretation across the management team. Rather than generally *improving sales,* a retail store might convey their intention to increase Conversion to 13.5 percent and units per transaction to 2.6. Targeted KPIs leave no ambiguity about what's important.

Sharpen focus. Targeted KPIs provide focused guidance for the *how.* Without targeted KPIs management teams either collect little data or collect data regardless of relevance. They try to work on all things at once, resulting in disappointing progress. Specific targets help managers avoid distractions and wasted efforts by focusing on the most important metrics – the ones that lead to the best results or have the largest gaps to close. Because portcos in lower middle-market have limited resources, targeted KPIs enable better resource allocation and utilization.

Heighten motivation. Just the fact of having specific indicators with defined targets – aggressive yet achievable with specific accountabilities – discourages procrastination and heightens motivation. What gets measured gets attention and therefore has a more likely chance of getting accomplished. The *Hawthorne effect* (as it has come to be known) refers to the tendency to work harder and achieve better results while effort and outcomes are being measured – not unlike the common saying of "shine a spotlight on it."

Characteristics of Effective Indicators

Forward-thinking PEGs avoid adding measures simply for measurement's sake but rather measure with intent. The overarching considerations for each indicator are availability, appropriateness, and accuracy. Because each requires time to measure, record, analyze, and present, and then to review, interpret, and discuss, each one must provide useful and actionable insight. Consider the sample KPI Report shown in Figure 7.1 for a hypothetical retail store in light of the following five characteristics that reflect different aspects of measuring with intent.

Specific and Quantified

A goal to *improve sales* is directionally helpful, but it's more helpful to get to the specifics of the underlying goal. That goal in our retail store example relates to store traffic and conversion rates among other things. In addition to being specific, targets must be quantified – the store intends to increase traffic from 12,325 people per month to 13,000 and improve conversion rate by half a percentage – from 13.0 to 13.5 percent.

Another, more generic example relates to the ubiquitous goal of *enhancing customer satisfaction.* A certain company might articulate that goal more specifically and quantifiably: *Enhance customer satisfaction by improving on-time delivery five percentage points to 95 percent for the top 100 customers before the end of the second quarter.*

It's even worth adding the stipulation that these improvements should not come at the expense of current delivery performance for the rest of the company's customers.

Cause-and-Effect Logic

Perhaps nothing is more intellectually satisfying than truly understanding cause and effect in a business context. A well-constructed set of key indicators should employ such logic. Consider again Figure 7.1 for March: Starting with a certain amount of customer traffic (12,090), if the store converts so many (12.1 percent) from a casual shopper to a buyer, and each buys on average a specific item quantity (2.0), having an average unit retail price ($62.60), then we should expect a certain sales revenue ($181k). The first four indicators – traffic, conversion, units per transaction ("basket size"), and average unit retail – are *leading* operational indicators. The final figure, sales revenue, is a *lagging* indicator for EBITDA. During any given month, we can target leading indicators to affect lagging ones.

Monthly KPI (Store Location)	LY	Jan	Feb	Mar	Target	Responsible Functions
Traffic (Shoppers)	12,325	12,200	12,250	12,090	13,000	Store Ops, Visual Design
× Conversion Rate (% Traffic)	13.0%	12.7%	12.0%	12.1%	13.5%	Store Ops, Merchandising
× Units per Transaction (# Items)	2.5	2.2	2.1	2.0	2.6	Store Ops, Merchandising
× Average Unit Retail ($/Item)	$62.00	$63.10	$66.00	$62.60	$62.00	Merchandising, Product
= Sales ($000)	$248k	$215k	$204k	$181k	$283k	(Same as Above)
× Average Unit Margin (% Sales)	50.2%	51.1%	51.2%	51.0%	51.0%	Merchandising, Product
= Gross Margin ($000)	$125k	$110k	$104k	$93k	$144k	(Same as Above)
Avg. Store Staffing (# Employees)	4.3	4.3	4.4	4.4	4.3	Store Operations
× Average Hourly Rate ($/Hr.)	$14.50	$14.20	$14.60	$14.50	$14.50	Store Operations, HR
× Average Overtime (% Total Hrs.)	12.0%	12.2%	12.3%	12.0%	9.0%	Store Operations
× Key Retention Rate (3 Mo.)	75.1%	75.1%	76.0%	78.0%	85.0%	Store Operations, HR
= Total Store Labor ($000)	$34k	$33k	$35k	$34k	$32k	(Same as Above)
– Store Opex Rate (% Sales)	25.2%	24.9%	24.9%	24.8%	25.0%	Store Operations
= Controllable Margin ($000, %)	$29k, 12%	$23k, 11%	$19k, 9%	$14k, 7%	$41k 14%	(Same as Above)

Note:
Note: Blue text are operational key performance indicators (KPI); LY = last year; YE = year end
■ Green is favorable; ■ Yellow is slightly unfavorable; ■ Red is unfavorable

Figure 7.1 Key Performance Indicators (KPIs)

Aggressive yet Achievable

Targeted KPIs must be set such as to make them both aggressive and achievable. If they are too easy, portco teams won't put in the extra effort, but if they're too difficult, they will give up before even starting. Some PEGs push for outrageously aggressive targets, hoping to get "half a loaf." They think excessively lofty targets are motivational carrots when in fact unachievable targets serve as a disincentive. Wiser PEGs partner with their portcos to generate aggressive yet achievable targets to which the management team can commit. Commitment can only be achieved through management involvement in defining KPIs and setting realistic and inspirational targets having at least a reasonable chance of being achieved.

In our store example, while at first a reduction of overtime percent from 12 percent to 9 percent seems like a large chasm, the team knew they had achieved 8 percent in previous years and so felt comfortable in setting their target at 9 percent.

Timely and Indicative of EBITDA

Because they are operationally focused, KPIs should be more readily available and reported more frequently than end-of-month financial figures. The portco team should be watching most leading indicators daily, and the equity partners – particularly the OP – should be looking at them at least weekly. The indicators selected should enable the company to roughly predict their monthly financial performance, including top- and bottom-line, as early as by the end of the first week of the month.

Back in our retail store example (Figure 7.1), at the end of each day the company publishes store traffic, conversion, and the other key figures – including their expected top and bottom line impacts – and compares them to the same period last year, last month, and to plan. If targeted daily traffic is 650 customers and targeted daily sales is $14,500, and the first three days of the week were above last year by 5 percent but below plan by 5 percent, the store managers know they're doing good but not good enough. They can extrapolate their EBITDA for the month, knowing clearly what they'll achieve unless they immediately address the specific underlying issues – actual traffic, conversion, units per transaction, or average unit retail. And they have all that detail to guide their focus. Having an ongoing pulse for how each month is shaping up is critical, enabling the PEG and portco team to intervene while there is still time to impact the month.

A Balanced Scorecard

Since the early 1990s, when Robert Kaplan and David Norton pioneered the topic, there's been an emphasis on selecting the KPI indicators around four "balanced" perspectives of historic business performance and drivers of future performance. It encompasses an appealing cause-and-effect logic, where infrastructure and team development lead to operational capability, which leads to customer fulfillment and finally to financial performance. Companies articulate their specific critical success factors and KPIs associated with each of the four perspectives.

In our example in Figure 7.1, the store understood that the *key retention rate,* or the retention of key-holders (managers, assistant managers, and other select employees entrusted with keys to the store) is linked to their ability to drive sales because key-holders typically are fully trained and have the most experience. So they've included key retention rate as a leading KPI.

The astute OP and CEO will increasingly include the balanced scorecard logic not only in KPIs but also as they refine and reload their Value Creation Program, as many initiatives will be focused on improving critical success factors and operational (KPI) performance for the company.

Because the right set of KPIs is so important to equity partners and management teams for managing their businesses, prioritizing their selection is critical. If the portco does not have a balanced and appropriate set of KPIs and targets for their business, or if the numbers are inaccurate or late in arriving, they should accelerate efforts to incorporate insightful indicators into their normal operating cadence.

Standardizing Operating Cadence

With KPIs in place, the PEG and portco now have quantified cause-and-effect logic as insightful guiding input to their normal operating cadence. Having a clear set of facts and trends is central to the routine of management review meetings – both the internal meetings and monthly business reviews with their equity partners. Shortsighted PEGs set no standard rhythm for operational meetings, giving neither ample warning nor specific expectations for what is requested at their ad-hoc meetings. Such actions disrupt the normal flow of portfolio company business operations instead of enhancing it.

Clear-minded PEGs understand their presence in the company, even in the best situations, can be disruptive and time-consuming. They're conscious of the impact those disruptions have on day-to-day business routines. They work with the CEO and management team to define a specific cadence for their interactions – including weekly, monthly, quarterly, and annual components – to review KPI, day-to-day operational, Value Creation Program, and resulting financial performance.

Establishing the right routine of who meets about what and when is important. The cadence pattern should include consideration for interactions among three specific subsets of the broader partnership: portco–internal, PEG–internal, and combined PEG and portco interactions. Internal portco communication is obvious for any company – it's what they do on a normal basis. Routine internal PEG communication is also a healthy routine, as the equity partners and their PEG colleagues need to stay on the same page regarding expectations and requests and communications to and from the portco. PEG and portco communication is the new addition and should be defined early in the investment period.

Weekly Routine

We've found that CEOs and OPs with the best relationships tend to speak, text, and email regularly – sometimes multiple times

Week Ending Friday, May X, 20XX	Revenue			EBITDA				Weekly Signal Discussion
	B	F	A/Est.	B	F	A/Est.	ΔB	
January	$0	$0	$0	$0	$0	$0	$0,0%	KPI Variances & Reasons:
February	$0	$0	$0	$0	$0	$0	$0,0%	• [Insert Here]
March	$0	$0	$0	$0	$0	$0	$0,0%	• [Insert Here]
Quarter 1	$0	$0	$0	$0	$0	$0	$0,0%	Revenue Variance & Reasons:
April	$0	$0	$0	$0	$0	$0	$0,0%	• [Insert Here]
								• [Insert Here]
May (Current Month)	$0	$0	$0	$0	$0	$0	$0,0%	EBITDA Variance & Reasons:
June	$0	$0	$0	$0	$0	$0	$0,0%	• [Insert Here]
Quarter 2	$0	$0	$0	$0	$0	$0	$0,0%	• [Insert Here]
July	$0	$0	$0	$0	$0	$0	$0,0%	Highlights & Lowlights Last Week:
August	$0	$0	$0	$0	$0	$0	$0,0%	• [Insert Here]
September	$0	$0	$0	$0	$0	$0	$0,0%	• [Insert Here]
Quarter 3	$0	$0	$0	$0	$0	$0	$0,0%	Plans for Next Week:
Quarter 4	$0	$0	$0	$0	$0	$0	$0,0%	• [Insert Here]
Total Year	$0	$0	$0	$0	$0	$0	$0,0%	• [Insert Here]

Note:
B is Budget; F is the latest quarterly forecast; A/Est is actual or estimate (latest weekly estimate); △ B is delta A/E vs. B
■ Green is favorable; ■ Yellow is slightly unfavorable; ■ Red is unfavorable

Figure 7.2 Weekly Signal Report

each day, depending on what's going on. As those relationships evolve, they may choose to bypass a standing weekly touch-base. But until that kind of unique relationship is established, the CEO and OP are well-served to continue having a standing weekly communication to simply catch up informally. The discussion agenda is kept fluid as necessitated by what happens in a given week but typically includes a review of a simple and concise Weekly Signal Report (WSR) – an example of which is seen in Figure 7.2.

The WSR is a one-pager consisting of an evergreen estimate of current monthly top and bottom-line performance as well as a perspective on future months. It shows management's best guess at how the current and future periods will shake out against the same period last year, the current budget, and the most recent formal quarterly forecast. Beyond the quantitative, the WSR should include a brief qualitative assessment. We recommend simple bullet points for which KPIs are tracking poorly and why, as well as reasons for revenue and EBITDA misses and planned mitigators for closing any gaps. Involved OPs will also appreciate seeing a summary of accomplishments from the week and important planned activities for the coming week to improve performance.

The purpose of the weekly cadence is to provide a "heads-up" perspective, enabling candid working exchanges between PEG and portco and an opportunity to influence the month while there's still time. Overly aggressive PEGs sometimes take management teams to task regarding weekly estimates, reprimanding instead of participating constructively. This results in portcos quickly retreating under a haze of nontransparency, resulting in time-wasting exercises in futility and damage to the PEG/portco partnership. Collaborative-minded PEGs treat the elements of the weekly routine as a valuable opportunity for informative and helpful discussions between the PEG and portco partners to brainstorm and adjust in real-time to impact the future in the best way possible.

Monthly Routine

The portfolio company will undoubtedly have a long-established month-end close process including an executive meeting to review monthly financials. We tend to refer to that meeting as the monthly internal review (MIR). It's typically best for the PEG and portco to schedule a joint monthly business review (MBR) immediately following each month's internal review. The company needs to have completed their own reviews and preparation before fielding a range of questions from its equity partners.

In the middle-market, companies often close their books mid-to-late month following any given month-end. PEGs typically expect a much quicker close, enabling the MBR to occur no later than the second week of each month so that MBR discussions can still influence the current month.

The MBR typically involves the equity partners, CEO, and CFO as standing participants, and perhaps others from the executive team – either as standing participants or available on-call. Efficient PEGs typically expect to cover several items at such a meeting: monthly state of the business, including highlights, lowlights, and upcoming actions, and Value Creation Program status, including a review of key initiatives and planned adjustments. Both financial and operating numbers should get covered, including KPIs (and commentary for outliers) and actual as well as projected performance.

We find a brief deck to be useful in guiding the MBR discussion that evolves to a standard format and set of contents. Companies will have their normal financial reporting routines in place, and the PEG should work to integrate their financial reporting requirements into what already exists. The CFO should ensure the updated standard monthly financial package (MFP) of all detailed reports (P&L, balance sheet, cash flows, and supporting schedules) is included as an appendix to the MBR deck.

As noted before, early in the investment period biweekly Value Creation Program executive steering group meetings are particularly useful. Chaired by the CEO with the PEG operating partner participating, and facilitated by the program manager, initiative sponsors and team leaders present a detailed status of each initiative, particularly those going off-track. Deeper individual initiative steering meetings (ISMs) for specific more complex initiatives requiring additional discussion with a smaller group are also scheduled, as required or during standing meeting times. Figure 7.3 illustrates an operating cadence for a portco, which has transitioned to a single VCP steering meeting each month but is supported by a couple of days earmarked for individual ISMs as required.

Operating Cadence and Meeting Expectations

The weekly and monthly cadence outlined above is certainly a model that performance-oriented PEGs use, but each PEG and portco partnership will gravitate to its own specific cadence with the meetings and reports that work for them. Because calendars move and fill quickly, these PEGs find having a standing but flexible set of meeting times is essential, balancing their needs for periodic updates with the higher priority needs of management running the obligations and surprises of everyday business.

Monthly	Monday	Tuesday	Wednesday	Thursday	Friday
Week 1					Weekly Touchbase (WTB), Signal Report (WSR)
Week 2	(Month-End Close)	Monthly Internal Reviews (MIR)	Monthly Business Review (MBR)	Initiative Steering Meetings (ISM) as Required	WTB & WSR
Week 3					WTB & WSR
Week 4			ISMs as Required	Value Creation Program (VCP) Steering	WTB & WSR
Quarterly			Quarterly Leadership Topic (QLT)	Quarterly Business Review (QBR)	
Annually					Annual Business Planning (ABP)

Note:
■ Represents days PEG-OP is On-Site; ■ Represents Portco-Internal Activity

Figure 7.3   Operating Cadence

It bears mentioning that smaller privately and closely held companies have had years of evolved informal yet efficient communications – brief, frequent individual exchanges with the founder, and rarely the need of larger (let alone formal) meetings. Over the years, they've simply gotten into a rhythm of efficient hallway exchanges that not only sufficed but were situationally ideal. A common complaint portco management has of their PEG partnership is that *there are so many meetings.*

Considering all the changes underway with the new PEG ownership, the need for more frequent and larger meetings is both certain and clear. There are new and more people in the mix (PEG team members and often newly added portco positions alike), an accelerated and larger program of value-creating initiatives requiring monitoring and cross-functional coordination, and fiduciary reporting requirements to the lenders, limited partners, and other investors. But underlying the complaints is a real issue, one we find centers not so much on the number of meetings but rather the quality and efficiency of those meetings.

It makes sense early in the investment period to have meetings over-attended, as everyone is getting to know each other and there are lots of overlapping discovery discussions. But once the partnership between the PEG and portco is running smoothly, meetings should be well-attended but not over-attended. Over time, meeting organizers can increasingly fine-tune attendance to just the essential players, because when a trusting teaming culture exists, people are comfortable only attending meetings where their contributions are specifically needed. Smart OPs and CEOs are adept at getting the right people involved in the discussion at the right time. For various meetings, they'll invite subject matter experts as needed. But they are also willing to be impromptu, asking others to join a meeting briefly to cover a certain unplanned subject.

Regardless of the meeting type or the participant list, OPs and CEOs should set an expectation of effective meeting cultures – professional yet informal meetings with specific meeting standards that serve to improve discourse and increase meeting efficiency. We'll mention some baseline expectations here:

Meeting preparation is important but too often overlooked. Each meeting needs a specifically assigned meeting leader who should send meeting objectives, the agenda (including timing and topical discussion assignments), and any materials that will be referenced to all participants at least a day before. With clear objectives, agenda, and meeting materials provided beforehand, meeting participants will have a chance to come properly prepared. Needless to say, meeting success is directly proportional to the level of preparation by both the leader as well as the participants. That said, managers should not overprepare, taking hours to create an elaborate presentation for a 15-minute update. Better PEGs would much rather have their portco teams focused on the business and not on the presentation. Materials are best when they're concise – as well as clear, fact-based, and informative.

Meeting discipline is equally important. We've all participated in way too many meetings where there was either no assigned meeting leader, the leader did not control the agenda, or the participants did not follow simple ground rules and basic etiquette. Participants should stick with the agenda topic at hand, listen more than speak, be candid but respectful, and follow meeting leader direction. The leader must take control – and be allowed to take control – of the meeting. He or she needs to keep the team on-point and on-schedule and use the "parking lot" concept expeditiously and generously.

Meeting conclusions are essential for effective meeting cultures. Before disbanding, the meeting leader should review the outcomes – decisions made, assignments committed, and next steps agreed to, including those related to parking lot topics as well as meeting logistics for the next time. The leader should then send meeting minutes or a summary of outcomes to all participants within 24 hours.

Regular Executive Feedback

A final element in the operating cadence is one that falls outside a weekly or monthly rhythm but is nevertheless essential in the spirit of partnership and continuous improvement: regular timely feedback.

Some PEGs provide little-to-no positive or improvement feedback for their CEOs and the rest of the portco executive team, or the feedback they provide is unbalanced or poorly timed. But responsive PEGs provide regular ongoing feedback and plenty of discourse so that individuals continue what is working well and make improvements on what is not.

Through their partnership, the OP and CEO should always be on the same page with what's going well and what's going not so well. And while it's up to the CEO to provide performance feedback to each of his or her team members, collaborative CEOs will solicit thoughts and input from their OP in preparation for that feedback.

Executive feedback discussions in middle-market private equity take on a different flavor than the reviews of executives in public companies and closely held private companies. Where the latter two largely have an indefinite time horizon, the condensed investment period means that feedback is keyed to fine-tuning people's approach to optimize the remainder of the investment period.

Particularly for the CEO and his or her executive team, helpful OPs will offer some variation of a "More, Keep, Less" feedback approach. Whatever approach is adopted, the intent should create a relaxed discussion atmosphere between the OP and CEO (or between the CEO and his or her team members) to offer candid and constructive feedback.

For example: To prepare for and develop a 360-degree perspective for a feedback conversation with the CEO, the OP will typically have preparatory discussions about the CEO with the board and (assuming prior agreement) his or her direct reports. The OP will compile that feedback in preparation for a one-on-one discussion covering the following:

Do more. What few things should the CEO be doing more of during the remaining investment period to help the team achieve the goals and initiatives and the business achieve its objective. An example could be to "spend more time speaking with and gathering ideas from junior staff."

Keep doing. These are the few things the CEO is particularly adept at – what they are doing that is especially effective and helpful – and positive reinforcement to keep these up. An example could be "continue investing in team dynamics and the teaming process as it's serving to improve the portco's culture and performance."

Do less. There will be feedback as well to the CEO to do less in certain areas. An example could be "reduce the level of micro-managing before board meetings and personally preparing the board document; let your team tell more of the story in their own words."

Incorporating the Board of Directors

While public companies must have a board of directors, private companies are not so obligated. That's not to say private companies should not have a board. In fact, whether for public or private, the board of directors has specific and important responsibilities.

The board represents the owners and their interests, while responsibly considering the interests of all stakeholders – not only company management and employees but customers, suppliers, lenders, government, and the public. They establish governance practices for monitoring the business, ensure the CEO is appropriately selected and operating effectively, and serve to elevate strategic thinking with a unique and detached perspective. The board effectively serves as the objective conscience of the company.

Shortsighted PEGs limit a portfolio company's board of directors to only the PEG's in-house team, failing to leverage external insight and perspective. They may demand the management team to cover the minutia with tons of reporting detail, or perhaps view board meetings as opportunities to trip up their management teams with unnecessarily detailed inquiries.

PEGs interested in both solid governance and strategic insight will not only properly staff the board of directors with the right balance of inside and outside directors, but they will also properly design the responsibilities, corporate authorities, governance cadence, and even board meeting material expectations. They will work hard to ensure the leverage expertise, perspective, and connections that come from constructing the right board membership.

Board Composition and Responsibilities

Unlike large public companies that may have ten or more directors, middle-market portfolio companies typically go with a smaller roster. Smaller private companies are typically better served with five to seven directors. The CEO and the private equity team members will serve as they are the individuals tasked with running the company on behalf of the investors, with one often appointed chairperson and possibly another as vice chairperson.

Likely they will have one-to-three outside board directors as well. Reasons for outside board directors are less obvious but certainly sensical. In fact, selected properly and leveraged intelligently, outside board directors can have a subtle yet significant influence.

Excellent outside board directors tend to embody the following characteristics:

Relevant expertise. Each outside board director (OBD) should have deep expertise specifically relevant to the portfolio company. Whether it's industry insight, functional knowhow, or strategic experience, the OBD will bring outside ideas and a breadth of experiences augmenting the executive team. The OBD in fact may serve to shore-in existing gaps in the executive team.

Independent perspective. In addition to insightful perspectives based on expertise, the OBD should provide insight characterized by independence and objectivity. He or she should provide varying perspectives not otherwise shared within the company. Each OBD should come removed from the personalities and politics of daily operations in both the portfolio company as well as the PEG.

Professional influence. With relevant expertise and an independent perspective, the OBD should be in the position to ask insightful and even provocative questions. He or she should challenge stale, sloppy, or lazy thinking. The right OBD should at various times serve as a confidant to the CEO, executive team members, and the private equity partners alike. The been-there, done-that coaching and coaxing they offer should serve to bolster confidence and mitigate risk.

As a team, the board of directors has several important responsibilities. Three are particularly relevant in middle-market private equity:

Strategy definition and execution. The board is responsible for providing input to the strategic direction of the portfolio company and approving the plans they make. The board is also responsible for guiding and confirming annual budgets, as well as approving significant strategic changes and expenditures outside of plan. The board is subsequently responsible to ensure the management team is executing properly against those plans and budgets.

Executive confirmation and accountabilities. Typically, the board is also responsible for evaluating to some degree the competence of the CEO and his or her executive team. It is responsible for suggesting when changes are needed and often participate in candidate evaluation and selection of new executive hires. A subset of the board will form a compensation committee and recommend annual changes for full board approval.

Fiduciary duty and oversight. Last but not least, the board is expected to execute responsibilities with the utmost of care, professionally monitoring the company and ensuring policies of corporate conduct are properly defined and enforced, including those associated with legal, regulatory, risk management, and financial compliance. A subset of the board will be assigned to an audit committee, which is responsible for the financial compliance and independent audit processes.

Expectations of Board Meetings

Depending on the approach, participants, and quality of the monthly operating reviews, the PEG and portco might forgo holding formal quarterly business reviews (QBRs). Still, many portcos do choose to conduct a formal QBR with the board of directors in attendance (and depending on the terms of the company's loan agreements, possibly a representative or two from the lender community as observers) – effectively making them quarterly board meetings.

From the portfolio company management team's perspective, the primary touchpoint to the board of directors is quarterly board meetings. They serve as an opportunity for the management team to update the board on primary aspects of the business, including the overall state of the company, financial performance and projections, and operational performance. Additionally, and importantly, the meeting also serves as an opportunity to receive director input on strategic topics and contemplated enhancements to strategic direction.

We find quarterly board meetings have an indirect but important secondary benefit in addition to the board director discourse. Quarterly board meetings serve as a "resnapping of the chalk line." They enable the management team to take a brief pause from the pace and the challenges of everyday business to reflect together upon what is going right and what needs more attention. The exercise of succinctly documenting the results of that reflection benefits not only the board but also the management team.

For new portfolio companies, equity partners often encounter management team frustration regarding the necessity and the time required to prepare for quarterly board meetings (and MBRs as well). Such frustration is understandable. The board's need for clear, candid, and complete updates is also understandable. Collaborative PEGs and management teams will work together to develop the right balance, considering the need for efficient preparation for an effective meeting.

It should come as a relief that from a board director perspective, the quality of board materials is not measured by the "thud factor." More is not better. A few dozen well-prepared pages are much better than a large data dump of materials that includes both the important and the trivial. Board directors will come much better prepared if they receive a manageably sized well-prepared board book at least a couple of days before the meeting.

Portfolio companies with proper financial and operational monitoring and reporting processes fare the best when it comes to board meeting preparation. Having accurate and available financial and operational metrics makes preparation considerably easier. We find portcos that invest early in establishing processes for such information are well-served indeed, not only in support of board meeting preparation but much more importantly for their own uses in targeting, tracking, and triaging company performance. Efficient and effective board meetings typically follow a board meeting agenda like that shown in Figure 7.4:

State of the business and financial summary is devoted to providing the CEO's perspective regarding the external and internal conditions, overall business performance for the quarter, and the business outlook for the rest of the year. The CFO will summarize recent financial performance, including highlights and lowlights of the recent quarter as well as projections for the coming quarters

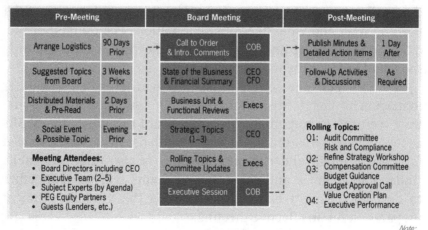

Pre-Meeting Social Event & Possible Topic – Sometimes a Dinner Event Combined with Quarterly Leadership Topic

Figure 7.4   Quarterly Board Meeting Plan

and the full year. Because the board will typically be receiving regular monthly financial updates, the quarterly board meeting financial review should typically not be a surprise but a reinforcing of key issues and opportunities and the chance for clarifying questions and comments.

Business unit updates are when each business unit and functional leader provide a brief update for their respective areas. Their updates would typically include their own set of highlights, lowlights, and upcoming actions, as well as key performance metrics and status of their VCP initiatives. Following business unit updates and functional reviews, the company will often wrap up the section with a summary of the company's entire set of KPIs and trends, as well as the full Value Creation Program initiatives and status, reinforcing the linkages to what the company is focusing on.

Strategic topics typically vary each quarter, depending on what's going on with the business and what opportunities are presenting themselves. The CEO or one of his or her executives will typically lead the discussion, particularly soliciting input and commentary from the board directors. The strategic topics section is an opportunity to specifically leverage the experience of the directors and to obtain either general confirmation for a direction or specific approval for a recommendation.

Standard quarterly board topics and executive session(s) typically follow. Standard rolling topics occur once-per-year at specific quarters. For instance, the audit committee might report the results of the audit during the first quarter meeting, the compensation committee might make recommendations during the third quarter meeting, and so forth. Attendees for standard topics are on an as-needed basis, and the executive session is for formal board directors only to debrief the meeting and various other topics.

In addition to the board meeting proper, many OPs and CEOs will plan a *quarterly leadership topic* to be covered the evening before the board meeting. The topic may include a formal presentation or a simple dinner discussion subject. It could be about market dynamics or recent competitive changes, or it could be a demonstration of a new business intelligence tool that an up-and-coming manager has spearheaded.

Overcoming Bumps in the Road

It's inevitable. There. will. be. bumps.

Some bumps are big and throw portcos off their game, but most are manageable and simply part of a normal private equity investment period. But it's only a matter of time before some aspect of the business – either day-to-day operations or VCP initiatives – will start to slip. While the goal is certainly to anticipate and avoid bumps, nimble PEG/portco teams not only recover quickly when they occur but do so by displaying resiliency, a positive attitude, and an eye for learning and leadership development.

We too often find that overly aggressive PEGs play the blame game. When their portcos encounter bumps in the road they intervene too quickly with presumption and make kneejerk reactions. They often revert to the we-say-you-do approach, which serves to disrupt any progress toward positive partnerships that might have been forming when the road was smooth and straight.

Indeed it's the way the PEG and portco partnership reacts to bumps that is important: Equity partners and portco executives should remain calm in challenging situations, evaluate options carefully, and make the best decisions possible at the moment. Rather than play the blame game, responsive OPs and CEOs use the past and the current to inform decisions for the future.

Reasons for Bumps

PEG and portco teams need to prepare to implement changes speedily to support strategies, deal opportunistically with new circumstances and evolved thinking, and react quickly and positively to the unexpected. Typical changes they should anticipate facing during an investment period include the following:

External disruptions. It was Mike Tyson who famously quipped, "everyone has a plan until they get punched in the mouth." It seems an ever-increasing number of external influences impact PEGs and their portfolio companies. Like a boxer in the ring, they get hit with a left hook, then after momentarily recovering get clocked with an uppercut. Disruptive technologies and out-of-the-blue competition seem commonplace while new government bureaucracies, stealthy system hackers, and Wall Street conundrums seemingly descend like locusts. Because we can rarely influence let alone stop these external disruptions, PEGs and portcos must position themselves to best react to external disruption as it comes. They must maintain a vigilant pulse on the industry and macroenvironment, stay nimble and migrate towards a variable cost structure, and always have multiple tongs in the fire to enable them to respond to various options and contingencies.

Leadership departures. During a typical several-year investment period, several portco leadership positions will have changed – both roles as well as individuals. Early in the investment period, OPs and CEOs may add new roles enabling the strategies and initiatives of the Value Creation Program, merge or split roles based on those same strategies and initiatives, and revise roles and assignments based upon the capabilities, interests, and attitudes of each management team member. Then later in the investment period the OP and CEO might find they need new roles as strategies shift or opportunities present themselves. And of course life happens: people retire, relocate, or move on. It's important to have ready a strong capable bench of executives and managers willing and able to stretch, step in, serve interim, and change their assignments. A deep bench in the lower middle-market is often unaffordable, and so having creative plans for key role succession is also important.

Initiative failures. Inevitably some initiatives will fail to materialize as originally envisioned. Some will fall short of plan and some will be canceled or suspended for one reason or another (perhaps to focus limited resources on even higher priority efforts). The Value Creation Program and the associated process of targeting, tracking, and triaging that program anticipates periodic shortfalls. In fact, the "off-track" (yellow and red) statuses are intended to provide early warning of a miss and to solicit sponsor, colleague, and even board involvement to help course correct. A large multi-initiative program will have misses. The key is to leverage the VCP approach in an established effective teaming environment to triage what's off course and continuously drive as much sustainable enterprise value as the team can.

Budget misses. In the best of worlds, all budgets would be both aggressive and achieved. As private equity lives in the real world, balanced PEGs want aggressive yet realistic budgets. As a result, even when properly balanced, perhaps 10 or 20 percent of the time (by design) the budget will be missed. This is not necessarily a cause for concern so long as the core business is sound and performing well. One typical yardstick in private equity is whether the business is at least performing better than last year. Making positive progress is always a good thing despite coming up short on the budget numbers. That's not to say missing plan is inconsequential or even acceptable. The key is for the portco team to have the company in the position to understand the reasons for any short-fall (e.g., underlying KPIs), and to provide their PEG partners with candid and timely warning as soon as there's reason to suspect a shortfall such that the PEG and portco team can take action to mitigate shortfalls.

Chronic resistance. Despite having achieved an effective PEG and portco partnership, an efficient operating cadence with solid financial and operational reporting, as well as broad agreement, preparation, and progress on the Value Creation Program, individual resistance sometimes perpetuates. Some portco managers just can't move on to the new reality of a new PEG owner or a new routine, to the point where they operate from the perspective of compliance at best and grudging reluctance at worst. Regardless of whether they are passively resistant or actively insubordinate, the time has passed for them to get on board. At this point the OP and CEO have let resistance go on for too long; now is the time remove chronic resistors so that the rest of the team can thrive.

Extended deterioration. Extended or prolonged deterioration marks a larger and more significant bump in the investment period road. As shown in Figure 7.5, the lifecycle of a company may pass through several stages. Better companies stay a long time (if not indefinitely) in the performing stage, perhaps bouncing briefly every so often into and then back from the underperforming stage. Sometimes of course companies will continue to underperform, passing into the troubled stage; if they don't turn things around quickly, they may then deteriorate into the crisis stage. If the PEG is large or tenured enough, it will likely have dealt with portfolio company situations in each of the four stages. By nature, one way or another companies don't last long in the latter two stages.

Troubled Situations

From our experience, troubled situations are most often rooted in ineffective management. It's not implausible that the cause could be

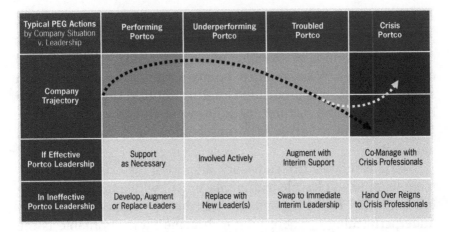

Typical PEG Actions by Company Situation v. Leadership	Performing Portco	Underperforming Portco	Troubled Portco	Crisis Portco
Company Trajectory				
If Effective Portco Leadership	Support as Necessary	Involved Actively	Augment with Interim Support	Co-Manage with Crisis Professionals
In Ineffective Portco Leadership	Develop, Augment or Replace Leaders	Replace with New Leader(s)	Swap to Immediate Interim Leadership	Hand Over Reigns to Crisis Professionals

Figure 7.5 PEG Actions During Deteriorating Performance

an unforeseen or unacknowledged external disruption, poor working capital controls, excessive debt burden, or some other reason. However, quite often trouble starts with leadership failures: not facing reality or failure to listen, accepting team dysfunction, or delaying switching out bad leaders. While troubled situations in portcos can certainly arise from external factors or various internal ones, it's the leadership factor that is typically at play.

Indicators of Trouble

Signs of trouble can come from the marketplace, including quickly shifting negative trends or increasing customer defections and complaints. Signs can be financial in nature: failure of the finance team to sufficiently explain financial underperformance, finance team frustration or defection, or unhealthily stretching of payables and drawing down the bank revolving credit facility. And often it comes from leadership signs: complacency despite rapid market changes, overconfidence despite a continuously deteriorating environment, or hesitancy to act despite general signs of stress and frustration. The indicators are not always clear at the moment, but in retrospect are like flashing lights in the rearview mirror.

Responses to Trouble

As shown in Figure 7.5, we identify three deteriorating stages of portfolio company trouble: underperforming, troubled, and crisis situations. What attentive equity partners should do in each situation and their approach to handling troubled situations should be based on three factors: mode (how intervention is handled), focus (profitability versus cash preservation), and pace (speed and approach).

Mode can range from advisory support of the existing management team to wholescale team replacement with a new one having full authority. Focus depends on whether the company is merely underperforming – where how to become more profitable is the goal – versus troubled – where the focus is on cash so the company has the time to evaluate stabilization options for the benefit of its creditors. Pace can range from measured to aggressive; the more trouble a company is in, the more aggressive decisions and actions need to be.

Underperforming companies. These companies have plateaued in performance and may be experiencing deteriorating results, particularly unexpectedly or inconsistent with management expectations or with the competition. Even if an effective portco leadership team is in place, the PEG and particularly the OP will become more involved. If the leadership team is generally deemed ineffective, the PEG will likely begin to initiate selective leadership changes as necessary.

Troubled companies. Certainly deteriorating and troubled companies usually have increased cash constraints and continued likely accelerated projections of poor performance. The PEG in this case (particularly the OP) will certainly become very involved and may decide to retain an interim leadership role – either personally or through retaining an external interim executive. If the CEO is deemed effective, the OP will work with him or her to make these and other decisions. If on the other hand the CEO or others on the team are deemed generally ineffective, the OP will likely replace certain executives with interim turnaround professionals.

Companies in crisis. These companies have begun to lose control and likely are in a liquidity situation and are quickly running out of both money as well as options. If things have gotten this bad, the PEG has no option than to bring in an interim crisis team familiar with bankruptcy administration practices to either work in conjunction with an effective in-place team or in place of an ineffective team. At this point, the banks and other creditors will likely be heavily involved, triggered by certain fiduciary responsibilities associated with the zone of insolvency.

Regardless of the particulars of a troubled situation, the best responses when faced with continued and accelerated deterioration should certainly include early recognition and admitting of real or possible trouble. As well, consolidating authority to a small core team empowered to respond with decisiveness and speed will typically improve the possibility of a positive outcome. They should engage in relentless triage, ongoing cash modeling, action planning and honest communication, with round-the-clock addressing of highest priority concerns to preserve value, focused now on maximizing expected creditor outcomes.

Day-to-Day Stability and Control

While the importance of initiatives and the VCP cannot be understated, day-to-day business operations certainly need continuous tending to throughout the investment period. It's important to recognize that the approach taken with initiatives – the careful planning and executing of them, with organized work plans and task lists – does not entirely translate to day-to-day business execution, which is much more nuanced, less stable, and less predictable. You can't create the plan for the day-to-day and then perfectly execute according to it – there's always fires in need of fighting. The best we can hope for is to "make 24 hours of progress every 24 hours."

The ability to react to disruptions is improved significantly in private equity middle-market when a regular oversight cadence is established. When we have a board of directors in place for objectivity and perspective, frequent, concise, and accurate reporting of cause-and-effect leading indicators for advance warning, and standard routines for candid operating reviews and addressing of issues, we're in better control of the day-to-day. Creating the most value during the investment period requires both stable day-to-day business execution as well as focused initiative execution.

The end of the first year together is approaching for Shed Cooper and GrammCo. They're in a position to look back over the year and take stock of their many successes as well as learn from those initiatives that failed to deliver as planned. But rather than simply sit on their laurels, they will also be positioning the company to grow and expand in new directions, leading them to significantly reload the VCP for Year 2.

Chapter 8
Quarter 4: Ringing the Bell

"By saying what his future was going to be like, he had created it. A plan is a real thing, and things projected are experienced. A place once made and visualized becomes a reality along with other realities."

John Steinbeck, *The Pearl*

Dianne Franklin wasn't performing her normal CEO duties. Neither was Operating Partner Shed Cooper performing his. At least, not their typical office roles – this was anything but office.

Dianne was crying with laughter and Shed was holding on for dear life. Ben Crawford sat in the back of the ASV trying to get Dianne to pay attention to the throttle. Careening through the woods of Northern Oregon out near Lake

(continued)

(*continued*)

Catherine, the head of field support at Bighill Mining, one of GrammCo's biggest customers, was eager to take back the reins. Remote and rough, an hour off the main highway, this was no place for a breakdown.

The lake came out of nowhere and Dianne reacted by cranking the steering stick hard. One side of caterpillar tracks slammed to a stop while the other accelerated full-go, effecting an impressive but unintentional donut maneuver just now on the sandy shores of Lake Catherine. Struggling to overcome the sudden inertia, Ben reached over to cut the engine.

"Okay... this looks like a good place for a break."

While Ben checked in with the office, Shed and Dianne had a moment for more typical discourse, albeit while skipping stones between sentences. These shores had certainly never before heard words like *budget* and *strategy* and *performance incentives.*

"It's amazing what the team has accomplished already in less than a year since we all came together. We couldn't have gotten here without you and Ocie."

Shed smiled warmly. "Thanks, Di. We did bring some ideas and a few tricks, but you and your team rocked it. I know there were lots of people nine months ago who didn't believe the team could ring the bell with over $4 million of new EBITDA, but that's the potential Ocie and I saw when we first proposed that Patterson Lake buy GrammCo."

"It's all come together quite nicely. And not just how the stalwarts at GrammCo have welcomed the new team members – our *teaming,* too." In the first year together, GrammCo and Patterson Lake had completed 12 significant initiatives, canceling only two once they realized the ROI wasn't going to materialize. Another 10 were in-process – five green, three yellow, and two in the red. "The Value Creation Program has really delivered," she observed as she reached down to pick up another flat stone, "and while Don has confirmed four of the five million the team has claimed, I'm confident we'll get the rest.

"Our operational cadence and KPI reporting are really clicking as well," she said as she inspected the stone for skipping perfection. "That's going to sharpen the budgeting process. And the new bonus plan – everyone will soon see why we were so excited to put that in place." Crouching and expertly skipping the stone into the lake, Dianne cried out, "Ha! That's eight, maybe nine if you count that little one at the end." Turning to Shed she smiled and pronounced victoriously, "I win!"

"You've been winning all year, Di. You're ahead of plan and with lots more to come. Congratulations!"

Dianne was pleased. "Tomorrow our strategic planning facilitator comes. Should be fun." They'd had several calls with the facilitator over the last couple of weeks and at 8 a.m. she'd be with them to kick off the day-and-a-half-long leadership offsite. Dianne knew the team would appreciate getting out of the office to refine their strategy and talk through some new initiatives in order to reload the VCP before starting in on budget season. Six initiatives were already waiting in the wings.

"Maybe not as adventurous as this little excursion into the boonies to experience our latest ASV firsthand . . . ." Shed turned, threw, and counted the skips, "Ten! Here comes Ben. Time to saddle up."

Confirming VCP Results

With the end of the first year in sight, there is a natural and correct inclination to reflect on what's been accomplished. But like with so many processes in middle-market private equity, there are better and worse ways to engage in such reflection. In a performance-based culture, the opportunity to reflect means devising intentional processes for confirming results and rewarding success. It also means reconfirming strategies, reloading the VCP with new initiatives, and memorializing commitments through the budgeting process. Each of these is a part of the broad continuous performance cycle that the company has been developing and nurturing. With the successful ending of the first year, the first full performance cycle will have been completed, making it an opportune time to step back and see it as a whole.

The first step in that reflection process is taking stock of results. As the first year of the investment period comes to a close, initiative leaders have completed initiatives and commenced new ones. Quick-win initiatives have long been finished, and by the fourth quarter more substantial initiatives will be crossing the finish line. Inevitably, some rather impressive claims will be made – teams proudly ringing the results bell for benefits achieved and ROIs exceeded. And in most cases they are right to be proud – accomplishing key initiatives in addition to executing day-to-day business is significant.

That said, benefits confirmation is an appropriate finish for any completed initiative. It's important from an accountability perspective and to reinforce a performance-based culture to check that "we achieve what we said we were going to achieve." Confirmation of actual results also informs the budgeting process, enabling specific benefits to be memorialized in business plans going forward.

Initiative ROI Confirmation

The process for confirming initiative results includes both operational and financial perspectives:

Operational confirmation. The VCP manager should ensure the physical or operational ramifications of completed initiatives are evident. For instance, for a sourcing initiative, perhaps reviewing the new vendor contract for signatures and terms and ensuring the master vendor file is updated; for an organizational initiative, confirming new headcount figures for accuracy and reviewing HR payroll rosters; and for a pricing initiative, checking that pricing tables have been updated in customer master files and accurately reflects newly published pricing sheets. Operational confirmation is a good practice and often serves to catch errors or oversights.

Financial confirmation. The CFO will want to evaluate three related questions: To what extent does the team's claimed impact correspond to the original plan (i.e., positive or negative variances to planned benefits and costs?); are claims of financial results making their way to the bottom line (i.e., is there evidence on the P&L or balance sheet?); and is there any reason to believe the financial results will unexpectedly deteriorate as time passes (i.e., are the achieved benefits sustainable?). The CFO will then update forecasts and budgets accordingly.

Memorializing impacts is not only a normal accounting practice but also further serves the goal of supporting the sustainability of initiative results.

Overall VCP ROI Confirmation

The executive team has been working hard to drive the milestones and completion of all initiatives in the Value Creation Program. As with individual initiatives, it's also important to confirm the Value Creation Program is achieving the benefits the executive team has committed to achieving as a whole.

Think of overall VCP ROI confirmation as a second level of ensuring benefits hit the bottom line. Once we do all we can to ensure each individual initiative achieves the benefits to which the team leader and sponsor committed, the executive team should feel a responsibility to fill in any gaps to achieve the total to which they'd jointly committed. The success of the investment period relies on

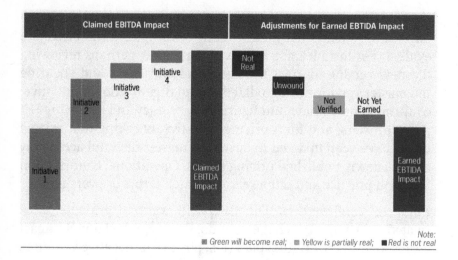

Figure 8.1   Confirming Value Creation Program Results

continuous VCP success and the ongoing culture of performance relies on making commitments and maintaining accountability.

Figure 8.1 provides an illustration of benefits confirmation for a Value Creation Program. In the example, four initiatives have been completed to date with a certain total "Claimed EBITDA Impact." Upon review, the CFO has determined only half of the claimed EBITDA benefits are actually hitting the bottom line. As that second level of benefits confirmation, he or she provides the feedback to the VCP steering team so they can work together with the initiative teams to close the benefits gap.

We typically suggest evaluating and tracking four types of possible deductions from claimed benefits:

Not real. This occurs when a claimed savings is overstated or unsupported. This deduction is not uncommon, and in our example represents some 20 percent of the total claimed benefit. Calculation and assumption errors are often the issue. For example, an initiative team claimed to have reduced 20 full-time equivalent (FTE) headcount, but because some were part-timers the CFO made the adjustment and confirmed a total reduction of 15 FTEs.

Unwound. This represents initiatives where all or part of the benefits deteriorate or are dissipated post-implementation. Some "unwindings" are straightforward albeit disappointing – for instance, if after opening a new sales territory the management team later decided to close it for lack of progress. Some are unsuspected leakages, as in the case of an initiative "resulting" in the elimination of field inspection and associated headcount, only to later realize the inspection workload simply transferred to the field training team, causing their costs to increase.

Not verified. Not verified indicates that the CFO has not yet been able to confirm one way or another if the claimed impact is real. Perhaps he or she has not had time to complete their review or there has not been enough "run-time" for the financial impact to begin to materialize on the bottom-line. The not-verified category is temporary because the eventual final disposition of those claims is only a matter of time. Many but perhaps not all of the claims in this bucket will soon be verified and moved to their appropriate final category.

Not yet earned. Not yet earned means that the benefits are confirmed but have not yet hit the bottom line. It's simply a timing issue based on the initiative's effective date and the reporting period. For instance, assume Figure 8.1 reflects a claimed and confirmed EBITDA for a certain month and three of the four initiatives had been completed before that month. Because the fourth initiative was completed mid-month, its full impact will not show up until the following month's report. This, too, is a temporary bucket because the claims are real and will soon be reflected on the bottom line.

The VCP represents a disciplined effort of authentic teaming, individual commitment, leadership accountability, and execution success. The approach is based on ownership and vigilance and critically examining, triaging, and augmenting results until the targeted benefits shows up on the bottom line. If the Value Creation Program is going to be all it can be, it should be approached with a zero-sum mentality. Achieving planned benefits means leaders hold themselves and their colleagues accountable for the growth commitments articulated in the VCP.

Rewarding Success

One of the most fulfilling parts of growing businesses is recognizing and rewarding success amongst the management team. For the right team, the biggest reward for success is success itself and the feeling of accomplishment, as well as having earned the opportunity for additional and new responsibilities.

Of course, personal pride in a job well done is not the only consideration for rewarding success. People appreciate being recognized by others for their accomplishments. Too often leaders forget to acknowledge the dedication and work and results of the people on their team. Strong executives – equity partners and portco leaders alike – take the time to regularly and sincerely recognize great work.

Executive Incentive Measures

In private equity, portfolio company executives typically receive annual performance bonuses based on achieving or exceeding planned EBITDA for the year, aligning their incentives to those of the PEG. While the CEO's bonus may often be calculated 100 percent based on EBITDA, the OP and portco CEO may choose to include additional performance measures in their management team's bonus structure.

Some portfolio companies will directly link the achievement of certain VCP initiatives to bonus plans. For example, a CFO bonus might be based 90 percent on company EBITDA and 10 percent on his or her specific initiatives achievement, whereas a business unit president might have 40 percent of their bonus tied to company EBITDA but 60 percent linked to business unit EBITDA. Other portcos will link other manager-controllable aspects to bonus plans. The VP of sales might have the bonus split three ways: 20 percent on company EBITDA, 50 percent on new customer margin, 30 percent on existing margin, whereas the calculation for the VP of operations might substitute operational budgets and specific initiative achievement for new customer margin and existing margin.

Performance Incentive Models

Just like there are many different potential measures for performance, there are equally many different ways of modeling those measures. For our purposes, it's important to distinguish between traditional models and what might be termed a continuous performance incentive model.

Traditional models. Traditional performance incentive models provide for a defined bonus payment upon achieving a certain performance level, usually as a percentage of base compensation. As shown in the left side of Figure 8.2, this model may drive unwanted behavior across the entire performance spectrum, with the single exception of when performance closely approaches the targeted level. For lower performance levels, the individual experiences little-to-no incentive, as he or she believes a bonus to be largely unattainable. Sometimes the individual may even be incentivized to hold back performance so that results might be applied to the next bonus period. A similar foot-dragging disincentive emerges after a bonus is earned and further performance levels will result in no additional incentive. Yet the very small period of positive incentive, when a bonus payment appears within reach, also generates its own issues: The final push for a bonus payment may drive aggressive and unwanted behaviors that have negative long-term consequences for the portco.

Continuous incentive models. Rather than the all-or-nothing approach of traditional models, conscientious PEGs advocate for models offering a positive incentive across a much broader performance spectrum that avoid zones of disincentive. As shown on the right side of Figure 8.2, continuous models are shaped like an S-curve, where earned bonus begins at a threshold level

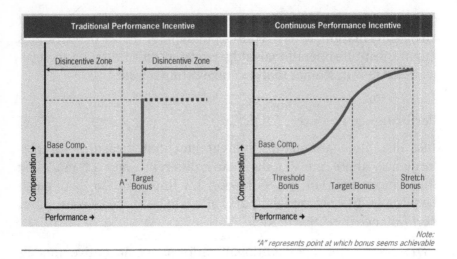

Note:
"A" represents point at which bonus seems achievable

Figure 8.2   Incentive Compensation Models

of performance – perhaps starting at 75 percent of targeted performance levels – and increases (at an increasing rate) until the targeted bonus amount is earned at the targeted performance level. After this point, the individual continues to earn an additional bonus for performance above target at a decreasing rate until the stretch bonus level is achieved (typically but not always capped at 25 percent or even 50 percent or more of their target bonus). Performance is therefore incentivized across the performance spectrum.

Planning Strategy Pragmatically

In Chapter 5 we argued for "suspending strategic planning formalities" because we didn't want portcos to delay in creating and accelerating the Value Creation Program and didn't want to get distracted from our new operating cadence. We also weren't prepared to jump into a strategic planning process so early in the new relationship. And perhaps most of all, we'd already pretty much gone through many components of strategic planning during diligence, onboarding, and creating the VCP.

Now that the year is nearing completion and the more obvious and high-priority initiatives are wrapping up, the time is right to conduct a facilitated but still pragmatic strategic planning process to confirm where we've been and where we're going, and to identify the next round of initiatives. Based on the six to nine months or more of specific hands-on experience, the PEG/portco team is well-prepared to now conduct a one- to two-day workshop to confirm their strategies and the overall Value Creation Plan. This will serve useful as preliminary input into the first budgeting exercise the PEG and portco teams undergo together.

Strategic Planning Workshop

Neither the OP nor the CEO should facilitate the session, as they will both want to be active participants. Instead, we like to hire an external strategy discussion facilitator skilled in managing these types of workshops. Their preparation should be limited to a week and include reviewing diligence materials and market studies, interviewing management team members, visiting an operation, and speaking with a handful of customers in a brief VOC.

Several overarching goals should be kept in mind when thinking about the outcomes of such a workshop:

Practical to investment period. By this time there are three to five years or so left in the investment period. Blue-sky ideas are worthy of discussion, but the focus should be on what the PEG and portco can accomplish during the remaining investment period as well as what they can initiate as a new runway for the next buyers. This should be thought of as an operational strategy rather than a 10-year strategy.

Added challenge. That said, it does make sense to discover one or two ideas that could be really exciting and perhaps transformational for the business. They should represent something the PEG/portco team could work toward, with the idea of putting some things in place that may make that transformational idea a reality still within the investment period or perhaps more likely for the next buyer (such that it would materialize in an increased sales multiple).

Informs add-on targeting. By this time, the PEG and portco team will likely be considering add-on acquisitions to support inorganic growth efforts. The workshop would likely be organized to have a session focused on add-on target characteristics and priorities – evaluating whether it is better to add a company that expands the platform company's geography, offerings, customer base, operational capability, or something else.

Input to the new budget. The workshop outcome is likely a refinement and clarification of the one-page VCP in addition to supporting initiative detail. It should serve as an invaluable input to the upcoming budgeting process, enabling the team to properly fund the reconfirmed or refined strategic priorities.

There are at least two simple but effective strategic planning tools we like to leverage in proceeding with pragmatic strategic planning: strengths, weaknesses,opportunities, and threats (SWOT) analysis and the growth opportunity matrix (GOM). Outlined in Figure 8.3, both are well-known and quite intuitive for a management team to apply. The facilitator will often want to work with the equity partners and CEO and the rest of the executive team using one or both as a basis for the planning approach.

The facilitated discussion regarding SWOT is particularly useful by way of evaluating against competition and disruptors. For instance, the SWOT session for a large real estate inspection company might include a lengthy discussion of how to respond to the threat of drone technology and its increasing impact on reducing some of the need for up-ladder roof inspection work.

In middle-market private equity portcos, the facilitated discussion utilizing the GOM will likely focus on the lower left of the right-hand chart in Figure 8.3, including better penetration of existing markets, product extensions, and market expansions. For instance, back in the days when there were copier repair companies,

SWOT Analysis	Helpful	Harmful	Growth Opportunities Matrix (GOM)		Products & Services		
	Strengths	**Weaknesses**			Existing	Modified	New
Internal	Capabilities, qualities & resources that are superior to your competitors	Limitations of your company compared to your competitors		New	Market Development	Partial Diversification	Diversification
External	**Opportunities**	**Threats**	Markets & Customers	Modified	Market Expansion	Stretched Extension	Partial Diversification
	Emerging needs, underserved markets, few competitors, creative ideas & new momentum	Emerging competition, changing regulatory environment & negative perceptions		Existing	Market Penetration	Product Extension	Product Development

Note:
Source: Growth Opportunities Matrix based on Ansoff Matrix first published in the Harvard Business Review in 1957
■ Yellow is medium complexity (GOM); ■ Red is negative (SWOT), higher complexity (GOM)
■ Green is positive (SWOT), current (GOM);

Figure 8.3 Strategic Planning Tools.

many a strategy session undoubtedly engaged in discussions about extending their services to printers and multifunction equipment. And while certainly a possible consideration, aggressive diversification into computer repair work was often likely dismissed. While differentiation into entirely new areas is certainly a possibility, it often involves more time and more risk than what a PEG and its portco are willing to take on during the remaining investment period.

Once the strategic planning workshop is complete, there needs to be concise documentation of any updates the team agreed to for the objectives, value proposition, strategies, and initiatives of the Value Creation Program. VCP has already been long up and running, and so it should be a seamless and relatively simple effort to progress from the workshop back to strategy execution mode.

Strategic Planning Rinse-and-Repeat Approach

Periodic reconfirming and refining strategies and adding new initiatives as others are completed should be part of the normal routine in a private equity portfolio company. These efforts should not be long, drawn-out, and costly ones, but rather pragmatic and periodic discussions about the VCP and the overall state of the business, with both eyes wide open and focused on the customer and the evolving marketplace.

Inattentive PEGs either never support their portcos in ongoing initiative planning, prioritization, and execution or only have a single major strategic planning session and let that serve as the strategic guidance for the entire investment period. Performance-oriented PEGs help their portcos learn to continuously reconfirm, execute, and reload the VCP. Not only does the latter approach drive the most EBITDA value during the investment period, but it also serves as the foundation for an ongoing culture of performance – one that will be attractive to the next buyer for sure.

The next and each subsequent year through exit will largely be a matter of this rinse-and-repeat approach. The PEG and portco team will continue to improve on their working rhythm and refine their operating cadence, but the bulk of their energies – in addition, of course, to managing the day-to-day – will be spent on executing initiatives, memorizing results into budgets, and reloading the VCP.

Integrating Plans and Budgets

One of the best ways a portco management team can hold themselves accountable is to memorialize commitments through the budgeting process. To that end, the CFO is responsible to ensure the targeted and achieved results of all VCP initiatives are properly integrated into operational forecasts and budgets.

Overly aggressive PEGs worry little about linkages of initiatives to budgets. Rather than supporting realistic budgets established from actual improvement initiatives, they pick a top- and a bottom-line number and communicate to their portcos that this is what they need to achieve. Unrealistic budget expectations and coerced numbers result in a lack of commitment and increase the risk of underperformance.

But clear-minded PEGs understand they cannot budget desires, and, rather, need to work with their management teams to establish realistic budgets based on market dynamics, internal capabilities, and prioritized VCP initiatives. They realize the annual budget – when developed jointly, candidly, and with trust – can be a realistic and specific motivating tool. Budgets so constructed serve as an incentive for the best possible performance from the combined PEG/portco team.

Typical Flaws in the Budgeting Process

Often in middle-market portfolio companies, and especially in first-time PEG-owned companies, we find operational planning and budgeting processes to be significantly lacking. The starting point in many companies having an unsophisticated budgeting process is an inflationary approach, whereby last year's actuals are adjusted up or down by rough percentages to serve as the new budget. The resulting budget lacks operational cause-and-effect logic, with neither supporting facts nor key operating assumptions to justify the numbers. Such an artificial process generates an unsubstantiated plan – one that no one can defend since no one has any idea what lies behind the figures.

Unsurprisingly, no one feels ownership of such plans, and virtually everyone yields to gamesmanship: Make as few commitments as possible but ask for as many resources as you can get. The age-old budgeting game of sandbagging is indefensible on its merits, but what's worse is the pernicious attitudes it fosters. Gamesmanship distorts what is achievable, encourages suboptimization of limited resources, and renders the resulting budget of little value in motivating and enabling performance.

Equity partners frequently find portcos undergoing the budgeting routine simply because somewhere, at some time, somebody drilled into them that they needed a budget and so they made a budget, checking that box once each year and disregarding the results after the first month or two. In these companies, most view the routine as an exorbitant waste of time, requiring multiple meetings and iterations while consuming weeks and months of what could have been applied to "real work" of the company – not realizing just how much real work is lost or inefficient without a realistic and motivating budget to guide them.

Top-Down, Then Bottom-Up Budgeting

Smart PEGs have budgeting practices that are the inverse of the approaches mentioned above, which were characterized by perceived waste, disjointed results, and gamesmanship. These PEGs will have long ago worked out preferred budgeting processes and corresponding templates to enable their management teams to build cause-and-effect logic into their plans. If the PEG has a finance director assigned to the portco, he or she will start the process by working side by side with the CFO. Undoubtedly, the introduction of standard processes and templates will result in a certain level of initial compliance frustration, but the result will be a marked improvement over prior years, characterized by the following:

Candid reflection of reality. Trust-based partnership between PEG and portco should position the management team to be candid about what they believe can be accomplished. There should be no coerced mandates from on high nor inflated numbers from below. This should be true between each level – from function to portco and from portco to PEG. Where significant uncertainty exists, the collective team should work through confidence ranges and incorporate various contingencies.

Efficient and collaborative. Rather than taking three or four months, the budgeting process should be designed to require only a couple at most. The finance organization should facilitate the process, incorporating historical and projected internal and external data and input from the team, using a predefined process with easy-to-use templates. Discussions should be candid and the process iterative. The exercise itself should be insightful, providing each participant with a better understanding of their business.

Linked and intelligent. Rather than simply starting from last year and adding a multiplier or "bumping it up a bit," the budget should be intentionally designed. The foundation should rest on explicit commercial and operational facts and assumptions with cause-and-effect logic. An industrial engineering approach is useful – standard rates and expected quantities, from which dollar figures are simply calculated outcomes of the inputs. Iterating through scenarios and sensitivities is useful, and relative accuracy trumps implied precision all day long.

Starting from a basic budget philosophy based on candor, collaboration, and logic, the portco management team is ready to prepare their annual budget, typically starting mid-fall for a calendar year-end company. The annual budget process should include both top-down guidance and bottom-up detail, following a series of incremental steps:

A kickoff meeting with all functional budget leaders and documentation describing the budget process, an explanation of the templates to be used, and a calendar of review dates. In the middle-market, the CFO typically leads this process.

Top-down guidance from the CEO, CFO, and the equity partners provide general guidance and standard expectations across the company, for instance, the handling of inflation for the year, or annual merit increase timing and average percentage to assume.

Early budgeting iterations focus on the top-line with the commercial functions because the other budget leaders will rely on monthly sale projections to guide their own assumptions regarding monthly activity level and required resources. The CEO, CFO, and equity partners sign off on this before distribution to the rest of the budget leaders.

Distribution of templates from the finance organization will typically be provided as in Figure 8.4 for each functional area and expense type combination. The standard template calculates the total draft monthly budget figures for each functional area and expense type combination, including an indication of the overall change from the previous year. The template will include

Budget by Organization & Expense Type	Budget Month												
	J	F	M	A	M	J	J	A	S	O	N	D	Total
Marketing, Salaries													
Prior Year Actual	$0	$0	$0	$0	$0	$0	$0	$0	$0	$0	$0	$0	$0
Adjustments to Arrive at Base Case:													
Full-Year Impact of Prior Year Changes	$0	$0	$0	$0	$0	$0	$0	$0	$0	$0	$0	$0	$0
Merit Increase (3% Avg. Starting 4/1)				$0	$0	$0	$0	$0	$0	$0	$0	$0	$0
Impact of Initiatives (I) & Other (O):													
Create New Analytics Team (I)				$0	$0	$0	$0	$0	$0	$0	$0	$0	$0
Outsource Graphics Function (I)			$0	$0	$0	$0	$0	$0	$0	$0	$0	$0	$0
Consolidate Administrative Roles (O)							$0	$0	$0	$0	$0	$0	$0
Total Adjustments & Impacts	$0	$0	$0	$0	$0	$0	$0	$0	$0	$0	$0	$0	$0
Budget	$0	$0	$0	$0	$0	$0	$0	$0	$0	$0	$0	$0	$0
Delta v. Prior Year $	$0	$0	$0	$0	$0	$0	$0	$0	$0	$0	$0	$0	$0
Delta v. Prior Year %	0%	0%	0%	0%	0%	0%	0%	0%	0%	0%	0%	0%	0%

Note:
See detailed assumptions regarding headcount, compensation, timing, offsetting costs, etc.
■ Green is very favorable; ■ Yellow is slightly favorable; ■ Red is unfavorable

Figure 8.4   Incorporating Changes into Budgets

prepopulated last year actuals and basic adjustments, including annualizing the impact of already completed VCP initiatives and other changes to start an upcoming year base case. Importantly, the budget leader will assemble supporting schedules specifying any additional assumptions and statistics.

Initiative incorporation by each budget owner will factor in the anticipated monthly impact of in-process or upcoming VCP initiatives and other efforts as well. For instance, a company having two initiatives impacting marketing salaries – *Create New Analytics Team* and *Outsource Graphics Function* – would incorporate forecasted monthly impacts into the budget.

Budget review starts with the finance organization assembling all input templates and rolling-up a budget review package for the company. They work with budget leaders for adjustments and assumption consistency across functions. The CFO then facilitates budget review meetings, leading to follow-up edits and iterations. The budget process is worked through until the company has the draft bottom-up budget ready for board review and approval.

When examining the proposed budget, the board will generally expect to see improved year-over-year top- and bottom-line growth rates, steady or improving gross margin rates, SG&A overhead increase rates less than top-line increases, improved working capital positions, and a conservative plan for capital expenditures. They'll also expect contingency plans with specific triggers (for example, if Q1 revenue growth does not materialize, certain planned Q2 spending will be canceled) that would be put in place should performance fall short of budget.

The outcome of the iterative process should be a reasonable but aggressive budget for the coming year, based on quantified logical cause-and-effect assumptions, including the impact of the Value Creation Program and containing stop-gap measures in the case of performance shortfalls. If the process is well facilitated and the resulting budget is detailed and defensible, the end result is an invaluable fundamental management tool to which the entire team can commit.

Embracing a Continuous Performance Cycle

Operational plans and budgets are integral to a company's overall continuous performance cycle: ensuring the right leaders are in place and properly supported, establishing and resourcing a prioritized Value Creation Program, integrating that into operational budgeting and reporting processes, and motivating and managing performance to plan. The continuous cycle starts again as operating results are realized and the equity partners and portco executives adjust their teams, update their VCP, refine operational plans, and continue executing according to those updated plans.

Shortsighted PEGs fail to institutionalize a continuous performance cycle in their portfolio companies, allowing gains to happen in starts and fits. Because they never ensure that the company embraces an efficient repetitive cycle of value creation, it's no

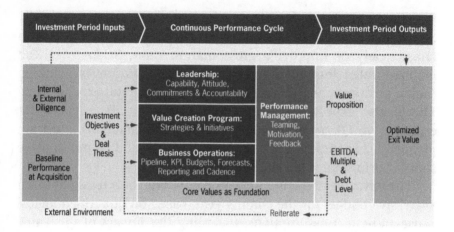

Figure 8.5   Continuous Performance Cycle

wonder they reward in fits and starts as well. Better PEGs realize they achieve optimized exit value by working in partnership with the portfolio company management team to create a continuous performance cycle and reward accordingly based on the intentional culture of performance built into such a cycle.

The continuous performance cycle summarizes many of the topics covered so far, from leadership and accountability through the Value Creation Plan and feedback. Figure 8.5 offers a comprehensive view of how all these components fit together: the "where we're starting from" of the investment period inputs, the "where we want to go" of the investment period outputs, and the "how to get to there" of the continuous performance cycle.

Investment Period Inputs

Investment period inputs represent key components for the OP and CEO as a starting point for the investment period:

Internal and external diligence is the plethora of data and information pulled together before the acquisition. These include reviews of internal details such as those associated with management team composition and capabilities, core business processes, systems and facilities, and their strengths and weaknesses. It also includes legal, financial, regulatory, and other topics. External diligence includes industry and marketplace research, customer interviews, and relative opportunities and threats. The resulting reports from external diligence providers, such as the market assessment and operational assessment, are prime fodder for continued use early in the investment period.

Baseline performance at acquisition serves as the starting point. This represents the key details of the company usually organized in an intelligent and usable form – financial details over time, organizational and employee statistics, physical asset listings and descriptions, customer and supplier master files, and related information. Ideally, if you were to gather the same data at the end of the investment period and "subtract" the baseline data from it, you'd end up with a detailed quantification of all the changes made during the investment period – everything from internal operating efficiencies to specific external revenue increases.

Investment objectives will typically come from modeling the investing partner and the PEG deal team completed to demonstrate to the PEG investment committee the ranges and likely outcomes of the investment. Often demonstrated in terms of anticipated EBITDA growth, exit multiple increase (or decrease), and levels of debt to be paid down based on free cash flow, these would typically include outcomes for a variety of scenarios, with a selected scenario as the targeted one showing a final expected COC return as well as the resulting proceeds that would be provided to each interested party – LPs, PEG, and portco management.

Deal thesis shows how the equity partners have originally intended to grow the business and create value. Typically, there will be several general initial value drivers that the team believes will deliver the necessary growth to achieve investment objectives. The deal thesis could include a variety of broad strategies as their hypotheses, which will be confirmed and refined early in the investment period. *Expand into New Geographies, Extend the Service or Product Line, Add New Customer Segments, Improve Four Wall Operational Efficiencies, Consolidate Manufacturing and Warehousing Operations,* and *Incorporate Add-On Acquisitions* are just a few examples of value drivers included in deal theses. The IP and deal team will model these improvements to support the viability of the investment objectives.

Together, these four components encompass a myriad of other inputs, financial models, discussions, and iterations that happened between the equity partners, their potential new portco management team, lenders, and the private equity firm investment committee. They comprise the starting point for the OP and the CEO to begin their work together once the portco has been acquired.

Continuous Performance Cycle

The elements of the continuous performance cycle all contribute to the growth of the portco over the investment period.

Leadership

Leadership includes capability, attitude, commitments, and accountability, among other traits. The OP and CEO work together and with the rest of the PEG and portco team to jointly onboard each other and to initiate true and lasting partnerships based on candor and trust. They agree to a core set of values as a foundation for all they do and begin to establish effective teaming across the entire management structure, including authenticity and trust, candid and respectful debate, a willingness to make commitments, and an expectation to hold each other accountable to those commitments.

Together the CEO and OP form an evaluation of each leader's capability and attitude and work with each to reduce any lingering consternation about the future. During this important time, the OP and CEO are evaluating any potential leadership gaps and considering options to shore-in the team when the time comes.

Value Creation Program

The OP and CEO waste no time, and within weeks of the acquisition they initiate the process of developing the Value Creation Program. They start with the original investment thesis and now work on a more exacting bottom-up collaborative approach of generating ideas, prioritizing opportunities, and profiling the highest-potential initiatives. They will have organized a couple dozen initiatives into perhaps three to six strategy buckets. Putting it all together – a one-page executive summary followed by the individual initiative profiles – they have a plan into which everyone had input and so can get behind. Over the course of this process they've succinctly articulated their value proposition for the customer and confirmed their quantified objectives for the investment period.

Armed with the initial Value Creation Program, the OP and CEO then work with their executive team to identify risks and gaps in the coverage model. They identify which initiatives require additional human resources to execute and then make necessary shore-ins – including modifying assignments, adding resources, or incorporating consulting support. They finalize all roles and responsibilities and accountabilities for the Value Creation Program and establish an approach to coordinate the VCP and to keep it on track, led by an assigned VCP manager and standing steering reviews.

Business Operations

Of course this is a broad bucket, but business operations certainly include KPIs, budgets, forecasts, reporting, and operational cadence. As the VCP progresses, the CFO and his or her team ensure all targeted results – both operational KPIs and financial outcomes – are memorialized in ongoing forecasts and eventual budgets. They expect reports regularly regarding the results of the VCP, which leads to improvement in KPIs, which in turn leads to achieving monthly and quarterly budgets. The PEG/portco team have iterated and evolved to an efficient reporting package and meeting cadence, enabling them to monitor and influence both day-to-day business progress as well as progress with the VCP's strategies and initiatives.

Performance Management

The PEG and portco team eventually settles into an effective ongoing approach of performance monitoring and management, ensuring prioritized, flexible, and actionable strategy alignment, operational alignment focused on capability and continuous improvement, and organizational alignment guided by clear and concise priorities regarding clear authority and decision-making. A well-managed integrated performance management cycle enables clear linkages between the current state of the business, strategic priorities, initiative execution, budgeting, planning, results monitoring, and performance adjustment.

The partners continue to hold each other accountable to VCP objectives and KPI targets and leverage effective teaming concepts and candid regular feedback as well as early successes for continued motivation. Toward the end of the first year, the team recognizes and rewards success, and also readily admits to and adjusts for setbacks.

Core Values

Supporting all of these elements is a well-articulated set of values to serve as the foundation for all decisions and all actions, as well as for the culture of the business. An important part of any effective and proud organization or leadership team is not merely to have core values, but more importantly to live them on a day-to-day basis.

As they begin a new year, the team reiterates its continuous performance cycle, which remains in place for the duration of the investment period and beyond. By focusing on the value proposition to their customers and incorporating any external marketplace changes, team members evaluate if they still have the right roles and leadership assignments, update and refine the VCP, and ensure all VCP initiatives and other growth efforts are budgeted and then reported against and forecasted. They stay true to their core values as they continuously manage performance and provide constructive feedback and support to the team, while making changes and enhancements where and when needed.

Investment Period Outputs

Investment period outputs reflect the ultimate measures for the OP and CEO to assess progress and results during the investment period and determine exit timing:

Value proposition. A well-defined, clear, and concise value proposition tells customers what the company stands for – what its intention is, how it will serve them, and how it is different from the marketplace. It conveys the underlying and unique value the company provides to its customers. Along with a company's core values, quantified business objectives, and primary strategies and initiatives, the company's value proposition sits squarely astride the company's one-pager summarizing its Value Creation Plan.

EBITDA, multiple, and debt level. These are the big three when it comes to optimizing enterprise value. EBITDA times Sales Multiple less Debt Outstanding and various other expenses is what will be distributed to the investors, PEG, and management team at the end of the investment period. These three are the ultimate lagging indicators, and together (minus the original enterprise value at the beginning of the investment period) form the total value created.

Optimized exit value. During each year of the investment period the PEG and portco team continue to grow EBITDA, improve the likely future exit multiple, and pay down debt levels. When the company has grown sufficiently to achieve its investment objectives and when the market conditions are right, the equity partners (led by the IP) work with the portco to identify the right investment bank to guide them through the sale process, eventually leading to an optimized exit value and providing a healthy return to the investors, PEG, and portco management team.

As the first year wraps up, it's natural for the equity partners and portco executives to reflect back. For successful and collaborative PEGs and portcos, theirs will be a reflection filled with pride and a sense of accomplishment. The relationship is positive and productive and they're making great progress.

Looking at the continuous performance cycle, one can see why Shed and Dianne feel there's much to celebrate and why there's such optimism looking ahead. While there's a correct sense of accomplishment, GrammCo is poised for even more transformative changes to continue improving their internal infrastructure and accelerate new revenue growth initiatives. It's exciting times ahead for everyone at Patterson Lake and GrammCo, full of new challenges and opportunities to continue to generate significant and lasting enterprise value, all with a successful exit in mind.

Chapter 9
Year 2: Improving Infrastructure

"The world breaks everyone and afterward many are strong at the broken places."

Ernest Hemingway, *A Farewell to Arms*

"That was really impressive."

"Are you kidding? It was awesome."

Two months into the new year and GrammCo was operating on all cylinders. The team was entering the second year on fire and just now had wrapped up a monthly full-team VCP steering meeting. Shed and Dianne were grabbing a coffee from the machine outside the maintenance crib with Sam Fredericks, VCP program manager.

"This was probably our tenth or twelfth VCP full-team meeting and the best one yet."

(continued)

(*continued*)

Dianne was proud of her team. "Lee hit it out of the park today – his Phase 2 Sourcing initiatives. People were excited – not only for the savings but for Lee. He did an excellent job and it showed. Everyone in the room saw that and genuinely loved seeing it pay off."

"Great for him; he's worked hard. His first sourcing effort got over two million. Don confirmed it."

Dianne remembered when Shed first discussed sourcing opportunities with the team, and everyone had been skeptical. GrammCo had a reputation as a great customer, and they had all heard stories from their suppliers about the high-pressure tactics other companies employed, only to have them backfire when there was a shortage. GrammCo was never short on materials, partly because of its excellent relationships with suppliers. But Shed had pointed out the different spend categories and that suppliers in each category can and should be approached differently. Lee had quickly embraced that analytical line of thinking and it proved out in spades.

"And then Jean. Did you ever see her so – I don't know – 'comfortable' is maybe the word I'm looking for – presenting in front of all 20 of us before? She was really into it."

Shed added, "Because she knows her stuff. Lean operations and project work is definitely her thing. The whole Houston gang loved the Kaizen process improvement event last week. What was that – her fourth probably?"

"At least." Sam chimed in. "The first thing she tackled was streamlining this maintenance crib right here," tapping the cage, "then she helped rethink the whole incoming receiving and parts storage process – then the locator system and bar-coding and scanning, which had gotten totally gummed up with so many extra steps and inefficiencies. And now this one at the Houston Depot."

Dianne had brought Sam on with Shed's prompting back in the summer. GrammCo had never had a program manager, but with so many things going with VCP it just made sense. He started as an independent contractor but had hoped it would turn into a full-time role, and after six months Dianne pulled the trigger. *He's paid for himself threefold*, Dianne thought.

There had been other organizational shifts at GrammCo as well. She and Shed had looked closely at the organizational chart and realized that the different plants had become their own silos, fraught with spans and layers and organizational complexities. Streamlining and right-sizing the company had taken some time, but the results were truly beginning to pay off.

So were the operational efficiencies from other initiatives. Things in the shop had never looked better – and the same was true based on the pictures from Houston. After Lee and Jean's status updates, three more team leaders provided similarly exciting updates showing great progress. But Don's new working capital initiative, *Reduce Slow Moving Inventory,* was itself moving slowly – too slowly.

"Hey, Sam, would you mind spending some time with Don next week? I'm sure he'd welcome a little of your insight to help get that inventory thing going."

"I'm on it."

Organizing Effectively

During the first year of the investment period, the portco management team will have implemented organizational and operational initiatives aimed at establishing more efficient and effective infrastructure. Yet as the PEG and portco team enter their second year together, there likely remains many more opportunities on both the organization and operational fronts. Funding these improvements can be expensive – be that new leadership roles or new systems, for instance – and so portcos likely will have addressed (or soon will be addressing) sourcing and working capital initiatives. These typically have high ROI that can serve to help fund the rest of the Value Creation Program.

There are certainly countless instances of specific internally focused improvement efforts that portcos can choose to pursue: organizational, operational, sourcing, working capital, or other types. This chapter just touches on a small number of them that are often relevant in middle-market private equity. But the point is clear – astute equity partners will expect their portfolio companies to have established an efficient and effective infrastructure within the first year or two of the investment period.

Getting the organization right is one of the most important things a PEG can do in partnership with its portfolio company, starting with the executive team. We've covered the leadership role in some detail previously, so this section will discuss the overall organizational structure – from functional silos to management spans of control to organizational layers and specter staffing.

Getting the structure right certainly improves efficiency. But the more powerful benefit of improving organizational structure relates to the effectiveness of the organization: getting the right things done in the right way, making better decisions faster, and reinforcing the functional teaming capability.

How a PEG goes about doing that – helping to improve structure – of course makes all the difference. Shortsighted PEGs micromanage organizational changes deep within the company without having had the experience of running the business and dealing with the realities of organizational change. Or they pay little attention to any role below the executive suite, not recognizing the need for broader and deeper organizational shifts to generate the gains they are after. As a result, their influence on organizational efficiency and effectiveness of portfolio companies is unproductive, nonexistent, or even harmful.

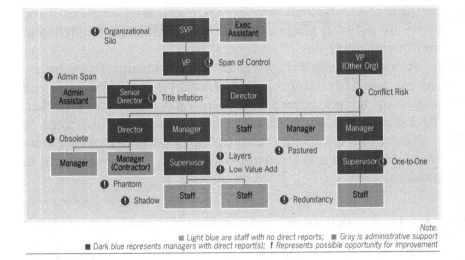

Note:
■ Light blue are staff with no direct reports;   ■ Gray is administrative support
■ Dark blue represents managers with direct report(s);   ! Represents possible opportunity for improvement

Figure 9.1   Organizational Structure Improvement

Forward-thinking PEGs appreciate well-designed and carefully nurtured organizational structures and realize organizational efficiency and effectiveness are influenced by proper structures. They also understand that simply moving boxes on a page results in nothing. Organizational design requires careful contemplation of individual relationships and experiences – of what's transpired in the past and what is needed for the future. These PEGs work with their management teams to continuously hone organizations and reporting relationships.

Figure 9.1 is representative of any number of organizational charts in middle-market portfolio companies. Organizations evolve, and while each particular change likely made perfect sense when it was implemented, decisions become obsolete and new changes are overlaid. Poor organizational design typically means more reporting, more meetings, more hand-offs, and slower decisions, placing decisions too far from the customer. The result is a misaligned organization with inefficient and excessive staffing.

Lean organizations, by contrast, are nimble and effective. They have fewer reports to interpret, meetings to attend, hand-offs to decipher, and hierarchies to manage. They make efficient fact-based decisions and swift progress based on the best and often firsthand information available.

Periodically most companies need a full organizational review and clean-up. But fixing a long-neglected organizational structure should not be tackled as a headcount reduction exercise. Rather, the focus should be on streamlining activities and decisions to accelerate and improve the customer experience. To that end, there are several things that forward-looking PEGs and portcos ought to consider.

Silos, Layers, and Spans

Organizational silos. In middle-market companies, typical structural hierarchies start at the business unit level, followed by function, department, and perhaps cost center. Each represents the possibility of an organizational silo emerging. With that comes the risk of inefficient and ineffective decision-making, with information flows going up, across, and then down another silo (then back again). They also risk sub-optimization, where one unit operates for its own betterment at the expense of the broader company. Symptoms include hoarding of personnel, secreting of information, or unfairly competing for limited shared resources. Smart PEGs work with their management teams to reduce the number of silos or make them permeable and fluid units by reducing the barriers between them.

Layers of hierarchy. Within any silo reside multiple levels of authority. Each organizational layer adds more complexity to the organization – more meetings, more reporting, more interpretation. Layers within silos tend to recreate the old telephone game we played as kids – with the more people playing the funnier the end result – but such communication distortions and delays in a portco are anything but funny. Flatter organizations instill better communication and improve collaboration. Fewer layers enable faster decision-making that's closer to the customer. Better PEGs work with their management teams to reduce hierarchy and flatten structures.

Spans of control. Management spans refer to the number of direct reports for any given manager and administrative spans refers to the number of people an administrative assistant supports. As with the number of organizational silos and layers of hierarchy, the proper number of spans of control is not an exact science and differs according to industry, company, function, and specific individual manager. Other factors influence span decisions, including the degree of work standardization and level of automation, staff role variability and interdependencies, as well as the pace of external change and manager tenure, experience, and capability. Span of control tends to be smaller for smaller companies, mostly because each function or department has fewer people on the roster to begin with. But as a rule of thumb, we'd say middle-market portfolio companies should target an average span in the range of four to eight direct reports per manager.

Specter Staffing

Issues with spans, layers, and silos can lead to another phenomenon often found in portfolio companies, which we call *specter staffing*. There are two types of specters – shadows and phantoms – and while neither is scary, both can be problematic.

Shadow staffing. These are roles within specific functional organizations that would better reside in others. They propagate when the first isn't receiving the support it expects from the second. Redundant shadows typically relate to support roles such as IT, finance, and human resources. For instance, shadow staffing occurs when a manufacturing department hires its own financial analyst because they're unsatisfied with the support they receive from the finance department. Perhaps 10 to 20 percent of staffing in some companies are shadows.

Phantom staffing. This is a term for people who are working in a company but their names do not show up on company payroll files. They look and act like employees, performing typical roles of employees, but they're long-term consultants or interim contractors. We also place excessive or perpetual overtime in the phantom bucket, because like other phantoms, overtime masks true headcount. We estimate phantoms represent the equivalent of 10 to 20 percent or more of total payroll "staffing" in some companies.

Phantoms and shadows are not necessarily bad, but they often do represent a large, less efficient, and perhaps unnoticed expense. Attentive PEGs work with their management teams to remove specter staffing or at least bring them out of the darkness.

Title Inflation and Pastured Roles

Equity partners often hear, and make, the argument that "titles are free," but in truth *title inflation* can eventually cost a company up to 30 percent more than the same person with the same skillset holding a more appropriate title. Increased cost pressures come from new salary expectations associated with the new paygrade and colleague comparables, along with increased expectations that more senior roles have for support staff and expenses, increased sense of inequity across the organization as others expect similar considerations for themselves, and pressure to backfill the position of the promoted individual. Prudent PEGs work with portco executives to carefully consider unintended consequences of title promotions.

Separate but related to inflated titles are two organizational phenomena that fall under a concept we call *pastured roles,* and such roles not only result in unnecessary costs but contribute to organizational dysfunction:

Sacred cows. These can come in several varieties but share a common characteristic of being deemed "untouchable," meaning company leadership considers his or her employment as non-negotiable. These individuals could be a family member or a long-time friend of the CEO, a former rainmaker with presumed priceless relationships, or a well-respected long-tenured employee nearing retirement. It could be that the individual's continued employment is valid, but it could also be that the role has been a long and unnecessary one requiring candid reconsideration.

The ignored. Perhaps people are ignored because they are difficult to deal with, having such a negative attitude that few want to manage them. Maybe they do just enough to get by and fly under the radar, so any decision about them gets "kicked down the road." Or maybe they're organizational chameleons or politicians, slippery or dangerous enough to warrant distance. For whatever reason, despite their expertise or institutional knowledge, these people have become marginalized and are not pulling their weight in the role they're occupying – consuming resources and denying opportunities to more deserving team members.

Both types can be costly and frustrating for the rest of the organization, inappropriate considering the fiduciary responsibility that equity partners and portfolio company managers have to their investors, and arguably negative for the individuals involved as well. Conscientious PEGs challenge their executive teams to evaluate roles frequently, not only for cost reasons but to open opportunities for more deserving candidates interested in working with the rest of the team in creating real enterprise value.

Excess Staffing and Obsolete Needs

Beyond these staffing issues, organizational inefficiencies manifest themselves in a variety of ways, and each type detracts from organizational effectiveness. PEGs should work with their portcos to identify obsolete roles performing activities that are no longer as relevant as they once were, redundancies where two groups of people are doing virtually the same thing, and even conflicting dual reporting relationships which may hamper both efficiency and effectiveness.

It's important to remember these issues did not spring up spontaneously or all at once. They've evolved into the organization one at a time over the years as capable managers reacted appropriately to internal and external pressures and did what they could with the resources they had. Understanding PEGs do not place blame on working through reorganization activities. They acknowledge the realities that drove past decisions while working with portco leadership to adjust to new realities and new structural needs. They make changes not simply with the bottom line in mind but with an eye on improving the culture of the organization, streamlining communication decision-making, and accelerating execution velocity.

Operating Efficiently

Especially in the lower middle-market, it's often the case that before the PEG's involvement, company management had simply been too busy with the day-to-day growing of the business to tackle many improvement efforts. As a result, safety, quality, and efficiency may have been overlooked to some degree. But now their equity partners will be challenging the team to make the time for operational excellence and to "lean-out" their business. Opportunities abound for a metrics-based, continuous improvement, and company-wide performance culture including the relentless pursuit of safe, streamlined, and efficient business processes.

Unfortunately, some PEGs have a low tolerance for systematic process improvement. Operational excellence is a journey, and lacking patience their blood boils when they hear the word associated with improvement, taking the word *journey* as an indicator for wasted time. They want immediate results – take out costs *today* or eliminate overtime *now* is their mantra. They hesitate to invest resources and time to enable embarking on (let alone traveling far along) the path of operational and organizational excellence.

Practical PEGs understand that while some improvements can be accomplished quickly, achieving true operational and organizational excellence is a process of months and years. Authentic gains that truly improve exit value tend to be systemic and deep and require time to introduce and realize. These PEGs and portcos have the patience to continuously drive excellence throughout the investment period, but they start early because they know the compounding benefit it brings in both year-to-year EBITDA growth as well as the ultimate exit multiple.

Process Devolution

Operational excellence is closely tied to process efficiency. A process is a series of related and typically cross-functional activities, executed over time and consuming certain resources, resulting in specific outcomes, preferably valued by internal or external customers. Many business processes, even those outside of manufacturing, consists of some variant of the following sequence: move, wait, prepare, process, inspect, correct, place, and store. A business represents a collection of many related processes, and just about every activity in a business is a part of a broader set of processes.

With positive attention, processes can evolve to become more effective and more efficient. Left untended, processes *devolve*, becoming more complex, tangled, and inefficient over time. Well-intentioned leaders often notice symptoms of process devolution but choose to apply quick remedies without addressing the underlying causes. For example, to overcome process errors someone may add an inspection step instead of addressing the root cause for those errors. Such bandages and workarounds accumulate over time, and are themselves open to devolution – and further "solutions" like one more "final" check. Process complexity and operational inefficiency self-germinate rapidly.

Not only do process inefficiencies spread, but such complexities and inefficiencies are sticky. Their persistence stems from status quo bias and pride of authorship. It's difficult to let go of an even complicated process once painstakingly created. Understandably, change is feared, because it involves risk and breaking something that (kind of) works. Improving complicated inefficient processes is difficult and the fear of failure is ever-present. Yet just like a garden will become overgrown with weeds, eventually bearing little of value if left untended, so, too, will business processes. They become increasingly complicated and therefore increasingly costly

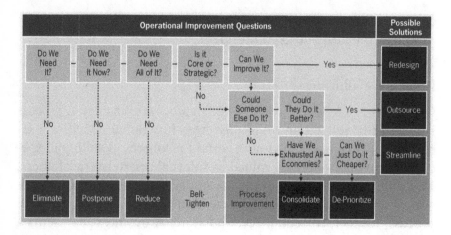

Figure 9.2   Operational Improvement

over time, detracting from value. While pruning the process garden takes hard labor, the bounty is well worth the effort.

Before jumping into the details of operational excellence, it's worth looking at a simple model of operational improvement focused on a basic logical thought process. Figure 9.2 shows a progression of questions and the associated likely solutions that can be applied to a variety of situations – related to operations, processes, and organizations alike.

The first three questions we often ask at the beginning are *do we need it, do we need it now,* and *do we need all of it?* If the answer is no to any of those three questions, there likely exists an opportunity for straightforward belt-tightening, either through eliminating, postponing, or reducing the target of attention. Such belt-tightening is usually quickly achieved without a lot of process or systems work.

The second set of questions relates more to a broader adjusting of operations, processes, and organizations. Opportunities here might relate to consolidation, streamlining, outsourcing, or redesigning. These solutions usually require a more formal process improvement approach, including current state review, future state design, and development followed by implementation.

Lean Operations

Within the huge field of ongoing business improvement models there exist a multitude of related concepts, from broad philosophies to specific techniques. We've all heard terms such as Masaaki Imai's *Kaizen,* Edward Deming's PDCA (Plan-Do-Check-Act) cycle, and Toyota's production management system. We've been exposed in various degrees to the likes of just-in-time, total quality management, Six Sigma, value stream mapping, 5S, continuous improvement, business process reengineering, and dozens of other concepts.

These concepts all have similarities as well as specific and sometimes important differences. *Lean operations* is a useful overarching term to describe the commitment to systematic improvement regardless of the particular "flavor" your organization pursues. What's most important is the common philosophy driving these changes:

Unceasing focus on value. Focusing on value means addressing internal and external customer needs and wants, but always with an eye on company profitability. It means understanding what the customer is willing to pay for and what that same thing costs the company. Lean operations start with the customer in mind and have an unceasing focus on value as it relates to both the customer and the company.

Organization-wide commitment. An improvement mentality cannot reside solely within a process engineering or operational excellence department but must be company-wide. While such departments may certainly serve to introduce better practices and facilitate improvements, successful portfolio companies will have an ingrained improvement culture – up, down, and across the entire organization.

Employee engagement and opportunity. In a positive, improvement-focused culture, success breeds enthusiasm, which breeds commitment and engagement, and then more success. It's a strong reinforcement cycle. Better companies focus not only on the customer but also on their team – introducing cross-functional opportunities and the chance to participate in true value creation to everyone.

Relentless improvement regimen. The culture should always look for simplification and elimination of waste. Complexity and wastefulness breed process inefficiency, excessive costs, and customer dissatisfaction. Simplification is the first step in continuous process improvement, followed by standardization. Once a process is in control, we can then systematically and continuously improve it.

There are clear steps that portcos can take to achieve the operational improvements embodied in the philosophy above. They first have to understand where and how the waste or inefficiency is happening and then tackle the problem in a logical order through simplification, standardization, and automation. By seeing the issue as an opportunity, they embrace an outlook of systematic and continuous improvement that is ongoing and ingrained in the company's culture.

Identifying Wastes

Inefficiencies and wastes run rampant across the processes of many middle-market companies. Wastes are anything that falls into the category of non-value-added effort, meaning effort expended as part of a process that a customer is not willing to pay for. Waste occurs at any stage of a process, and typically results in one of the following:

Overproduction. Overproduction means securing too much output too far ahead of when it's needed. It uses up resources prematurely, consumes cash unnecessarily, and risks significant loss if requirements change. While manufacturing-related examples are plentiful, overproduction also occurs in the service world – for example, developing costly systems, methodologies, and capabilities long before they're needed. Overproduction can be caused by poor planning, inaccurate forecasting, unreliable processes, and disproportionate focus on output metrics.

Inventory. Wastes related to inventory are obvious if you walk through an overflowing warehouse, but can occur in other less obvious ways as well. While raw materials and finished goods are the classic examples, inventory also includes work-in-process (and not just on the manufacturing floor). Stacks of piled paper awaiting an administrative process, digital files awaiting analytics, and reports needing review: All these are work-in-process – the "inventory" accumulated before processing. Inventory is costly when you consider the cash that's tied up in it, the space required for it, the effort to track it, and the cost to rework it if it becomes obsolete. Excess or wasteful inventory arises from unbalanced process flow and inaccurate forecasting. Like overproduction, it can mask other wasteful inefficiencies.

Transportation. Transportation wastes can involve both macro issues like trucking and shipping as well as micro issues like departmental hand-offs. Both forms involve moving from one place (where something is harvested or created or produced) to another (where it is consumed or enjoyed or used). There's a great deal of waste when it comes to simply shifting stuff around a factory floor or in terms of inefficient hand-offs from person to person in fragmented administrative or managerial processes. Transportation wastes are the result of multiple locations and multiple steps, and result in a variety of extra costs and delays.

Motion. Motion is different from transportation in that it generally concerns the individual – walking, bending, and stretching on a repetitive basis. Motion waste involves any extra movement that hinders productivity or increases the risk of repetitive injury. Motion waste is a consequence of poor work-center design and poor methods engineering. While each individual episode may be small, motion waste can add up to significant process inefficiencies and lasting personal injuries.

Waiting. The cost of waiting would be even more staggering if we could only quantify all of it. Simple measurable examples include waiting because of process bottlenecks, waiting for equipment setups, or waiting for paperwork. Waiting not only includes the literal sense of thumb-twiddling, but also the more rampant but harder-to-track waste of slowing pace to adjust for reduced input flow. Waiting comes from poor planning and forecasting, excess capacity, and upstream process inefficiencies.

Defects and inspecting. Defects arise from when a product or service doesn't perform as intended. It causes costly re-working or wasteful scrapping when caught internally before reaching the customer, and significantly more when caught by the customer. In-field performance failures can result in large-scale recalls, lost business, legal implications, and even consumer safety issues. Because of the cost of poor quality, companies will often install multiple redundant inspection activities. Defects (and inspections meant to catch them) are caused by nonstandard and poorly controlled processes.

Overprocessing. Last but not least is overprocessing – doing more than what is required for any given service or product. It means overengineering a solution, incorporating unnecessary features, stipulating excessive standards, or having too many parts or extra steps. Overprocessing results in unnecessary costs that are not being covered by the customer and their stipulated requirements. Painting materials that do not need protection, using high-grade steel when a lower-grade would suffice, or incorporating too many administrative signoffs are examples. Overprocessing emerges over time, where past one-off solutions for a specific problem become an unnecessary part of an ongoing process.

Focused Process Improvement

Some portcos seem to take it as a badge of honor that they are "too busy to do process improvement." Their attitude is shortsighted, as focused process improvement can have profound effects on safety, cost, productivity, and morale, and just about any other metric you care to think about. It also can serve to improve the eventual sale exit multiple.

Process improvement is separate and entirely different from the day-to-day business management and unending firefighting.

It means taking a step back and fixing a process rather than continuing to live with a broken, inefficient, or ineffective way of doing things. It involves a variety of prioritized actions to improve outcomes – first eliminating what's unnecessary, then simplifying and standardizing work, and ultimately automating where you can (in that order, as well to avoid automating unnecessary or inefficient process steps). Once improvements are in place, the final step is monitoring them and making enhancements as needed.

Most Value Creation Programs will include a variety of process improvement initiatives. While focused process improvement is just one type of VCP initiative, it typically progresses through the following five milestone phases:

Analyze current state. The current state review typically consists of accumulating and reviewing existing process documentation: policies, practices, metrics, reporting, and so on. The improvement team will then complete process walk-throughs to understand from a firsthand basis process inputs, flows, roles, systems, and outputs, as well as bottlenecks and issues experienced by those who work the process. In their review, the improvement team should typically follow two flows – how the product or service progresses through the process, and how paperwork and data move through the process. The team documents current state flow, cost, time, and quality aspects along the way, as well as inefficiencies and issues. From that, the team then establishes hypotheses for improvement opportunities.

Envision future state. Following the current state review, the team assembles the future state vision. This first involves researching relevant better practices and typical process benchmarks from similar industries and companies. It also involves reaching out to internal and external subject matter experts to explore the latest thinking in the targeted process areas. With various ideas to "seed" improvements, the team then discusses and augments ideas via multiple iterative one-on-one or small team meetings with process owners and other stakeholders. The team can then document enough details of the intended endgame to enable sponsor review and confirmation to proceed with detailed planning.

Plan and justify implementation. This phase involves documenting general business requirements, including those associated with changes to processes, systems, and organizations. It includes developing rough-cut workplans for design, development, and implementation phases, as well as identifying the necessary resources required for each phase. Development and implementation resources typically include internal team members and often external consulting support. As with any VCP initiative, the team should update their expected costs and benefits and planned ROI. The team compares their updated business case to the original VCP initiative profile and reviews the more detailed plans with their sponsors for formal approval to proceed with design and development.

Design and develop as agreed-on. After the team gets the go-ahead, the first step involves the critical step of carefully documenting *detailed* requirements. From those, the team designs all the necessary components involving people, process, and technology. The team then creates or develops all the enabling tools, techniques, processes, organizations, systems, and infrastructure to achieve the future state. Development may include efforts such as programming a new system, expanding a building, or crafting a new training program. The development of all the enabling components often takes considerable time and involves one-time costs in the process improvement effort.

Pilot, refine, roll out, and monitor. This final focused process improvement phase typically involves piloting the improvement, then after gathering sufficient data refining and enhancing the process before full rollout. Once that is complete, the team finalizes all documentation and prepares for the rollout across the company. After rollout and intense initial monitoring, the implementation team carefully hands the reigns off to the normal day-to-day operating team, who operate now under the new process. Together they continue to monitor things in case of unexpected consequences and look for further improvement opportunities.

After implementation, the team formally conducts a review of the effort – both what went wrong and what went right and whether the company received the expected ROI. At that point, as with the other VCP initiatives, the team should feel free (and in fact be encouraged) to ring the rewards bell!

Sourcing Strategically and Spending Economically

Until benefits materialize on the bottom line, portcos need to fund those process and organizational improvement initiatives upfront, and that can be expensive. Quicker payback initiatives, such as improved sourcing and controlled spending discussed in this section, can be an excellent funding source for longer payback initiatives.

Sourcing strategically and spending economically are two different but certainly related topics because they're both associated with money going out the door to suppliers, vendors, and providers. Sourcing practices and spending controls typically offer excellent near-term as well as ongoing opportunities.

But achieving sustainable gains is not simply a matter of picking up the phone and twisting arms to get a decent price reduction (despite what overly aggressive PEGs might think) – nor will that happen every time a company pursues such tactics. Prudent PEGs know such actions will harm the supplier relationship in the long run. They also recognize that strategic sourcing and cautious spending is not simply about getting better prices and reducing budgets.

Sourcing Philosophies

Oftentimes, lower-to-midsized private companies have not investigated bringing on board professional sourcing expertise. It makes sense for PEGs to introduce such expertise during the first year or two of the investment period. Whether the portco chooses to bring that talent in-house, leverage external sourcing consultants, or take a blended approach, the first thing qualified sourcing experts will do is to introduce basic sourcing philosophies to help position the company for near-term sourcing initiatives. This section looks at three of them.

Total Cost vs. Cheapest Price

Total cost of ownership (TCO) involves not only the initial purchase price (IPP) of a product or service but also all the operating costs associated with it. In sourcing and purchasing decisions, TCO should be considered alongside IPP.

Automobiles illustrate this idea clearly. If offered the choice in purchase price between a $25,000 vehicle and one twice as much, individuals with an IPP mindset would immediately gravitate to the cheaper of the two vehicles. But if the cheaper of the two vehicles requires four times as many service calls as the more expensive automobile and has a life span half as long, the TCO of the "cheaper" car can actually run 20 percent more than the expensive brand. While there are certainly instances when IPP should be considered over TCO, PEGs with short-term thinking will too often automatically put IPP over TCO to the detriment of ongoing company value.

True Requirements vs. Presumed Needs

The voice of the customer (VOC) is a fundamental and extremely important concept in all businesses. VOC involves having a clear understanding of customer needs associated with company offerings – products and services – as well as to their expectations, experiences, and wants. VOC helps companies design specifically to actual customer requirements (and for which customers are willing to pay). VOC is used to find and incorporate features that best address customer needs as well as to eliminate or simplify features for which the customer cares little – and to continuously improve according to the market. Focusing on true versus presumed customer needs is an important philosophy for sourcing professionals.

Let's consider an example. A certain company had always applied a high-quality cardboard backing painted to match the components they produced. During a simple VOC exercise they realized the cardboard backing was no longer a customer requirement and in fact hadn't been for years – the customer simply ripped it off before installing the component. By understanding true versus presumed needs, the company saved not only the cost of glue and cardboard and labor to apply it, but also the cost of purchasing and inventorying paints for all the various color options. And the customer benefited as well, as they no longer needed to take the extra step to remove the cardboard, handle and dispose of the waste, and clean off the adhesive before installing the component.

Continuous Process vs. Episodic Bullying

As budget season comes near or as margins deteriorate (or when someone simply says it's time), many companies resort to demanding from their suppliers unsubstantiated price reductions. The approach is shortsighted and fraught with disappointment. Better PEGs help their portcos become skilled in strategic sourcing which seeks win–win opportunities for them and their vendors and suppliers. They realize that having a continuous and professional process for sourcing and purchasing produces the best outcomes.

As an example, consider two apparel companies, both using tons of cotton fabric. The first company uses a sourcing manager, who analyzes historical spending details, studies the cotton marketplace, attends cotton conferences, joins a cotton-purchasing peer group, visits customers to understand their expectations, and conducts a detailed supplier study. The second company has a purchasing agent whose experience (and interest) is limited to purchasing transactions, and who on occasion puts the hammer down demanding discounts. While the latter strategy might work once, or twice, is there any question which company will wind up having better pricing, terms, quality, and service when it comes to their sourcing?

Sourcing Strategies

Putting these philosophies to work results in effective and efficient sourcing strategies. It will involve resource and talent development, category analysis of the marketplace, voice of the customer, detailing supplier and internal capabilities and cost structures, and understanding the value chain of industry inputs and economics of what comprises the purchase price. These strategies are reinforced by subscribing to the philosophy of TCO, and continuously improving partnerships with suppliers – all with an eye to holding suppliers accountable to service levels, terms, and pricing to which they've agreed.

For each category of spend – be it specific direct materials, indirect materials, or service categories – companies should have strategies and approaches by which to evaluate more specific levers of improvement. Category strategies can be measured against several factors. As an example, Figure 9.3 shows just two possible axes: external supply availability and internal importance to the business. Each of the four resulting quadrants represents a particular strategy to keep in mind when sourcing.

Common Quadrant

The term *commodity* is well-known – interchangeable and uniform cost-transparent products and services readily available across many suppliers. Commodities (and more broadly common off-the-shelf items) include raw basic inputs such as standard bolts, aluminum sheeting, and cane sugar; basic replacement parts, operating supplies, and lubricants; or everyday office supplies, overnight deliveries, and temporary unskilled labor.

But just because these items are common doesn't mean there isn't opportunity – quite the opposite. While many companies have long focused their sourcing efforts on components core to their businesses – specific materials and specialized labor – many have overlooked common categories. Consolidating and leveraging

Sourcing Strategy by Internal and External Dynamic		Sourcing Opportunity and Improvement Levers	Vendor 1	Vendor 2	Vendor 3
		Annual Spend	$0	$0	$0
		Ours as % of Their Business	0–0%	0–0%	0–0%
		Purchase Terms	0% Net 0	0% Net 0	0% Net 0
Strategic: Partnerships, Supply Continuity	**Leverage:** Utilize Leverage, Active Sourcing	Length of Relationship	0 Yrs.	0 Yrs.	0 Yrs.
		Contract End-Date	0/0/0	0/0/0	0/0/0
		Last Re-Bid Date	0/0/0	0/0/0	0/0/0
		Sourcing Opportunity	High	Medium	Low
		Redesign Product Specification	Yes	No	No
Unique: Watch Carefully, Hold Extra Supply	**Common:** Price-Focus, Opportunistic	Adjust Business Requirements	Yes	Yes	No
		Consolidate Volumes (Int/Ext)	No	No	No
		Renegotiate or Re-Bid	Yes	Yes	No
		Improve Price Consistency	Yes	No	No
		Control Scorecard Performance	No	Yes	Yes

Importance to Our Business → (y-axis)   Supply Availability → (x-axis)

Note:
X-axis: High Supply Availability means many suppliers for the category, low supplier rivalry, low technical knowhow required, etc.
Y-axis: High Importance to Our Business means high annual volumes, high criticality, unavailability of alternative components, etc.
■ Green is high priority; ■ Yellow is medium priority; ■ Red is low priority

Figure 9.3   Strategic Sourcing Improvement

such purchases across manufacturing facilities or office locations is usually an easy place to start for multifacility portcos. Price monitoring and opportunistic buys are also typical opportunities.

We often suggest PEGs and portcos focus early attention on common purchases because they're usually unemotional purchases with little design differentiation and are readily substitutable, so implementation risks are low. Creating early and quickly achieved successes will "get points on the board" for near-term and highly visible EBITDA impact, helping achieve early momentum in the Value Creation Program. Near-term benefits from common quadrant sourcing opportunities also serve to fund other efforts, including more complicated sourcing efforts and other VCP initiatives.

Unique Quadrant

The "unique" quadrant consists of items that individually are not necessarily or particularly important to the buyer because purchased volumes are low, the items are not highly visible to end customers, or the items are purchased only infrequently. But unlike the common quadrant, such items have either a lower need or availability of supply or an otherwise higher level of sourcing complexity. These items and services may have a specific market differentiation, or they're particularly complex or customized, or have long lead times. For one reason or another, they are truly unique.

Of the thousands of items and services possibly found in this quadrant, consider just a couple: a small replacement electrical connector of unique specifications used only in punch press equipment made from a manufacturer in Dusseldorf. This 90-cent part only needs replacing every so often, but when it fails the equipment is unusable. The metal stamping company relying on this equipment would be well-served to have a healthy stock of these connectors to avoid a shutdown.

Or consider a long-established field services business having a local marketing firm it has used forever. The firm knows the company well and the two work almost as one, each filling in gaps where the other falls short. There are dozens of other capable marketing firms in the city, but to lose this intricate relationship would generate a considerable headache. The company is well-served to monitor and nurture this relationship carefully.

Strategic Quadrant

The strategic quadrant is by definition a very important one. Like the unique quadrant, here the importance to the company is high and the ability to secure can potentially be challenging – either availability is low or the difficulty is high. Continuity of supply is similarly critical; without it a company may even find itself in the predicament of having to shut down operations entirely until they regain the required part or material. For these categories, companies are well-served to establish and monitor long-term supply agreements.

In the strategic quadrant, supply is so important that establishing trusting partnerships with suppliers and providers is critical.

Each portco and strategic supplier pair should consider establishing regular direct CEO-to-CEO contact and creating mutually beneficial joint councils to work on continuous improvement opportunities that create practices to ensure capacity and work priorities beyond simple long-term contracts. They ought to also integrate value chain systems, including ordering, scheduling, invoicing, and service systems, and establish inter-business scorecards.

Because of the importance of these items, portcos are also well-served to establish alternative sources of supply *before they need them*. True partners will understand that such moves are both pragmatic and sensical. To mitigate risk, responsible companies will have qualified at least two suppliers for strategic items, perhaps divvying purchase orders 80/20 to keep both as viable options. For highly proprietary purchases, they may want to work on designing and qualifying substitutions and having specific contingency plans in case of supply source disruption.

Leverage Quadrant

Products and services in this quadrant are also plentiful; these are items particularly important to the buyer typically in that the associated annual spend is high. Unlike in the strategic quadrant, buyers have leverage because of their high purchase volume, abundant availability of alternative sources, and usually plenty of accessible inventory in the value chain. It's a buyers' market for leverage quadrant items, like certain basic grades of resin to a plastic wares manufacturer, general telecommunications equipment and services to a call center business, or small standard-sized off-the-shelf electric motors to a knit and sew operation.

Particularly in the leverage quadrant, there are several improvement levers the buyer can use for sourcing leverage. These scenarios allow for adjustments to business requirements relating to terms, lead times, packaging, time-of-day delivery, returns allowances, and so on. Tracking supplier price and service levels also engages the Hawthorne effect, illuminating performance and thereby tending to improve it or providing negotiation leverage. For example, companies can recover and avoid overcharges when they have transparent price details and systematically audit and track for consistency over time. Companies can also consolidate volume internally from multiple company locations or externally by through fewer suppliers, and push for product or service changes that reflect true requirements by simplifying unnecessary components or features.

All these and other improvement levers are available to portfolio companies to improve both their cost structure as well as their operating performance. The important part is to take a methodological and fact-based approach, look for productive partnerships, and be respectable and fair in all business dealings.

Controls on Indirect Spending

Though a portfolio company might achieve true sourcing expertise, there's usually still opportunity (and often easier to be had opportunity) in controlling *usage* – particularly for indirect categories. Usage or spending control represents a stand-alone opportunity that can be started before or after sourcing efforts, and the time it takes to implement spending controls is quicker than just about any other initiative a company might pursue. That's why they're often prioritized to start early in the VCP efforts, but in any event, conscientious portcos will eventually implement a spending regimen as part of their overall culture of accountability and performance.

Despite what might appear as "draconian" enforcement, having a clear set of reasonable policies consistently applied and regularly enforced serves to improve company culture rather than detract from it. Especially in middle-market portcos, we find pent-up frustration about inequities and favoritism, often evidenced by inconsistent policy application, enforcements, and selective "looking the other way." Improving this and focusing on impartial application goes a long way to remedying the situation.

Indirect categories are the individual items no one ever really thinks about because each is seemingly inconsequential – office supplies, travel and entertainment policies, overnight deliveries, home office expense, leased vehicles, mileage reimbursement, mobile devices, meeting meals, printers and copiers, discretionary spending, company events, subscriptions, procurement cards, temperature and lighting management, etc. The list goes on and on – in fact it's so long that it turns out to be a surprisingly large amount when you add up everything and all the individual spending for these indirect items by everyone in the company across all locations every day. Spending controls on indirect items therefore represent a quick way for portfolio companies to self-fund other capital-intensive VCP efforts. Controlling such costs also supports a culture of performance and accountability.

Controlling spending of indirect costs is a relatively simple effort, particularly compared to other possible VCP initiatives. The approach consists of straightforward steps that are rarely pursued in the middle-market until someone simply expects it: documenting and publishing policies for each spending category, clarifying and tightening them where needed, actively monitoring and reporting spending and usage by individual, and consistently enforcing policies and holding everyone accountable with chargebacks and other consequences for noncompliance. Often, simply enforcing policies that are already in place is a great place to start.

There are numerous commonsense areas in which greater clarity regarding policy and enforcement would result in savings, whether it's travel and entertainment (enforcing travel approval, limits to out-of-town travel, standardization of carriers and hotels, chargebacks for out-of-policy expenses), vehicle leases and phones (tighten participation, changes to monthly allowances/fixed monthly reimbursement on personal vehicles and phones), or employee programs and relocation expenses (central coordination and tightened budget control by HR, fixed policy for maximum amounts). Even utility management in the form of centralized outsourcing of temperature and lighting controls can save portcos money that could be better invested in revenue-producing streams.

As one CEO we know well repeatedly declares to his team, "A dollar is a dollar." Spending controls are an essential part of having a well-run portco that respects the value of a dollar and acknowledges there are more effective places to spend those dollars. Companies can achieve anywhere from 10 to 25 percent savings on average across relevant indirect spending categories on which they focus – a surprising amount for such little effort.

Financing Internally

Running the day-to-day business requires working capital – how quickly a company can convert activity and inventory into cash – and running a fast-growing business requires ever-increasing working capital. Many companies can fund normal growth through corresponding increased operating cash flow. But for accelerated growth – when we add a series of EBITDA growth initiatives on top of normal growth rates – cash flow from operations will likely be unable to keep up. Rather than cancel or delay growth initiatives, the portfolio company will need to find other funding sources to support their growth.

In the short-term and particularly in companies where working capital has not previously been actively managed, it's often possible to make significant improvements in a manner of weeks, not only in adjusting policy and practices, but importantly in monitoring and enforcing compliance for things already in place. That's why opportunistic PEGs will often launch focused SWAT-like working capital efforts early in the investment period.

Some PEGs advocate an approach to working capital management that is unsustainable. They push management teams to "simply" collect receivables faster, stretch payables longer, and reduce inventory further. While perhaps resulting in short-term improvements, these directives are often short-lived and fraught with negative repercussions if ill-conceived and poorly executed.

Astute PEGs work with their management teams to fully understand the sources of working capital and sustainable improvements to help finance new EBITDA growth initiatives. They help their teams understand that self-funding growth initiatives through operating cash flow and working capital management are less expensive and less risky than financing growth with more debt. Considering the typical number of Value Creation Program initiatives underway and requiring initial investment, working capital funding is an important source of funds.

In fact, these PEGs will encourage portco management to include a series of working capital initiatives as part of their overall VCP. Sequenced precisely and executed proficiently, working capital initiatives may even make it possible for the entire VCP program to be self-funding, resulting in spending no net new dollars on value creation.

Working Capital Improvement Levers

There are four primary components of working capital – cash, receivables, payables, and inventory. Depending on the industry and the company, the balances of each can vary widely from one to the other and over time. Aggressively addressing these four components can have a positive near-term impact on working capital. But depending on how those four are managed and the extent to which underlying processes are addressed, benefits may be fleeting and have associated unexpected negative consequences.

As shown in Figure 9.4, components of working capital are determined by their associated business process cycles. Three of the four are typically considered in implementing traditional working capital improvement efforts:

Accounts receivable cycle. "Collecting faster" is certainly one improvement lever, but more sustainable systematic improvement levers across the entire invoice-to-pay process will result in long-term gains measured in days sales outstanding (DSO). Everything from customer selection, credit and commercial terms, sales order processing, and payment terms and deviation approvals to pricing structure and practices, invoice policies and procedures, invoice accuracy, and invoicing frequency and mode can lead to gains. Changes to negotiation practices, collection

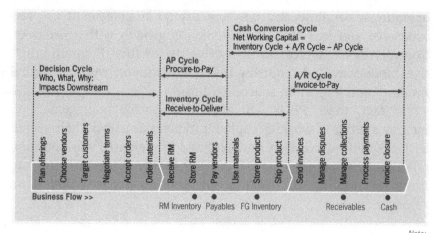

Figure 9.4   Working Capital Improvement

practices, and proactive letters and calling practices can impact cash flow, as do improvements to delinquent account processing, cash application practices, banking and lockbox practices, and sales team incentives.

Accounts payable cycle. "Paying slower" is an available but typically unsustainable lever. Instead, responsive PEGs and portcos work together to implement more long-term systematic levers across the entire procure-to-pay process, calculated as days payable outstanding (DPO). They examine vendor selection, vendor payment terms, negotiating practices, and purchasing practices. They put in place three-way match procedures, payables policies, and dispute resolution policies. They critically assess payment processing frequency and practices, float and banking practices, credit management, and cash payment, rebates, and discount policies.

Inventory cycle. "Hold less" is a natural if unspecific request of those responsible for inventory. But instead of pursuing general mandates, forward-thinking PEGs help their portcos make improvements to the receive-to-ship process by closely examining days inventory on-hand (DIO). They look at forecasting accuracy, vendor and internal lead times, quality and variability inputs, and internal capabilities and flexibility. Inventory itself gets investigated, resulting in slow moving and obsolete inventory management policies as well as improvements to inventory accuracy, supplier location, and distribution network optimization. Everything from SKU rationalization and part standardization to consignment and vendor-managed inventory to supplier scorecarding and sales, inventory and operations planning practices are reviewed for potential improvements.

The combination of inventory, receivables, and payables is the cash conversion cycle (CCC) – a useful indicator for how well a company manages their working capital. For example, if a company has 60 days-worth of inventory on-hand and it takes on average 40 days to collect from their customers, but they pay their vendors in 25 days, the total CCC is 75 days. A lower CCC typically means the company is efficiently managing inventory and collecting receivables while carefully managing payables, and improvements to any combination of DSO, DPO, or DIO will improve the CCC.

Working capital initiatives can have a dramatic effect on a company. If it can improve its CCC by just a single day, that's worth a one-time benefit of up to a full day of sales. For instance, if a company has $365 million annual revenue and it decreases DSO by a single day, it puts $1 million in the bank (or has $1 million available to invest in VCP improvement initiatives). And depending on the industry and cost structure, decreasing DIO or increasing DPO by one day could well be worth $500,000.

Decision cycle. Not considered as often as the first three, the decision cycle is a fourth working capital–related business cycle that is just as important and influential, but often requires cross-functional efforts and longer implementation timelines. It consists of the entire set of historical and everyday decisions across the entire plan-to-order process, including upstream business design choices and commercial decisions. These involve decisions that have been made over the years associated with which products and services to offer to the marketplace. These include decisions about the types, numbers, and quality of the customers they've chosen to pursue over the years and are pursuing now, and the ways and means in which they interact – pricing, terms, contracting, order management, and relationship management. It also involves those same decisions – type, number, quality – made over the years about their suppliers, vendors, and providers. The decision cycle involves implicit and explicit as well as historical and current decisions about with whom and in what manner a portco executes business with their business partners.

Sustainable Solutions for Working Capital

Contrary to popular belief, working capital management is not an exclusive activity of the accounting team. For example, many of the policy decisions related to the payables, receivables, and inventory cycles call for the significant involvement (if not a sponsorship or leadership role) by the commercial and operations teams. Indeed, opportunities to influence sustainable working capital improvements exist for most functional areas and across all four cycles.

Overly aggressive and superficial working capital efforts often lead to disappointing results that deteriorate quickly, slipping back to the status quo and soon unwinding any fleeting benefit. When companies fail to address fundamental practices and eliminate root cause issues, and when implementation plans are limited to simply working harder, collecting faster, paying slower, and storing less stuff, lasting results will not take hold.

Sustainable improvement involves addressing root causes and making fundamental process, policy, and system changes to operationalize the improvements. Changes need to be documented carefully and trained fully. They need to be carefully monitored through clear metrics and performance indicators and need to be supported by the executive, commercial, and operations teams, not just the accounting team.

Improvements to infrastructure can significantly improve EBITDA growth capabilities, and as everyone at GrammCo knows by year two, EBITDA is the name of the game. But if the combined effects of organizational streamlining and implementing operational and sourcing efficiencies are to prune away bloated costs and business wastes, the next step is often to leverage that efficient and effective infrastructure for new organic and inorganic growth.As Dianne and the whole team at GrammCo will discover, add-ons offer tremendous growth potential for an organization but come with their own set of challenges and opportunities.

Chapter 10
Year 3: Expanding Beyond

"Man, unlike any other thing organic or inorganic in the universe, grows beyond his work, walks up the stairs of his concepts, and emerges ahead of his accomplishments."

John Steinbeck, *The Grapes of Wrath*

"And without further ado, I'd like to introduce Dianne Franklin and Shed Cooper – recipients of this year's *Patterson Lake Capital Award for Excellence!*"

As they approached the stage, the clapping reverberated around the ballroom, drowning out Dianne's accelerating heartbeat. Glasses clinked and hoots hollered. Dianne and Shed reached the stage simultaneously and shared a smile as Shed gestured for Dianne to take to the stairs first.

Every year, Patterson Lake Capital conducted a formal event at Chicago's beautiful Carter House. It was a chance for all Limited Partners, PLC team members, and portco

(continued)

(*continued*)

senior executives to celebrate accomplishments from the previous year and offer exciting hints about the coming year. The Award for Excellence was given to the Portfolio Company CEO and PLC Operating Partner best demonstrating Patterson Lake's core values – how working in collaborative partnership generates some of the highest value in PLC's portfolio of companies.

Dianne and Shed were beaming and obviously thrilled to be on the stage. It took a while for the assembly to quiet down and retake their seats.

Dianne leaned toward the microphone and started, breaking the momentary silence, "It's hard to believe three years ago I hadn't even heard of Patterson Lake Capital. And I certainly didn't know my good friend Shed yet. I now know both well and am truly proud about what we've accomplished together," smiling broadly at her GrammCo colleagues seated at the eight-top close to the stage. "But while proud of what my team has done," she said, turning to face the assembly again and elevating her voice, "I'm particularly excited about what we're still planning to do over the next few years!"

After an enthusiastic second round of clapping, Dianne continued for several minutes highlighting GrammCo's core values, describing their culture of accountability and performance, and explaining GrammCo's Value Creation Program. She mentioned some of their earliest successes – bringing on new leaders to fill a few key roles, streamlining the organization, and making significant progress on their journey of operational excellence. She pointed out how they had self-funded their VCP initiatives through early work on sourcing and working capital wins.

She continued with more recent successes: optimizing their product, service, and customer portfolios, enhancing their approach to pricing, and improving sales force effectiveness and opportunity pipelining. She touted how simplifying their offerings and streamlining customer interactions actually led to *better* customer satisfaction and greater profitability. And she recognized the whole sales team, who embraced the new pricing discipline while simultaneously accelerating sales through their smart application of a fresh sales pipeline approach and a newly documented Sales Playbook.

At the end, Dianne looked over at Shed, feigning a true question because it'd been preplanned. "And finally, I'd like to announce... Shed, should I tell them?" Shed smiled and nodded. Dianne raised her hand, shielding the light as she glanced around the ballroom and saw Ocie Carter, PLC investing partner for GrammCo, who was nodding her head and smiling broadly.

"Just this morning, we closed the deal to buy Rochfield Vehicles!" Some *oohs* and *aahs* and another round of applause. "Together with Rochfield, GrammCo is today 30 percent bigger than it was yesterday. We have a lot of work to do, but the entire GrammCo team cannot wait to embrace our newest colleagues! Thank you, Ocie – you and the PLC gang worked extremely hard over these past weeks to complete the deal. It was truly impressive to see it all come together so quickly," Dianne laughed, knowing just how much time it took to fully vet Rochfield to ensure that they would lead to a successful integration.

"And Shed, my partner in crime. Thank you. We've been through a lot these past couple of years, but we did it together. It's been a heckuva lot of fun – so far – and GrammCo couldn't have gotten to where we are today without you."

Optimizing Profitability

During the first and second year of the investment period, the portco management team will have implemented extensive organizational and operational initiatives aimed at establishing more efficient and effective infrastructure. The internal focus has its complement in considering external factors to fuel EBITDA growth, which the management team will have been increasingly exploring as their own house is being put in better order. They will be attending to profitability, pricing, and pipelining, as well as searching for acquisitions to leapfrog growth. With new scalable infrastructure, the team will be looking to significantly accelerate revenue growth.

Although all PEGs embrace growth, some PEGs push their portco teams to such an extent that they take on sales they'd be better off not taking. Because profitability reporting systems in middle-market portcos are often poor, excessive pressure to make the next sale may well result in toeing the profitability line (if not coming up short). Excessive pressure for top-line growth can result in literally unprofitable decision-making about pricing and related underlying activities like customizations, distant deliveries, and service obligations.

Even without excessive pressure, well-intentioned smaller companies sometimes reach for every sales dollar, inadvertently taking on work beyond their profitable core capabilities. Some companies try to be all things to all people – ever trying to please customers and address all requests – but forget that pricing needs to offset the true investment in resources and added complexity. Astute PEGs realize that while all services and products sold contribute to revenue, not all contribute to profit. From their proper perspective, not all revenue is good revenue worth taking.

It turns out that "give the people what they want" is a costly mentality. Its two cousins – do "anything for our customers" and "the customer is always right" – while certainly sounding like virtuous philosophies, can in fact be quite costly if left unchecked. Particularly in the lower-middle-market where opportunistic growth is so important, it's essential to understand the impact of each business decision, including company offerings, pricing, targeted and accepted customers, customizations, and specialized services. Only by continuously (or at least periodically) challenging and correcting past decisions will the company stay on the path of profitability.

Cost of Complexity

Often 10 to 30 percent of a company's cost structure is direct labor – typically well-understood and well managed since the days of Frederick Taylor and scientific management. Another 30 to 40 percent may be direct materials, also well-understood since the era of Carnegie, Rockefeller, and Ford.

But indirect and overhead costs, representing between 30 to 60 percent of a company's cost structure, are often poorly understood and rarely attributed properly to specific products, services, and customers. Many companies use only intuition to make critical business decisions regarding these costs – decisions that are often incorrect and pile up over time, resulting in business complexity.

One prolific root cause of complexity relates to customers' ever-increasing demand for choices and options, immediate satisfaction, and perfect service. For example, consider the general store of the 1930s. Ike Godsey's small country store aside, Walton's Mountain from the long-running TV show *The Waltons* offers a fictitious but representative picture of the time. He sold only a few hundred grocery items and various other sundries. Today most grocery chains offer literally tens of thousands of well-stocked options, plus in-store specialty counters to customize items that can be made while you wait or delivered directly to your home within hours.

Unrestrained customer choice perpetuates with no end in sight, and the resulting complexity and "cost-to-serve" proliferate across the entire value chain. As complexity and cost increase, companies need to continuously account for the impact on their business. Instead of the traditional peanut-buttering of a single overhead percentage across offerings and customers, better PEGs work with their portcos to directly assign "overhead" costs specifically to their products, service, and customers – especially those consuming more specialized activities, thereby illuminating true profitability.

For example, engineering design, specialized equipment, high scrap rates, setup efforts and line changes, unique materials, extra components, lead time, and raw material inventory are all classic examples of "hidden" overhead costs that can and should be associated with specific products and services. Nor should customers get left off the hook: Actions like customizations, expedited or change-orders, unique setups, materials, colors, and packaging requirements, inventory holding requirements, multiple or far freight drops, after-sales support, warranties and returns, and collection efforts can all "silently" but significantly impact the bottom-line of customer profitability.

Certainly not all complexity is bad, and in fact some industry complexity helps limit new competition. But as a general rule when companies get too complex bad things happen – including bad things happening to EBITDA.

Product, Service, and Customer Profitability

Especially in the lower middle-market, companies haven't historically had the costing systems or resources to develop proper insight into the true cost and profitability of their offerings and customers. But standard costing and activity-based methodologies are long-proven, and today practical systems and business intelligence tools are available to even the least sophisticated of companies. Once a company understands its costs, it becomes clear that not all revenue is good revenue (or at least the resulting profits from each of those revenue dollars are extremely different).

Once armed with true cost and profitability details of their offerings and customers and segments, companies will often discover that perhaps only one-quarter to one-third of their offerings and their customers are truly profitable. Another half or so may only be marginally profitable, falling below desired hurdle rates and often hovering near simply break-even. And typically to everyone's surprise, often one quarter or more of all offerings and all customers *detract* from company profit.

This level of insight can put a company on an entirely new thought path and trajectory. Management is now able to refocus on core capabilities and make informed fact-based decisions on what to offer to which customers at what price and in which way.

Intentional Portfolio Management

The resulting discoveries by portcos naturally lead to a discussion of portfolio management – the company's selection of offerings (their portfolio of products and services) and their portfolio of customers. Managing these is an ongoing process of making tradeoff selections for which products, services, and customers to dedicate resources. These resources include management time and attention as well as investment dollars, all of which are limited.

Companies constantly experience the opportunity to add new offerings and new customers. Armed with profitability data, they can make informed decisions about what to include in their offering and customer portfolios. They can also make informed decisions about eliminating or repricing lesser-profitable offerings and customers to make room for more profitable ones. Management teams need to continuously rationalize and reconfirm which products and services they'll continue to develop and provide to which customers and in which channels, markets, and geographies.

Just as processes pile up over time, so do the offerings and customers in their respective portfolios – the good, the bad, and the ugly. Therefore, management teams should regularly take a step back to evaluate and take specific action adjusting their portfolios. Take, for example, the customer portfolio shown in Figure 10.1. This company serves some couple hundred customers, plotted here by true profit margin (taking all cost-to-serve and cost of complexity into account) and annual revenue. The resulting plot is an insightful one – showing four quadrants of customers (which could have easily been offerings), each with associated specific implications:

Capture. Quadrant 1 (Q1) customers represent those whose individual profit margins are quite nice, in fact above the hurdle

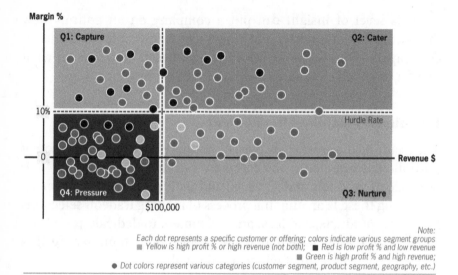

Figure 10.1   Customer Portfolio Optimization

profit margin (10 percent in this illustration). Each is a valuable small customer and the portco would like to get more of their business – thus the term *capture*. A fruitful exercise for the sales team is to evaluate all Q1 customers for their "share of wallet." For those Q1 customers having a fat wallet but not currently spending much with the portco, the sales force will likely focus on growing those relationships.

Cater. Customers in Quadrant 2 (Q2) represent the portco's biggest and best customers. They meet the profitability hurdle and represent significant sales volume (at least $100,000 of annual sales in this illustration). Portcos want to continue to cater to their needs and treat them particularly well. These customers should receive special attention and platinum-level service because losing even one of them significantly impacts the bottom-line.

Nurture. Quadrant 3 (Q3) customers are large but of marginal profitability. Because of their sales volume, they still represent important consequential customers. Portcos need to continuously try to nurture them above the profitability hurdle mark through actions like managing their pricing, nudging them to a more profitable set of products and services, and/or carefully refining business practices and services to reduce their cost-to-serve.

Pressure. Customers in Quadrant 4 (Q4) are each small and either only marginally profitable or unprofitable. These customers sneak in because the company didn't have an understanding of their true cost and profitability, or perhaps because what was supposed to "eventually become" an excellent customer never did materialize and no one ever stopped the experiment. Portcos can be quite aggressive with taking action on Q4 customers (especially the unprofitable ones) in terms of immediate price increases to get them at least above the zero line (if not the hurdle), recognizing that if they balk at their price increase and opt out, the company is better off anyway.

Segmenting and analyzing customer portfolios in various ways like customer size versus profitability enables management to load up their sales reps with specific plays for each customer, segment, and subset. The company in our illustration will be working to move as many as possible of their customers up and to the right of the chart toward Q2.

Pricing Intelligently

If profitability is the ends, pricing is the means – or at least one important means. Shortsighted PEGs insist on frequent list price increases without fully understanding the marketplace. This pressure inadvertently instills a kind of internal pricing black market where portco sales managers are compelled to creatively apply price adjustments, off-invoice reductions, and side-agreements to maintain sales volumes, thereby making pricing less transparent and more difficult to manage, often resulting in reduced margins over time.

Savvy PEGs understand market dynamics and appreciate the unfavorable impact of on- and off-invoice adjustments to price and margin realization. The leakage from list price to pocket price to pocket margin is usually significant in middle-market companies. These PEGs therefore work with their portco management teams to illuminate causes, quantify leakages, and plug holes so the profit ship can sail higher.

Power of Pricing

It seems obvious if you think about it, but most portcos don't think about it enough: Properly planned and executed, pricing initiatives have the potential to drive more relative value than almost any other initiative a company can undertake. In Chapter 4, we compared the relative impact of various 5 percent improvement scenarios, including price, volume, margin, and cost. Pricing made it to the top of that list because it drops to the bottom of the P&L dollar for dollar. In fact, in rough numbers pricing initiatives are worth two to five times more than many other initiatives. It all starts with PEGs and portcos understanding both the psychology and economics of pricing.

Prudent equity partners and portfolio company managers make it their business to understand pricing dynamics so they can properly leverage it not only in their Value Creation Program but also into their everyday thought processes. Price management is much more than simply raising prices now and then, or "strategically" lowering prices. In fact, that time-honored (though often ill-conceived) tradition of reducing prices to increase volume requires enormous if rarely achievable offsetting increases in volume.

Consider a scenario in which a $350 million revenue company rolls out a 5 percent price reduction across the board. That reduction in price goes immediately against the bottom-line to the tune of $17.5 million. Assuming even a 40 percent gross margin, the company would have to sell another $44 million just to break even, meaning it would have to grow sales by 12.5 percent in the short-term to make up for that price reduction. While limited and precise price reductions are at times warranted, broadscale price reductions are enormously risky. The potential for long-lasting negative consequences of even small but broadly applied price reductions is significant.

Clear-minded PEGs instead base pricing on standard processes with specific algorithms. Rarely should pricing be a one-off intuitive decision outside standard flows. Even for companies with "customized" offerings, these should typically be developed by combining standardized options (along with standard pricing algorithms) such that the result has the resemblance of a customized and specifically priced product or service.

Price and Margin Realization

Those processes and standards begin with list price, but that's only the starting point when it comes to the amount of money a company puts and keeps in their pocket after conducting business. Companies effectively have holes in their pockets – some larger than others – from which money leaks. Price and margin realization are about sewing up those holes and keeping as much of a company's targeted price in its pocket as possible.

We'll use the price-to-margin waterfall shown in Figure 10.2 (inspired by McKinsey & Company *The Price Advantage*) to illustrate price and margin leaks and how big the opportunity can be to fix them.

Could-Be Price

Unlike list, the could-be price is conceptual. Think of could-be price as the price a company could set if it fully understood and properly assigned value to all components (products, add-ons, services) a customer might be willing to pay for. Many valuable and specific product and service features (as well as cost-to-serve activities) never get included into list price. Achieving a justifiable and defensible higher starting price point often represents an excellent margin-generating opportunity even before plugging price leaks.

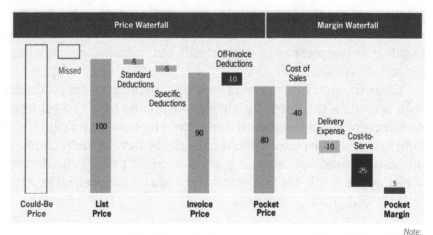

Figure 10.2   Price-to-Margin Waterfall

List Price

List price is the price reflected on a company's catalog – the price the common customer walking in the door would pay. Most buyers understandably do not like to pay list, and many will work very hard to enjoy discounts from it. List price typically includes the price of the base product or service, plus incremental pricing for various additions – options, special features, and extras – associated with the base (which are often not insignificant). But for many companies, these components are insufficiently identified, valued, priced, attached-to, and charged-for, yet could be high-margin adds.

Invoice Price

Invoice price is calculated from list price less standard and customer-specific deductions. Virtually any customer can receive a standard deduction, such as a basic discount (by simply requesting one), cash payment discount, and early payment discount. Standard deductions can easily add up to 5 percent or more of list price and represent a near-term leak-stopping opportunity.

Unlike standard deductions, specific deductions are associated with specific customers and the "deal" they have negotiated. For instance, a repeat or large customer might negotiate another 5 percent discount off list price. A company sales team could make dozens or hundreds of such deals each year, accumulating like a confusing spaghetti bowl of formally contracted, informally emailed, or simply verbally acknowledged special discounts. These can remain in place for years until someone works specifically to stop these leaks.

Pocket Price

This is the amount of cold hard cash the company puts in its pocket after selling its product or service. In addition to standard and specific deductions, pocket price is net of off-invoice deductions. As the name implies, these are effectively price reductions that do not show up on the typical invoice and are much harder to spot. Examples of off-invoice deductions include annual volume rebates, advertising allowances, price guarantees, and product sample allowances. While off-invoice deductions vary widely by industry, they could easily represent some 10 percent of a company's list price.

Price realization is about minimizing the number and size of deductions – off-invoice deductions, as well as standard and specific deductions – to maintain margins. The example in Figure 10.2 shows a pocket price that is 20 percent less than list price, including a stealthy 10 percent off the invoice. Price realization involves eliminating price leaks and getting as close to list price as possible. It would not be surprising for a company that learns to focus on controlling price leaks to enjoy a 5 percent revenue improvement (and therefore a 5 percent bottom-line improvement, too).

While certain price adjustments are sometimes necessary to win or keep business, too often adjustments are made with insufficient thought or controls. When not strategically determined, carefully evaluated, and consciously applied, price adjustments quickly become price leaks. With insufficient monitoring, controls, and sales force incentives, leaks perpetuate over time and add up quickly. Like a dripping faucet, price leaks might start slow but soon become a real and costly problem.

Pocket Margin

Starting from pocket price, pocket margin is calculated by subtracting cost of sales (including direct labor, direct material, and manufacturing or service overhead), delivery expense, and customer cost-to-serve. There are multitudes of examples where companies have overlooked direct value-adding activities in arriving at price, effectively giving away for free various production, service, and delivery operations customers value (and would be willing to pay for). We can't even begin to count the examples of associated possible margin leaks from unique parts, custom finishing, special packaging, extra inspections, free deliveries, and on and on.

Similarly, customer cost-to-serve represents a significant set of activities – and possible margin leaks – that are specific to individual customers. Cost-to-serve is often treated as general *overhead,* so companies fail to identify and apply these costs to the customers they specifically serve. For instance, customer-specific engineering, training, and support can easily represent 25 percent or more of list price. Much of cost-to-serve is value-added and represents significant margin leaks.

After applying cost-to-serve and all other costs and deductions in the example, the result is only a 5 percent pocket margin. Compare that to the 44 percent gross margin that many would incorrectly assume is the profitability in this example ($40 gross margin from $90 invoice less $40 COS and $10 delivery). The difference includes a significant number of price and margin leaks, many of which could potentially be plugged.

Price Setting and Pricing Discipline

Effective price setting requires an understanding of the price and margin waterfall and all possible associated leaks, in addition to understanding the marketplace and competition, the customers and their requirements, and their perception of value. Relatedly, pricing discipline is achieved through an ongoing process of subsequent policy and measurement, training and incentives, and dedicated management. There's an entire science around pricing, but fortunately companies don't need a PhD to begin; they just need to begin. This section discusses some of the most important considerations and practices associated with effective price setting and pricing discipline.

Price Considerations

Pricing should be determined based on several factors such as customer knowledge of what they're buying and their level of sophistication in the buying process, level of differentiation and perceived value compared with competitive offerings, availability of supply, customer switching costs from one provider to another and features and benefits Consideration should also be given to volumes and terms and other obligations required to achieve certain pricing, contracts and commitments already in place, pricing history, and of course the true actual cost to make and deliver and service the offering.

Fair Pricing

The right price is not necessarily the absolute *minimum* price. Rather, customers most often care about a fair price based on relative perceived value. Consumers and corporate buyers alike detest being taken advantage of and the sense that they are being ripped off. They largely want a fair price – not necessarily the lowest price – compared to similar buyers. Customers and buyers alike welcome not having to shop – whether for the best sticker or the best request-for-proposal response – and would rather trust that they are buying smartly and equitably from fair, honest, and capable sellers.

Pricing Analytics

Analytical inputs for pricing include customer segmentation for a deep understanding of the market, voice of the customer for clarity of value in company offerings, waterfall reviews for various price adjustments and price leaks, price variability reviews for gaps in policy consistency, price elasticity analyses for price and volume trade-offs, and conjoint analyses to understand customers' relative valuation of features.

Pricing Policy and Communications

Pricing policy should specifically cover discounts, rebates, freight, returns, and all other price adjustments as well as escalation, approval, and sign-off authorities. Pricing policy should sound like a single and consistent voice and be regularly communicated not just to the sales force but to everyone involved in pricing and customer management, including customer service, customer billing and collections, and the executive team. It should be simple, clear, and well-documented.

Pricing Process and Authorities

Companies need efficient and accurate quote processes because quicker quotes often mean more wins. They need clearly defined decision authorities and escalation rules for nonstandard pricing approvals, as well as price steering committees to periodically review and update list prices, price adjustment policy, and pricing processes. These processes should include the entire quote-to-cash cycle, ensuring invoices accurately reflect price policy (invoice leaks represent a separate but related opportunity to plug leaks). Like policy, pricing processes should be clearly documented and well-understood.

Realization Tracking and Motivation

Companies need to establish price realization tracking and associated reporting to enable management to actively monitor and regularly manage pricing. They should be continuously tracking pricing history and variability as well as monitoring the competition and the marketplace.

Companies need the right sales force and customer service incentives in place to ensure maximum price and margin dollar realization – and clear consequences for noncompliance or "going rogue" outside of policy and procedure.

Confidence in Price and Value

Last but not least – but often overlooked – companies should ensure that *everyone* understands the company's overall value proposition as well as the many benefits their products and services provide to their customers. They need to understand how the company's value-based pricing is justified and applied fairly – for the good of the customer, their company, and themselves personally. Like communicating features and benefits, communications regarding pricing should be straightforward, direct, and nonapologetic.

Pricing is not just a marketing job or a sales team job, nor is it finished when a price table is updated. Rather it's the job of every customer-facing individual in the company to be able to communicate confidently about value to customers. Only when the entire internal team understands and believes in the value they are providing will customers also understand and believe.

Pipelining Systematically

Even with the right value-based pricing in place, selling still needs to happen. Less-capable PEGs assume and at times perpetuate the myth that selling is the result of a mysterious and higher-level art performed by magical rainmakers. They believe that if you find the right rainmaker and pay them enough commission, you've identified your sales function. They place rainmakers on pedestals and coddle them, treating them as untouchables.

Performance-oriented PEGs appreciate the importance of systematized and customized sales processes implemented by the sales team that evolves according to market and company characteristics. While appreciating the individual high-performing

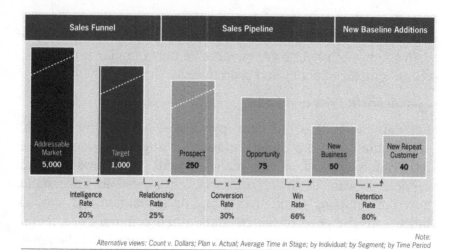

Figure 10.3   Sales Funnel, Pipeline, and New Baseline Additions

salesperson, they also understand that selling is a process that can and should be codified, trained, and managed.

Sales Pipeline

Central to managing the selling process is a well-tuned and carefully managed sales pipeline. Figure 10.3 shows an example, expanded to include the earlier sales funnel and resulting established baseline additions. Effective PEGs ensure that their portcos develop a firm grasp of the sales pipeline and apply it rigorously.

The sales pipeline shows both numbers and dollars of potential customers as they move through the pipeline to become real customers over time. The pipeline consists of several stages with associated rates of progression to subsequent stages. Companies typically will track actual pipeline performance against planned performance at the company, business unit, region, and individual territory levels. They'll also track average time potential customers stay within a certain stage and study the characteristics of those who have been successfully moved from one stage to the next. All this information, including the underlying potential customer-by-customer detail, is central to sales management.

Sales funnel. The example begins with Addressable Market, multiplied by Intelligence Rate to result in the Target stage. The Addressable Market is a rough round number and the Intelligence Rate is the portco's estimate of the percentage of the market that the sales team knows about and may target as potential prospects. This company has a target set of 1,000 specific and tracked possible new customers meeting specific criteria as a formal starting point for the main pipeline.

Sales pipeline. Of those 1,000 known targets, the sales team has personal relationships and ongoing dialogue with 250 potential customers, whom they call prospects. These prospects – the company name and also specific individuals within the company – are recorded in the portco's CRM tool. The company converted 30 percent of the prospects into 75 opportunities (by their definition, the prospects requested a proposal from them). Of those 75 opportunities, the company subsequently won the business of 50 companies. So its win rate was 66 percent.

Established baseline. In addition to new business, this company also analyzes the retention rate of the new business it has won. Over time, the company retained 80 percent of new business customers as repeat customers. The company is intimate with all the characteristics and each detail of those customers won (and lost) and can leverage that information for continuous sales process improvement.

The sales pipeline is an important tool because executives and sales management can and should be analyzing every aspect of their targeted new business and the performance of their sales team. Sales management has clear visibility into quantified data for the entire process and can analyze (for instance) who's better at opening doors and who's better at closing deals (and to what extent and why). The tool and associated sales pipeline management processes are invaluable for training salespeople and then monitoring performance, refining focus, coaching improvements, and improving results.

Sales Playbook

The sales pipeline tells the quantified story and enables portcos to focus on a critical component of a portfolio company's overall growth approach. When coupled with a standardized selling process and documented Sales Playbook, pipeline quality and velocity will improve and result in sales growth.

The Sales Playbook is a practical internal document, describing in detail the standardized, formalized, and company-specific selling approach and related tools and techniques that a company's entire sales force uses to grow the top line. Used properly, the Sales Playbook is a living document, regularly augmented and enhanced. It needs to be consistently and meticulously applied by everyone involved in sales, residing in the back pocket of every sales rep and sales manager of the company.

While Sales Playbooks are tailored to each individual company, we often find the following three topics detailed in better playbooks:

Value proposition. Each salesperson should have a comprehensive understanding of the company and its value proposition. A detailed playbook likely covers company and customer-level topics such as company history, values and folklore, value proposition and unique capabilities, go-to-market channels and strategies, product and service offerings, unique features, fit and functionality, descriptions of customer segments and customer personas, needs and wants, and typical customer journey by persona.

Selling process. The playbook will have sections describing the specific selling process, typically including CRM tools and process, sales pipeline stages, transitions, and associated statistics, sales channels, and sources for leads. It will have tailored sales model and selling processes including tools and talk-tracks by persona, guidelines for overcoming rejection, discussing competitors, and other situational vignettes, pricing strategies, controls, and decision authorities, pricing mechanics by option, feature, and add-on, and basic processes and procedures for order taking, scheduling, and change requests.

Supporting tools. In addition to the process, the playbook will provide details relevant to the sales team members themselves, including sales organization, roles, responsibilities and accountabilities, territory plans and cross-sell and support practices, sales reporting, data analytics, company commission and incentive policies and calculators, tips for arranging individual selling and account management plans, company sales reporting tools, and a listing of supporting sales tools and documents and where to obtain them.

In short, if the right person studied the playbook and knew it inside and out, that person could be the leading salesperson in the company. The playbook should be that specific and specially customized according to the company, their customers, their offerings, and the competition. Along with the Value Creation Program, the Sales Playbook represents another key piece of the recipe for where the company is going and how it's getting there.

Sales Excellence

The sales model is an important component of a solid playbook. There are dozens of general selling models, ranging from consultative selling, solution selling, and Socratic selling. The base model a company chooses probably doesn't matter as much as the effectiveness to which the company tailors it for their specific market and customers, the consistency in which the company implements it across the selling organizations, and the level to which the company embraces and enhances it over time.

Most models follow a similar sequence of steps from prospecting leads, planning calls, and conducting meetings to following up afterward and maintaining documentation. And most sales job descriptions articulate a consistent set of requirements, such as know your company and represent them well; understand your offerings, the competition, and key differentiators; know your customer by addressing their needs and preparing for their objections; achieve your targeted sales at the right margins; and enjoy a nice performance-based compensation.

But sales *excellence* requires companies to significantly up their game beyond the basics of developing a sales pipeline and a standardized Sales Playbook. Better PEGs might also expect to nurture the following practices in high-performing middle-market portfolio companies:

Cadence for Sales Skill Building

Many companies hire sales folks, arm them with a couple of days training, and then send them out alone into the wild with the simple mandate of "go sell." But merely providing a good set of offerings and a long list of targets will not result in sales excellence. Even the best salespeople not only need but want a weekly cadence with their sales manager – one-on-one meetings focused on their pipeline metrics and targets, frequent training and retraining, various scenario roleplaying and practicing, and thoughtful personal coaching. Often overlooked or trivialized, these activities are an important and safe way for even the most successful salespeople to continuously hone their skills.

Maximum Selling Time

It's not uncommon to find 25 percent of a sales rep's time spent on travel, 25 percent on administration, 25 percent on post-sale service and issue resolution, and only 25 percent on actual selling. In fact, that final 25 percent "selling" time is likely half spent on planning and prospecting, and the other half spent on true customer relationship-building and high-value-added selling. Better companies regularly look for ways to improve those figures.

Companies might add an inside sales team to contact and schedule sales visits, or sales administrators to handle planning, prospecting, and follow-up. Focused post-sales service reps might hand-hold the customer or incorporate new tools like online catalogs and product and price configurators and automated sales order entry.

Incentives for Priority Levers

Despite having been long aware of superior margin-based incentives, middle-market portfolio companies often have a stale, static, and exclusively revenue-based sales compensation model. But even in the absence of perfect data, many companies can still design effective margin-based incentive models. In addition to their basic models, companies should regularly enhance incentives based on business priorities and opportunities to temporarily target certain products, services, or add-ons, or perhaps certain customer segments.

Better sales managers can properly and consistently motivate their teams for the right behaviors – including plugging existing price and margin leaks and actively avoiding the creation of new ones – to optimize high-margin revenue growth resulting in optimal EBITDA growth.

Revenue Cycle Process Optimization

The revenue cycle and its related pseudonyms – quote-to-cash, order-to-invoice, or service-to-collection process – represents one of the most critical cross-functional processes within any company. It typically includes customer-touching activities such as requirements definition, solution configuring, pricing, quoting, credit checking, negotiating, contracting, customer setup, initial ordering, and scheduling; and after the product is delivered or service rendered, it then includes servicing, invoicing, and collections.

Especially in lower-middle-market portcos, this important process is often manual and disconnected. When companies standardize, integrate, and automate their revenue cycle, visibility increases, price leaks reduce, collections increase, and sales velocity increases.

Integrating Pragmatically

Talk of portfolios, pricing, and sales pipeline all are premised on there being goods and services on offer. Typically by this time in a growth-oriented company's development, the company is considering expanding capacity or offerings by purchasing an add-on company. While inorganic revenue growth is certainly a driving factor in that decision, add-ons present just as many challenges as they offer opportunities.

Impatient PEGs have unreasonable expectations for huge and immediate synergies from add-on acquisitions, pursuing a strategy of simply jamming things together and letting management teams work out the mess. Everything is clean and easy on paper, and they typically just ignore the sticky issues, preferring instead to merely count the gains that naturally flow (they hope) from the addition.

Pragmatic PEGs realize that things get muddy and messy when dealing with the complicated realities of integrating two sets of employees and cultures who've never even met. They realize that successfully executing add-on acquisitions is hard and complicated work, requiring careful planning, excellent execution, strong will, and a lot of patience. There are no plug-and-play solutions to acquiring and integrating add-ons; portco management and the equity partners will need to be creative and flexible when incorporating a new company into the platform.

Rationale for Add-Ons

Middle-market growth-oriented private equity loves add-ons. It seems not even a month will go by following the platform acquisition before the investing partner is out scouring the marketplace for companies to bolt-on. For many reasons it makes sense for the PEG to at least begin looking even if the original honeymoon is far from over and the intimacies of the platform company are not fully understood. The right add-ons are few and far between, and finding, courting, and consummating the purchase takes time.

The private equity team will expect the management team to participate actively in the search for add-ons since they know the industry well and have contacts within it. They'll be familiar with the companies out there and those that when integrated would lead to significant gains and synergies moving forward. Starting early and incorporating management's attention in finding the right add-on acquisitions is one of the best ways to leapfrog value during an investment period. That surge in value typically stems from one or more of the following five sources:

Commercial growth. Additional revenue comes immediately and automatically when one company's revenue is added to the other. In addition, further growth typically comes from leveraging synergies of the sales teams of each company to multiply that growth, and from introducing the market, customers, offerings, and distribution channels of each company to the other.

New capabilities. With new add-ons comes new capabilities and talent. The combined company now has a variety of new resources – new facilities, equipment, systems, providers, and people – and importantly new leaders and experts from whom to leverage energy and expertise. The add-on also offers new methodologies, processes, and practices from which to draw to arrive at the best of both.

Operational synergies. The new larger company will likely now have redundant resources, positioning management to pick and choose the necessary and best resources for its future, including facilities, equipment, systems, providers, and people. This is usually (at least in the near-term) the most visible and sensitive effect of integration and requires particularly careful management to navigate successfully surprising for a company that learns to focus.

Scale economies. Economies of scale are a specific type of synergy related to a larger structure. With integration, the two companies can combine their two sets of spending and two sets of suppliers into single larger spend pool with a consolidated set of suppliers, enabling better partnerships and improved purchasing power.

Multiple accretion. Larger more established companies usually sell at higher multiples than smaller ones in the same industry. Multiple accretion occurs when a larger platform company, having for instance an expected exit multiple of 8× EBITDA, purchases a smaller add-on company (say a $10 million EBITDA company at 6×). The new combined company is presumedly worth 8×, reflecting an immediate "multiple accretion" value of $20 million ($10m at 2×). Even better, multiple accretion applies not only to "purchased EBITDA" but to all future EBITDA growth from all add-ons during the investment period.

When you consider all these factors, it's no wonder why private equity is so interested in add-on acquisitions. But while add-ons represent a fantastic potential source of investment period value creation, add-ons should by no means be considered a slam-dunk. Although add-ons can represent one of the best value drivers of an investment period, they can also represent one of the biggest risks a PEG and portco team can undertake.

Integration Failure

It's a common observation in the business world that most company integrations fail. What is meant by that differs, depending on whom you ask, but one all-encompassing explanation is to say that the preponderance of integrations fail to deliver full value as promised on paper. In fact, a not insignificant number of integrations end up destroying rather than generating value, having been ill-conceived, poorly executed, or both. And as a result of the relative brevity of the investment period, a PEG and its platform portfolio company rarely have time to fully recover from an add-on acquisition gone wrong. The risk is real, and the implications are significant when it comes to selecting and integrating add-ons to platform portfolio companies.

There are at least three primary points of possible add-on acquisition failure: ill-conceived strategy execution, transaction process complications, and ineffective integration execution. While the final cause comprises the bulk of the reason for most add-on failures, the first two are not insignificant and certainly worth examining as well:

Ill-conceived strategy. This typically relates to either fit or timing. The PEG/portco team may have been too aggressive and purchased an add-on early despite the platform company being unstable – either with poorly functioning systems, out-of-control processes, or insufficient leadership. Or perhaps the fit wasn't perfect – the target company's core business was too far astray from the platform's core competencies or the target's processes and cultures were too different to warrant the risk.

Transaction complications. The transaction or "deal" typically progresses from management presentations through letter of intent, due diligence, ROI/business case, PEG investment committee approvals, financing, offer letter and negotiation, term sheets, lawyers, and closing. The process can easily take several months, and each step is fraught with the risk of derailment. Risks include the possibility of anti-trust issues, deterioration in operating performance, executive attrition, financial integrity problems, or unresolved legal risks and environmental issues.

Ineffective integration. Post-close integration can take anywhere from a few months to over a year, and represents the riskiest component of add-on acquisition failure. As if the addition of organizations, processes, systems, and facilities weren't complicated enough, the integration of personalities and cultures often poses the largest and most unpredictable hurdles. Risks include poorly articulated vision, insufficient or noncandid communication, substandard integration planning, and, of course, poor execution. Failure can also arise from "failure to mind the store" during integration – inattention to basic operating performance, customers, suppliers, and other stakeholders of either legacy company.

Despite the myriad risks that can befall the add-on process, the value creation opportunity of well-conceived and well-executed add-on integration that mitigates these risks can be well worth the effort.

Pragmatic Integration Process

The best way to mitigate integration risk is to develop and execute a well-planned pragmatic approach focused on business stability and sustainable value creation. The right plan will identify those actions that need to be done quickly and then allow more time for those actions that can afford or that need more time – managing the urgent, the important, and the necessary in their own ways. For instance, clarifying organizational reporting relationships should be accomplished first and immediately, whereas eliminating organizational redundancy can occur over some (limited) time, and harmonizing job titles and pay grades across both legacy companies can catch up as we go.

Relatedly, we have found it beneficial to consider three phases when integrating add-ons, related to planning and preparation, "first" integration, and full integration.

Preparing Pre-Integration

Proper preparation cannot be overlooked or minimized as it identifies the pathway for a successfully integrated company. This phase starts during diligence and accelerates as the acquisition closing date approaches. Preparation includes arranging inter-company functional teams, each typically consisting of just a few people representing both companies, conducting detailed planning for what the integrated business will look like, and developing the process to get there.

It's particularly useful for each functional integration team to create a model showing the starting point of the two companies' functions and the vision for what the combined function will become. As Figure 10.4 shows, the vision considers all the key components – operations, organizations, processes, and systems as well as metrics and impacts. Needless to say, planning at this level requires the attention of the senior-most executives from both legacy companies as well as the equity partners.

Function-by-Function Integration Synergies	Functional Area A			
	Starting Point Pre-Integration		Post-Integration Company	
	Company 1	Company 2	First Integration	Full Integration
Summary of Operations	Description	Description	Description of Changes	Description of Changes
Organization	Leaders, Structure, Locations, Comp, etc.	Leaders, Structure, Locations, Comp, etc.	Leaders, Structure, Locations, Comp, etc.	Leaders, Structure, Locations, Comp, etc.
Processes & Systems	Flow, Key Attributes, Providers, etc.	Flow, Key Attributes, Providers, etc.	Flow, Key Attributes, Providers, etc.	Flow, Key Attributes, Providers, etc.
Key Statistics	Headcount, Operating Expense, KPIs, etc.	Headcount, Operating Expense, KPIs, etc.	Headcount, Operating Expense, KPIs, etc.	Headcount, Operating Expense, KPIs, etc.
Total Impact	Total Headcount, Locations, Systems, Costs		EBITDA Benefit A	+ EBITDA Benefit B

Figure 10.4 Acquisition Integration by Function

Completing First Integration

The second phase, typically requiring 60–90 days, is where critical components of the business are integrated to make it into a single company. First integration includes high-priority items that need to get done early, typically consisting of communications, expectation setting, preliminary reporting structures and assignments, preliminary policies and practices, legal and compliance topics, and early financial consolidation practices. These activities focus on establishing, protecting, and stabilizing the new single company. For example, there often needs to be early agreement regarding how mutual customers and suppliers will be handled going forward.

While the company should realize some immediate benefits during first integration, the immediate priority should not be optimizing synergies and leveraging economies. Instead, the focus should be on preserving while uniting the strengths of the core businesses. In addition to the high-priority integration activities, the key is to continue serving all customers without hiccups and maintaining business stability and control. During first integration, the company teams begin to get to know each other better and jointly plan the details for full integration.

Achieving Full Integration

With first integration, the team has completed the urgent integration activities aimed at looking and acting like a single company. It has stabilized and protected the combined business. The team now attends to achieving the integration synergies and benefits to which it has committed as justification for buying the company, such as further consolidation of functions, process, and systems, supplier consolidation, harmonization of offerings, branding and market messaging, and uniting commercial activities.

Unsurprisingly, the best way to achieve these ends is to have the combined team launch a series of new VCP initiatives focused on integration. Leveraging their (now well-oiled) VCP approach, the VCP program manager and steering team have new team members to onboard into the VCP process. New integration efforts should roll right into the standard process of opportunity identification, initiative profiling, and ongoing targeting, tracking, and triaging results to the bottom line.

Improving the Odds for Integration Success

Carefully executing a well-planned pragmatic integration process is the best way to improve the odds of integration success. That's easily said, but PEG and portco teams can take several steps to avoid the typical pitfalls that plague integration efforts:

Focused team. Designing and managing all the integration details at the same time as the running day-to-day business is a recipe for disaster, or as the old adage observes, "If everybody does both, nobody does either." The majority of each combined team should be focused on the daily execution of the business, while a small, dedicated, and well-led team should be working on the integration details.

First do no harm. The worst thing that can happen during an integration is to damage either of the legacy businesses. First integration should therefore be focused on doing no harm – to perpetuate the value propositions of both companies and to continue to serve customers well. Most of the team's attention should remain on day-to-day business and maintaining top-flight customer interactions. Integrations require time, and having to deal with an unexpected drop in business performance or deterioration in incoming revenue would significantly disrupt the process.

It's about the people. Companies are collections of individuals with emotions, needs, and desires. The employees of both legacy companies require careful handling during add-on integrations. The entire teams from both companies need to understand that leadership is committed to them and is working hard to take careful consideration regarding everybody's role. The combined management team needs to remember they are dealing with people's livelihoods and lives and must act with empathy and compassion.

Candor and honesty. Equity partners and management teams inexperienced with integration sometimes espouse an extreme "need to know" philosophy and avoid all communication despite a proliferation of circulating stories. But people need to hear what's going on directly from their leaders and not from the rumor mill, so they can internalize the changes underway and more quickly accommodate to the new reality. While speed is not a top priority for all aspects of integration, it is important to communicate quickly. Although not everything can or should be communicated, leaders should default to sharing "what we can, to as many as we can, as soon as we can."

Individual role clarity. As a natural and immediate consequence following the announcement of an acquisition, first on everyone's mind is what will happen to their job and role in the combined business. It is important for management to address these questions as soon as possible, even if the answer is an interim one. Management needs to ensure everyone knows who they're reporting to and what role they are serving at least in the near-term until things are sorted out. Particularly preacquisition, careful attention needs to be given to leadership and other key roles, including developing creative solutions for key people who's legacy role may be redundant and future role may be unclear. Overstaffing during first integration to maintain valuable options is a wise course of action.

Distinguishing first from final integration. While a speedy integration is certainly important, what really matters is a swift but well-executed *first* integration focused on urgent topics. Too often well-intentioned integration teams attempt to organize everything at once, failing to differentiate what needs to happen first from what can happen later. The necessary details of integration add to an extremely long list; integration leaders can do themselves and their company a significant risk-mitigating favor by separating that exhaustive integration list into a shorter group of first integration steps and a longer set needed to achieve full integration. Achieving full integration is better arrived at through measured and controlled process improvement versus hurtling toward the end goal.

Best of both worlds. Wise PEGs understand that an authentically genuine integration will transform both the target and platform companies. Integration failure happens when the buying team – those from the original platform company – assume their world will change only a little and that the add-on company and their team will be the ones doing most of the changing. The newly combined firm should be looking to absorb the best of both legacy companies – the best capabilities, resources, and assets, no matter from which legacy group they originated.

An extremely important part of acquisition integration involves the commercial side of the businesses – the offerings, customers, and marketplace. Fortunately, at least the original platform company team members have already honed their skills in optimizing profitably, pricing intelligently, and pipelining systematically, because they're now going to be doing it all over again!

The external growth portcos experience during this period creates lasting value when add-ons are properly integrated, matching the gains they've experienced in the internal organizational and operational initiatives they've put in place. As the management team at GrammCo discovered, a sharpened focus on profitability, pricing, and pipelining means the portco is positioned to capitalize on its revenue growth. Tending to the patterns of efficiency improvements and external growth means that in short order GrammCo will be poised for the final step in the investment period – the exit.

Chapter 11
Year X: The Exit

"We can't ever go back to old things ... We have them as we remember them and they are fine and wonderful and we have to go on and have other things because the old things are nowhere except in our minds now."

Ernest Hemingway, *Selected Letters, 1917–1961*

Colorado Route 301, and Bruce Springsteen's *Born to Run* comes on the radio at 7:10 a.m. on a beautiful sunny Monday morning. As Yogi Berra would say, it was déjà vu all over again for GrammCo CEO Dianne Franklin on her drive into work.

In what felt like decades but in truth was only a few short years ago, Dianne had heard this same song on this same stretch of the road looking into this same orange sunrise. But as she thought about everything that had transpired, she had to admit that the similarity ended there, because everything felt different today than it did then.

(continued)

(*continued*)

Then she had been heading in to start her first day of work under the ownership of Patterson Lake Capital, which had closed the deal to purchase GrammCo. At the time, Dianne was anxious about what the next few years would hold both for her executive team and the company in general – not to mention herself. Private equity was new to Dianne and everyone else at GrammCo back then.

But today the investment period was old hat. Dianne and her leadership team were now in their final weeks of being under the vigilant eye of PLC. At first, some saw Shed and Ocie's attention as oppressive, but that – and in some cases they – didn't last long in the new environment. For those who recognized that what Shed and Ocie wanted most of all was a collaborative partnership with a capable can-do team, these past few years had been some of the best of their professional lives.

Like the last go-round – when GrammCo was sold to PLC – the GrammCo leadership team has been working for weeks with prospective new buyers as they evaluated the business, conducted due diligence, and positioned themselves for purchase. The process and preparation for the exit came back to them pretty easily, although they had forgotten how distracting it could be from day-to-day operations.

The idea that they would again be sold became a reality several months ago when PLC Investing Partner Ocie Gleason first suggested the time might be right. While there had never been any secret that PLC was eventually going to sell the company – indeed, the intensity of the investment period was premised on that very idea – Dianne had still been surprised because the entire team had really been rocking. They were in a good operational groove, showing double-digit organic growth numbers year-over-year, even before factoring in the impact of the two companies they'd acquired. Their Value Creation Program had been loaded and reloaded several times, and their plate was full with even better things on the horizon. So why sell now?

Dianne remembered how Ocie had agreed that the business was in fantastic shape – in fact, pointing out that it was a driving motivation for selling GrammCo at the present time. Dianne and her team had plenty "left on the plate" for the next buyer, and the strong tailwinds in the market showed no signs of weakening. She and Shed both suspected that buyers would be "frothy" for the opportunity to purchase a company as valuable as GrammCo had become.

Dianne kept smiling as her thoughts moved quickly back to the present. The entire executive team had a lot to be proud of. They'd built such a great business these past few years – much bigger and better than anyone (even Dianne) would have guessed. A dozen of her managers had flourished dramatically during this time – the capabilities and experiences they had gained had been multiplied considerably by the accelerated pace of the investment period. She had learned a ton herself while staying true to her values – a purposeful, practical, and principled leader. Together they created value *and* opportunity – and lots of it. They all felt proud of what they had accomplished.

Dianne remembered another term Ocie had used that first day – "monies moving." In just a few short weeks, monies would all but certainly move again. PLC's investors will be thrilled to discover that the value of the company materialized even above expectations. Dianne and many of the best value-generating leaders on her team would be handsomely rewarded for their efforts as well.

"This was a lot of fun," she said out loud to no one. She knew she would keep up with Shed and Ocie for the rest of their respective careers. They were great partners and even better people, and together they had accomplished a lot of great things.

Exit Timing

The investment period culminates in preparing for and executing a successful sale of the portfolio company from the PEG to another owner. After multiple cycles of reloading the VCP, completion of internal improvements, and integration of add-ons, there comes a point when the PEG and portco recognize that it's time for "the exit."

The exit may consist of one of several types, most typically in the middle-market selling to another PEG or investing group, or perhaps to a strategic buyer – typically a larger company where the portco would now be integrated as their add-on. Other less frequent exits include completing an initial public offering (IPO) or in rare instances exiting through bankruptcy administration or another salvaging process. While the exit transition results in a change in ownership, it can also involve significant financial rewards as well.

This culminating phase of the investment period is both exciting and challenging. It poses its own hurdles while offering both qualitative and quantitative rewards to key participants of the journey. Not only does management need to continue to run the business – now even more flawlessly than ever – but it must demonstrate that the fruits of their past labors are impactful and sustainable. They also need to initiate preparations for the sale process, which involves considerable effort by the management team. What the PEG/portco team do at the end of the investment period will have a large impact on the company's final enterprise value and the associated proceeds from the sale. Now is not a time for either the PEG or the portco to rest on their laurels.

Factors Affecting Exit Timing

The typical investment cycle of raising a fund, deploying the capital, and "harvesting" returns is often three to seven years, and that window serves as a broad starting point for determining the investment duration of any particular portfolio company. But the right time for a PEG to sell their investment in a portfolio company to the benefit of all investors (including management team option-holders) is not formulaic. In addition to the typical expectations associated with fundraising, the decision regarding exit timing involves key factors including company progress since purchase, current company performance, and overall market conditions now and looking forward:

Company progress. Company progress involves all aspects of portfolio company changes and improvements discussed in this book – the extent to which the portco has improved infrastructure and capability, built a better and oftentimes bigger company, and created sustainable EBITDA growth and new enterprise value. The amount of new value the company has created is probably the most important of timing factors. If the company has not grown to the extent that it will generate expected returns to investors, the propensity will be to continue operating and growing the business until it can.

Company performance. Current company performance is also an important input for exit timing decisions – if not from the formal enterprise value calculations including EBITDA and multiple and debt level, certainly from buyer perception and buyer confidence. The portco should have a healthy budget compared to the previous year, illustrating the favorable trajectory the company is on, and should be achieving or exceeding those plans and budgets. A buyer does not want to pay for a company based in part on its recent successful past performance and trajectory only to struggle to overcome immediate company underperformance post-transaction.

Market conditions. Despite all the excellent historical progress and sustained current performance a company may proudly offer a buyer, current and anticipated market conditions significantly impact exit timing decisions. After all, it is in that projected market that the new buyer will own the company, and it is in those market conditions that the new buyer will be expected to continue and even accelerate past growth trends for its investors. A seller will certainly think twice, for example, about putting a spec home construction business on the market at the beginning of a recession.

Consider a situation where the company has made excellent progress quickly. It has grown significantly to warrant outsized investor returns, has a full-contingent management team performing well against an aggressive plan, and is enjoying strong market tailwinds promising ever-expanding opportunities in the foreseeable future. In this case, the PEG will likely consider selling the portco early, maybe even after the third year or so. On the other hand, those with a longer time horizon may very well opt to keep that gem in their portfolio a bit longer.

Alternatively, consider a polar opposite situation where the portco has significantly underperformed since its purchase, still doesn't have the right management team in place, is currently performing poorly against an unimpressive plan, and is facing market headwinds all but ensuring even more difficult months and years to come. In that unfortunate situation, the PEG may consider not selling until it can enhance the management team, right the ship, and weather the approaching storm. That is, unless it doesn't have the confidence, courage, or stomach to continue – in those cases the PEG will likely decide to cut its losses, avoid the distraction, and transact immediately. In fact, some PEGs will proactively choose to cut their losses in a difficult situation early and point their attention and resources to other portfolio companies that can achieve compensating gains.

In the end, exit timing is largely based on maximizing the return for investors. Roughly speaking, the LPs will want to see at minimum a 2× cash-on-cash (COC) transaction for the sale – particularly if it's an earlier sale generating a higher IRR. A 3× COC would be quite respectable and a 4× or more COC would be considered a very good return for a timely sale of a growth-focused middle-market PEG. A five-year investment period with a 3× COC, for instance, could mean a healthy 15–30 percent IRR to investors.

The Exit Process

Although the discussion of timing might make it sound like the actual sale follows quickly on the heels of the decision to sell,

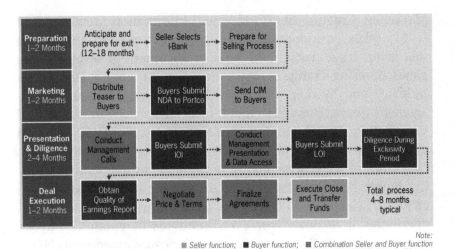

Figure 11.1   Portfolio Company Sale Process

nothing could be further from the truth. Equity partners are constantly evaluating the market and modeling various exit timing outcomes. The critical importance of timing becomes all the more clear in the context of the entire exit process, which typically takes anywhere from 4–10 months. The process can be divided into four phases as shown in Figure 11.1.

Preparation. Preparing for the exit with general timing in mind starts percolating maybe a year or more out. The kickoff to the more formal process is typically earmarked with the selection of an investment bank by the PEG and portco to facilitate the sale. The PEG will have worked with many banks in the past and will introduce a few most relevant candidates. Once a bank is selected, the portco selling team – consisting of the investment bank, the IP and his or her deal colleagues, and the portfolio company CEO, CFO, and various others as needed – will establish expectations of the process and arrange the calendar and work plan. The OP typically serves in a supporting role in the exit process, remaining focused with portco management team on continued company performance through the exit.

Marketing. Creating the Confidential Information Memorandum (CIM) takes considerable time from everyone on the portco sale team. It's a crucial and detailed document of several dozen pages, covering a range of topics including Investment Highlights, Industry and Market, Offerings (Products and Services), Management Team, Business Operations, Historical Financials and Financial Projections, and various appendices. The CIM is created to highlight both the company and investment opportunity. It's chock-full of facts, presented in favorable light intended to entice the buyer. After weeks of CIM development, the selling team creates a brief, two- to three-page CIM summary or "teaser" and distributes it to dozens or even hundreds of potential buyers. Interested buyers then provide a nondisclosure agreement (NDA) in exchange for the full CIM, which they'll then study in detail to confirm their interest.

Presentation and diligence. Shepherded by the investment bank, potential buyers schedule conference calls with portco leadership to review the investment highlights and ask preliminary questions. Interested parties then model preliminary valuation ranges and submit an indication of interest (IOI) with an estimated purchase price. From IOIs, the selling team selects the most promising handful with whom to schedule management presentations for which they will have been preparing meticulously. Each presentation, typically on-site and requiring an entire day, serves as the opportunity for the leadership team to market their company. Interested potential buyers then submit letters of intent (LOI) with a refined nonbinding purchase price. The selling team selects one or possibly a couple of most likely buyers to continue diligence and provides full access to the data room as well as significant access to the management team.

Deal execution. Following weeks and months of diligence – an arduous and time-consuming process for both buyer and seller – the buyer(s) will confirm for themselves their interest and obtain a quality of earnings analysis from a qualified accounting firm. Buyer(s) submit their offer letter with specified terms and pricing, based on detailed discounted cash flow modeling and past transaction comparables. The seller then negotiates with the selected buyer and they move to drafting a definitive purchase agreement. Finalizing the agreements can take several iterations between buyer and seller and their attorneys. Once finalized, and as the agreed-upon closing date approaches, both buyer and seller accelerate preparations for the transition. Just like purchasing a home, on the closing date funds are transferred and the buyer effectively takes the keys.

Exit Preparation

In a quite obvious sense, all the hard work discussed in the previous chapters was done in preparation for the exit. That said, even more focused preparation of the company with a specific exit in mind should begin a full 12 or more months prior to the start of the process.

At "*t*-minus 12 months," the PEG and portfolio company should begin devoting increasing attention to the factors on which potential buyers will soon focus their attention. The portco should begin preparations early, as perceptive buyers know and discount last minute window-dressing compared to ingrained sustainable improvements.

In addition to the most important priority – continuing to deliver consistent company performance and positive growth trends – we suggest the PEG and portco team specifically ask questions of themselves that they know buyers will ask, and have their answers ready, along with ample supporting evidence. Buyers will be most interested in a variety of factors, including the following:

Full-contingent leadership. Buyers will be watching carefully for evidence of a full and effective leadership team during every interaction. They'll be looking for leadership coverage, role clarity, authentic teaming, performance management, and a culture of accountability and performance. They'll want to know the level of commitment each leader has to the company post-transaction and viable succession plans for executives that will be leaving the company post-sale.

Truly compelling story. The CEO and the leadership team must tell a compelling story of company progress, starting from early in the current investment period. They need to proudly share what they've done and why – and in addition need to clearly and passionately articulate the continuation of that story and their vision for future chapters under new ownership. The future story should be just as (if not more) exciting than the past, and include growth continuation or even acceleration and hopefully one or two big and bold game-changing aspirational opportunities.

Perpetuating accomplishment. Intrigued by the company story, the buyer will be looking for evidence of continuation or stickiness of results achieved to date. They need to be convinced recent accomplishments will not unwind, currently underway initiatives will not derail, and future opportunities will not evaporate. They'll want to see longevity in all aspects of the business – the customer base, pricing integrity, margin consistency, and operational capability. Portco management should have case examples and illustrations at the ready.

Strategic execution acumen. Realizing continued growth is largely a matter of strategy execution – the ability to line up initiatives, knock them down, and line up new ones. Buyers will be on the lookout for a well-honed, ingrained, and continuous Value Creation Program. They will want to see a clear history of successfully completed EBITDA growth initiatives, a continuous process of targeting, tracking, and triaging initiatives, and evidence that the results of those efforts make their way to the bottom line.

Repeatable growth practices. Buyers will have expectations of real progress having been made on commercial capabilities and sales force effectiveness. Buyers will be comforted to see a well-used Sales Playbook, excellent sales pipeline management, analytical capabilities such as pricing and customer profitability optimization, and repeatable acquisition integration toolkits.

Buyers realize developing repeatable growth practices takes time, and the more they can buy the quicker they can leverage those practices for immediate post-purchase growth.

Stable scalable infrastructure. Similarly, buyers will have expectations of systematic ingrained business stability: business continuity, systems security, regulatory compliance, financial controls, operational process controls, operational cadence, management and KPI reporting, disciplined contracts, employment and HR policies, noncompete agreements, effective union relations, and so on. Buyers expect fully scalable infrastructure: capable ERP and other systems, available operational capacity, supplier agreements and continuity of supply, variable cost structures, access to labor, and so on. They place value on being able to scale quickly without pausing to address infrastructure issues post-close.

Operational excellence. In addition to scalable infrastructure, buyers expect operations that have well-established safety and quality programs. They'll expect clear evidence of a culture of operational excellence to be in place, with lean processes and a continuous improvement mindset. Like with purchasing a car, the buyer wants to be confident of driving off the lot (and safely going miles and miles in comfort and at great speeds) without things breaking down.

There is one final factor the PEG and portco should address prior to exit. While savvy sellers will leave exciting future opportunities on the table for the next buyer, they will also want to avoid leaving money on the table – any remaining short-term bottom-line improvement opportunities undone. These include any final sustainable quick process improvements, accelerated working capital efforts, selling off unusable items (obsolete inventory, scrap equipment, and clutter), and better managed spend controls. Every dollar – cash or EBITDA – is an improvement and part of proceed calculations, and every additional EBITDA benefit achieved even now at the end of the investment period still will be part of what's used in the calculation with the multiple in just a few short weeks or months. The team has long been well-practiced in value creation and should make a final push before the exit.

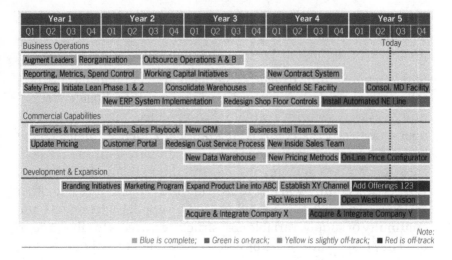

Figure 11.2　Investment Period Accomplishments Timeline

As the PEG and portco look back they should prepare a summary of their accomplishments. Part of that summary should typically include something similar to Figure 11.2 that captures in snapshot fashion the operational improvements and growth highlights during the investment period.

As the PEG and portco team head towards exit they'll need to be – and really should enjoy – reviewing and revisiting their past few years: what they originally intended to do, what they did well, and even what did not go so well. The team should look back and feel proud of what they accomplished together through their new Value Creation Program, enhanced operating cadence approach, and enriched culture of accountability and performance. This review additionally serves to help line up what the portco will plan to accomplish during the next investment period, as they will need to clearly and enthusiastically communicate that during the selling process.

It's therefore obvious that in reality, exit preparation began on Day 1 of the investment period – the team has been doing this all along. Throughout the entire investment period, the PEG/portco team members have been urgently, unquestionably, and specifically working for the day of sale – the day their hard work finally pays off.

Enjoying the Rewards

The best portco executive teams will realize that the day of sale is the day they've worked so hard for - a rewarding conclusion and a new beginning. Of course, for some their personal rewards are merely good but not great, and for others the gains are minimal. But for teams that have grown the company as expected, it's not just this day that is the reward – it's been a rewarding journey for the successful team, resulting in both professional and financial benefits:

Engagement. Growing a business and creating opportunities is a wonderful and truly rewarding thing. Executives and managers who put their hearts and souls into the investment period will look back on it with exceptional pride. Any investment period is filled with ups and downs – numerous successes where ideas went according to plan, as well as lots of challenges and hurdles to overcome. Those who stood tall for the trials and tribulations – who checked their egos, teamed authentically, maintained strong character, toiled endlessly with a positive attitude, and embraced company values throughout – deserve to be very proud indeed. These leaders created opportunities for everyone, grew the business, and generated new jobs and opportunities. They impacted lives by serving as a positive influence on everyone they touched – not only their colleagues and stakeholders but also their families.

Development. Four, five, or six years of working hard with a great team, in a performance-based culture under high pressure, while having a specific end result in mind and on the line, undoubtedly builds capability in addition to character. Middle managers and less-experienced leaders who step up and embrace accountability while making and keeping commitments during an investment period grow to be extremely valuable and proven business leaders.

An investment period represents a fantastic opportunity for people to accelerate their careers, and some will have progressed through two or three promotions and increasing responsibility. It's no exaggeration to say that thriving during a successful five-year investment period is equivalent or better than having experienced 10 years in a more "traditional" corporate environment. And those with the best attitude and work ethic will be provided ample future opportunities to continue to grow and develop their capabilities as well as their careers.

Opportunity. The kind of experience provided by an investment period is invaluable to a wide range of future employers. The most obvious opportunity is to continue with the portco and do it all over again with a new ownership team. Other opportunities often arise across the rest of the portfolio of the PEG with whom you've just made excellent relationships. And leaders who thrive in one or more private equity investment periods tend to get plenty of recruiting eyeballs on them as well. While some might be concerned that portfolio company career opportunities may be short-term compared to the presumed security of traditional corporate jobs, it's more clear today than ever before that such jobs are rarely a sure thing. Being a leader in a PEG-owned company is a great opportunity for those who thrive in dynamic, fast-paced, high growth environments.

Financials. Like any industry where talented people do great things that others value, private equity offers not just career growth but significant financial rewards. The private equity industry as a whole and particularly forward-thinking firms work hard to ensure that investment period financial rewards are aligned to opportunity and value creation – including specifically those who incurred the highest financial risk (investors), those who identified and shepherded the investment (PEG), and those who drove the most enterprise value (successful portco leaders).

While every situation is different, rather than "peanut-buttering" a few stock options across a large set of individuals, performance-oriented PEGs typically award options to portfolio company leaders by focusing on those who can drive the most value during the investment period as well as those who understand and are motivated by stock options. Doing so allows them to award options in meaningful quantities that serve to inspire the best out of those executives. But they also recognize that key roles in the organization go beyond simply the top three to five executives, and they look to include individuals from the top two or three organizational layers where possible. Prudent PEGs also encourage co-investing (an often-undervalued opportunity) where portco senior leaders are provided the opportunity at the beginning of the investment period to put their own money in alongside the LPs (and incur the same upside potential but also downside risk as other investors).

An illustration of potential financial rewards for executives leading successful investment periods can be found in Figure 11.3, which shows a hypothetical example of a portfolio company CEO. In this case, the CEO having 30% of the management option pool received $8.5 million for taking a $20 million EBITDA company valued at 10× to a $50 million firm valued at 11×. Actual proceeds, of course, depend on numerous assumptions not shown, including the impact of option value, strike price, vesting, changes in debt level, and so on. That said, it's worth considering some of the details:

% of Portco Option Pool			
Portco Role	People	Each	Total
CEO	1	30%	30%
CFO	1	15%	15%
CCO	1	15%	15%
COO	1	15%	15%
Other Exec	3	5%	15%
Other Key	5	2%	10%
Total	12	–	100%

CEO Proceeds Scenarios				
Multiple x EBITDA $	9x	10x	11x	12x
$20m	$0.0m	$0.0m	$0.5m	1.0m
$30m	$1.5m	$2.5m	$3.0m	$4.0m
$40m	$4.0m	$5.0m	$6.0m	$6.5m
$50m	$6.0m	$7.0m	$8.5m	$9.5m
$60m	$8.0m	$9.5m	$11.0m	$12.5m

Note:
Illustration only; based on numerous assumptions not shown (option value and vesting, strike price, changes in debt and cash, etc.
■ Sample exit scenario; ■ Proceeds if exit scenario equaled purchase scenario

Figure 11.3   Management Proceeds

Ownership. The private equity firm allocates a pool of options to the portfolio company team at the beginning of the investment period. The awarded pool varies significantly but may effectively result in the portfolio company's participating leadership having ownership in the company. This serves to help align incentives between LP investors, the private equity firm, and the portco leadership team.

Distribution. The equity partners will typically award the CEO's amount of the total pool first, and then work with him or her to allocate the remaining options to those leaders in the company who will drive the most value. They may award the entire option pool at once or may choose to maintain a portion in reserve for future executive hires or for later distribution. The CEO grant and other grants vary widely, depending on the industry, company, and situation.

Outcome. Astute PEGs closely link long-term incentives to portfolio company performance and exit value. If the company doesn't grow, the CEO and executives understandably do not garner much if any upside financial benefit. But if the CEO and his or her team significantly grow the company, they will likely be well compensated for their efforts (on top of whatever co-investment they might have made in the business). It is not hard to imagine that motivated executives will roll over much of their proceeds into the next investment period, hoping for (and planning to work extremely hard for) another two or three times COC outcome.

In the end analysis, private equity is an exciting place to be. Whether you are an investor putting your money at risk, an employee at a PEG finding, analyzing, placing, and managing portfolio bets, or a part of portfolio management growing the company, private equity offers opportunities for engagement, development, and financial gain unlike any other space in the corporate world.

Chapter 12

Conclusion

Restructuring the Hold is a two-way street – private equity firms improving the way they work with their portfolio companies and portfolio companies improving how they work with their PEGs. The median between the two is a constructive partnership – equity partners and portco leaders working side-by-side to optimize outcomes and opportunities for investors and the management team alike.

Constructive partnerships are effective at optimizing enterprise value because they are collaborative and complementary – the right marriage of positive attitudes and unique capabilities. Performance-oriented PEGs ensure their portcos have the right leadership team in place – those with the attitudes and capabilities necessary to achieve a successful investment period. Just as important, these PEGs also ensure that they bring *their* best to the table – highly collaborative and extremely capable investing and operating talent.

Capability, confidence, and collaboration lead to authentic partnerships and positive teamwork, which in turn leads to trusting relationships. With trust and authenticity, both PEG and portco are keenly aware of each other's capabilities as well as limitations, and work to shore each other up. In *The Winter of Our Discontent*, John Steinbeck said: "When two people meet, each one is changed by the other so you've got two new people." And in private equity, those two new "people" are all the better for it, achieving much more than either could on their own. That's the result of a genuine constructive PEG/portco partnership.

The investment period demands strong partnerships because the objectives and pace are difficult and challenging. It's not for the faint of heart, and the inevitable bumps in the road and periodic missteps along the way lead to more than a few moments of consternation. But consternation and missteps can be minimized without resorting to the worst stereotypes of private equity and business leaders in general. It requires both the PEG and the portco to *decide* to embrace the partnership, because constructive partnerships and authentic teaming do not just happen – in fact, they require specific commitment and unrelenting work.

The work of the investment period is both complicated and complex. But together PEG and portco can engineer the complicated and manage the complex to improve the likelihood of outsized outcomes.

The investment period is complicated because it involves many interrelated components that nevertheless have a logical order. As a result, the investment period can be dissected, analyzed, and improved. It can be engineered to some degree and made less complicated through (for instance) consistent reporting, a standard operating cadence, and active management of a well-organized value creation program. This book includes our attempt to address the complications posed by the investment period by applying systems thinking to meet the challenge.

The investment period is also complex because despite being logically complicated it is also unpredictable. The complex aspects of the investment period – people and external circumstances – cannot be engineered and then periodically monitored but must be managed incessantly with continuous proactive efforts and reactive adjustments. We can reduce the impact of investment period complexity through collaborative partnering, authentic teaming, and a commitment to holding one another responsible and accountable. This book is equally our attempt to address the complexity posed by the investment period by showing how principled leadership can be applied to meet the challenge.

Over the course of this book, we've offered several suggestions regarding how to restructure the hold period. In the end analysis, we believe success or failure rests on a few foundational principles:

Hard work. An investment period comes with lots of pressures requiring a considerable amount of effort to succeed. Even for PEG and portcos having excellent constructive partnerships, the steady drumbeat is fast-paced and never-ending – relentless, in fact. Especially in the middle-market, where things change quickly and resources are few, executives are pressured from all directions. One day they're envisioning the future with the board of directors, the next day they're responding to KPI inquiries from equity partners, and the following day they're sleeves-up with the team – analyzing spreadsheets of warranty returns and moving boxes around the plant floor. It's not for everyone, as it involves a dedication and commitment to doing whatever it takes, all the while focused on performance feedback and continuous improvement – for oneself and one's team.

Healthy egos. The roles of CEO, portco executives, and equity partners naturally draw type-A individuals – hard-charging, no sleep types. Those same types by nature also have a disproportionate amount of ego. But being a hard-charging type-A personality does not require an *oversized* ego. Someone can have a healthy sense of their own self-worth without it leading them to be arrogant, conceited, or condescending. Constructive private equity and portfolio company partnerships in fact require feeling confident and taking pride in one's accomplishments. But an exaggerated sense of one's importance will ultimately undermine those partnerships because the qualities associated with an outsized ego are fundamentally destructive.

End-in-mind. Success during the investment period hinges on being able to clearly and specifically paint the picture of the endgame: the ability to articulate what that future company will be and the specifics of how to get there within the remaining investment period. Indeed, it's a finite and short game, with the inevitable ending getting one year closer with each passing year.

Those who flourish in private equity operate with an impatient mindset that says "time's-a-wastin'." They know what they want to get done and relentlessly make 24 hours of progress every day towards that vision. What might start as an initial sketch of that endgame will be continually fleshed out, revised, and refined as the exit approaches. It's important that PEG and portco partnerships have a bottomless well of motivation and momentum to get there.

Act like owners. Finally, when a portfolio company and the equity partners think and act like owners – when the entire team believes in the vision and feels empowered and responsible to do their part and then some – that's when things click. Genuine owners know their business inside and out, and as a result can get more things done faster and better. Owners know the value of a dollar, relish paying attention to the details, and have the passion to get things right. When both the PEG and the portco act this way, that's when sustainable value creation is just everyday "runnin' the business."

In the end, we hope the lessons of *Restructuring the Hold* will encourage private equity firms and portfolio companies to increasingly embrace collaborative and constructive partnerships as they work toward better and more successful investment periods. We hope we've demonstrated how management teams and their private equity partners can and should work together to achieve an efficient operating rhythm, institutionalize an effective Value Creation Program, accelerate sustainable EBITDA growth, and ultimately optimize exit value to the benefit of everyone – investors and their general partners, portfolio company leadership and their managers, and company employees and their families.

The opportunities for doing exciting and wonderful things in private equity-sponsored portfolio companies are plentiful, including building businesses, accelerating careers, creating jobs, and improving lives. We believe the right path forward for PEGs and portcos alike is marked by clarity of purpose, by practical solutions for complicated and complex issues, and by the principles of integrity, compassion, and authenticity.

References

Ansoff, H. Igor. "Strategies for Diversification." *Harvard Business Review*, September–October (1957): 113–24.

Baker, Walter, Michael Marn, and Craig Zawada. *The Price Advantage*. Hoboken, NJ: John Wiley and Sons, 2010.

Cooperrider, David. L., Diana Whitney, and Jacqueline M. Stavros. *Appreciative Inquiry Handbook*. 2nd ed. Brunswick, OH: Crown Custom Publishing, 2008.

"GE Annual Report 2000." Accessed April 4, 2019. https://www.ge.com/annual00/download/images/GEannual00.pdf

Kaplan, Robert, and David Norton. "The Balanced Scorecard – Measures that Drive Performance." *Harvard Business Review*, January–February (1992): 71–79.

Lencioni, Patrick. *Five Dysfunctions of a Team: A Leadership Fable*. San Francisco, CA: Jossey-Bass, 2002.

Panagiotou, George. "Bringing SWOT into Focus." *Business Strategy Review*, 14, no. 2, (2003): 8–10.

Stone, Oliver, dir. *Wall Street*. 1987. Los Angeles, CA: Twentieth Century Fox, 2000. DVD.

Index